WHERE'S THE RHETORIC?

WHERE'S THE RHETORIC?

Imagining a Unified Field

S. SCOTT GRAHAM

THE OHIO STATE UNIVERSITY
COLUMBUS

Copyright © 2020 by The Ohio State University.
All rights reserved.

Library of Congress Cataloging-in-Publication Data
Names: Graham, S. Scott, author.
Title: Where's the rhetoric? : imagining a unified field / S. Scott Graham.
Description: Columbus : The Ohio State University Press, [2020] | Includes
 bibliographical references and index. | Summary: "Draws on the works of Gilles
 Deleuze, Bruno Latour, Kenneth Burke, Carolyn Miller, and Henri Bergson to
 make connections between rhetorical new materialisms and computational
 rhetorics to provide the foundation for a unified rhetorical field. Demonstrates
 how disparate intellectual approaches within rhetoric can be put in conversation
 around questions of genre, media, and political discourse"—Provided by
 publisher.
Identifiers: LCCN 2020023019 | ISBN 9780814214534 (cloth) | ISBN 0814214533
 (cloth) | ISBN 9780814280782 (ebook) | ISBN 0814280781 (ebook)
Subjects: LCSH: Rhetoric—Philosophy. | Material culture—Philosophy. | Process
 philosophy. | Computational linguistics.
Classification: LCC P301 .G68 2020 | DDC 808.001—dc23
LC record available at https://lccn.loc.gov/2020023019

Cover design by Nathan Putens
Text design by Juliet Williams
Type set in Adobe Palatino

CONTENTS

List of Illustrations								vii
Acknowledgments								ix
List of Abbreviations								xi

CHAPTER 1	Disciplinary Fractures	1
CHAPTER 2	The Bergson Legacy	21
CHAPTER 3	Genre as Process	59
CHAPTER 4	People as Process	93
CHAPTER 5	Fit Forging	115
CHAPTER 6	The Science of Intuition	137
CHAPTER 7	Chasing Satisfaction	161
CHAPTER 8	Imagining a Unified Field	183

Appendix									195
References									199
Index										211

ILLUSTRATIONS

FIGURES

FIGURE 2.1	Bergsonian circulation map	27
FIGURE 3.1	Opening invitational tweets by Ellie Murray, Katja Thieme, and Kevin Kruse	83
FIGURE 3.2	Height of data dump among sample tweetorials	84
FIGURE 3.3	Murray tweet within data dump	85
FIGURE 3.4	Hierarchy of genre-ing processes within tweetorials and tweets	88
FIGURE 5.1	Graham and Whalen's (2008) schematic of e-card/game mode, medium, and genre interaction	129
FIGURE 6.1	Graham et al.'s (2015) genre fingerprint	154
FIGURE 7.1	Average sentiment score and trend of GOP primary debates, 2007–2016	169
FIGURE 7.2	Average sentiment score and trend of GOP primary debates, 2015–2016	177
FIGURE 8.1	Bergsonian legacies in new materialisms, RGS, and GAP	187

TABLES

TABLE 6.1	Coding Domains and Representative Content Codes	147
TABLE 7.1	Average Sentiment of Debate Season and Party	168
TABLE 7.2	Tukey's HST Post-Hoc Test Results for Primary Debates, by Season and Party	169
TABLE 8.1	Inquiry Traditions	188
TABLE 8.2	Foundational Concepts	188
TABLE 8.3	Core Constructs	189
TABLE 8.4	Meta-Methodological Resources	189
TABLE A.1	Works That Cite Bergson's *Creative Evolution*	195
TABLE A.2	Works That Cite Bergson's *Matter and Memory*	196
TABLE A.3	Works That Cite Bergson's *Time and Free Will*	196
TABLE A.4	Works That Cite Whitehead's *Process and Reality*	196
TABLE A.5	Citation Relationships Among Lessor-Cited Works in the Bergson-Rhetoric-New Materialisms Scholarly Network	196–97

ACKNOWLEDGMENTS

Anthropomorphized academic *mythoi* like to imagine that scholarship springs forth whole cloth (and perhaps unbidden) from the deeper recesses of a scholar's mind. This is obviously not the case. Academia doesn't happen without community, and scholars don't happen without social support. Recognizing this, I find it's hard to draw a line on where to stop thanking people who helped make this work and my professional life possible. What follows is the best I could do.

Roxi Copland, Odin Van Pooch, and Haggis McHound: Thank you for keeping me sane on this journey and in life, more broadly.

Ashley Mehlenbacher, Benjamin Harley, Bill Keith, Carl Herndl, Caroline Gottschalk Druschke, Carolyn Miller, Casey Boyle, David Gruber, Debra Hawhee, Jason Kalin, Jennifer LeMesurier, Kenny Fountain, Kenny Walker, Laurie Gries, Nathan Bedsole, Nathan Stormer, Nathaniel Rivers, Scot Barnett, Taralee Cyphers, Thomas Rickert, and Zoltan Majdik: Thank you for your feedback on early manuscripts and/or your generous engagement with the various ill-formed ideas that finally came (at least mostly) to fruition in the pages that follow.

Brandon Whalen, Christa Teston, Dan Card, Dani DeVasto, Fallon Bubacy, Kirk St.Amant, Laura Roberts, Michelle Olsen, Molly Kessler, Sang-Yeon Kim, and Seokoon Ahn: Many thanks—without each of you, the research that supports chapters 5 and 6 would not have been possible.

enculturation Anonymous Reviewer 2, who wrote, "I really enjoyed reading this engaging and lively piece. It was like watching someone attempt to jump over 22 cars with a motorcycle. Common sense tells you it can't be done, but you hold your breath and excitedly see what happens. Daring jumps are exciting, but crashes are exciting too." This is my favorite line in a reviewer report. Ever. Please tell me who you are, so I can buy you a beer.

Publication of this book was made possible, in part, thanks to a subvention grant from the President's Office of the University of Texas.

ABBREVIATIONS

ANT	Actor-Network Theory
CR	Computational Rhetoric
GAP	Genre as Process
GASA	Genre as Social Action
NM	New Materialisms
OBB	Original Bergsonian Burke
OOO	Object-Oriented Ontologies
RGS	Rhetorical Genre Studies
RNM	Rhetorical New Materialisms

CHAPTER 1

DISCIPLINARY FRACTURES

RHETORIC IS IN CRISIS. This statement is both shocking and banal. Rhetoric is always in crisis and has always been in crisis. From the sophism–Platonism debates of ancient Greece to the final rejection of rhetoric as "mere" in the modern era, rhetoric has always been marked by an enduring sense of anxiety. In many respects, that anxiety is an essential part of the discipline itself and may not be possible (or even desirable) to fully resolve. When I say "rhetoric is in crisis," I do not mean any of this. Perhaps what I should say instead is that "rhetoric is fractured." Unfortunately, however, this provokes another hedge. When I say "rhetoric is fractured," I do not mean the split between English rhetoric and speech rhetoric; I do not mean public address versus professional writing; and I do not mean any of the two dozen intellectual initiatives vying to be the One True Church of Composition. No, these fractures endure and, like the persistent state of anxiety, actually do much to keep the discipline together.

So, what do I mean? The crisis and the fracture to which I refer is occasioned by new fault lines—demarcations that cut through all the pre-existing divides. Here I speak of the recent emergences of rhetorical new materialisms (RNM) and computational rhetorics (CR). Unlike the administrative and pedagogical divisions that attempt to separate composition, professional writing, and speech, these new divisions drive at the very core of disciplinary identity. What is rhetoric? And, what does it mean to do rhetoric? These questions come to the fore every time the conversation turns to RNM or CR. And, of course, this is no surprise. Rhetorical inquiry has long defined itself as a humanistic practice devoted to the careful study of certain semiotic modes. We study *texts, discourse, words*. And *we* study texts, discourse, words. The critic has always been the instrument, and human communication the object of inquiry.

Materialist, computational, and quantitative rhetorics have been chipping away at or expanding (depending on your perspective) the edges of the discipline for quite some time now. In some respects, materialist rhetorical inquiry came into its own with Celest Condit's (1999) *The Meaning of the Gene*, and computational approaches have been an on-again/off-again fad since at least Roderick Hart's (1984) *Verbal Style and the Presidency: A Computer-Based Analysis* and Sandra Thompson and William Mann's (1987) "Rhetorical Structure Theory." Yet, at present, it seems like these two initiatives have never been stronger. In recent years, we've seen a veritable explosion of new materialist and computational approaches to rhetoric that have the potential to shake the very core of what it means to do rhetoric and to be a rhetorician. Posthuman and object-oriented rhetorics vie for attention with hedge-o-matics and writing analytics. In the most recent pages of our scholarly journals, we learn about the rhetoric of fish and explore the frequencies of Burkean ratios in the entire collected Congressional Record addressing climate change.

This shift is seismic. The schisms are real. And, a pressing question is: what's next? Not too long ago, Lisa Melonçon and I debated on Twitter as to whether we were witnessing a disciplinary speciation event. Are we watching rhetoric fracture into new areas of inquiry embarking on new projects so foreign to the core discipline that no connection can be drawn? As we tweeted back and forth, Melonçon called it "sad." I embraced the speciation and the new horizons of inquiry it might offer for the future. I have since changed my mind. If you know me and my work, that may well come across as odd. Indeed, I have been attempting to push at the disciplinary boundaries of rhetoric for quite some time. I push hard in both new materialist and computational directions. Nevertheless, I believe there is a rhetorical core that unites my work and the work of other rhetorical new materialists and computational rhetoricians. I hope it is the same core that unites rhetorical scholars who are less enthusiastic about these new directions for inquiry.

Ultimately, the primary purpose of this book is to think through one way we might forge new connections at the various points of apparent disciplinary fissure. Let me be clear: I will not walk back RNM or CR. Rather, I have become convinced that there is at least one way of understanding the contemporary diversity of rhetorical inquiry, at least as a continuity, if not a unity. Many of my readers will know of work on a unified field theory in physics. This is the pursuit—as of yet unachieved—of a single intellectual framework that accounts for both the fundamental forces in the universe (gravity, electromagnetism, strong, weak) and the interactions among subatomic particles. This is the effort to integrate general relativity and quantum mechanics. In much the same way, my goal here is to develop a unified field theory of rhetoric. In all honesty, this effort is partially a response to all the Reviewer Twos out there who have told me my work doesn't belong in this discipline. Additionally, it is an effort to forge a coherent whole out of a research agenda that has pulled me in two seemingly opposing directions. But I hope it is also more than that. I hope it is also a way to galvanize greater degrees of disciplinary cohesion. Cohesion, mind you, not agreement. At heart, I will always be an agonistic rhetorician. There's more Gorgias in me than Protagoras. But, no matter how you fancy your *dissoi logoi*, you must share an *agora* for argument to proceed.

Essentially, what I will argue in this book is that there already exists an intellectual thread that effectively binds more traditional approaches to rhetorical inquiry with RNM and CR. A cornerstone of this argument will be my contention that rhetorical inquiry has been new materialist for far longer than anyone has realized. In fact, I will argue that the earliest antecedents to RNM can be found in the scholarship of Kenneth Burke,[1] and that, furthermore, Carolyn Miller invented the very first fully formed RNM in 1984. In so doing, I challenge the notion that new materialism is "other" to rhetorical inquiry, or at least I reject the idea that it has been entirely "other" over the last eighty years. It will take me several chapters to make the case, but as I do, I will demonstrate that there is a heretofore unrecognized intellectual thread running through rhetorical genre studies (RGS), new materialisms, and CR. And that thread begins with a remarkably prolific and influential continental philosopher whose work is largely ignored in rhetorical studies—Henri Bergson.

Maddeningly, I must put a pin in this argument about rhetoric's hidden history for now. As mentioned above, it will take several chapters for my account to unfold. The proper task for this introduction is to better set the stage for my eventual argument. In so doing, I will detail my burdens

---

1. My work on Burke's new materialist tendencies is greatly indebted to Debra Hawhee's (2009) *Moving Bodies* and Chris Mays, Nathaniel A. Rivers, and Kellie Sharp-Hoskins's (2017) *Kenneth Burke + The Posthuman*—two texts that have really opened up this area of inquiry.

of proof (in full recognition that they are high). I will begin by tracing the default assumption that the new materialist project is profoundly "other" with respect to rhetoric. I will then outline some of the primary arguments for a computational approach to rhetorical inquiry. These arguments generally take the form of citing external nondisciplinary exigencies. I warn the reader in advance: the introduction will not end with an easy resolution or an obvious connection between these two emergent projects. (But I promise that connection is forthcoming.)

The Loci of Boundary Work

In 1983 sociologist of science Thomas Gieryn introduced science studies to the notion of boundary work. Although his intellectual contribution was aimed at the demarcation problem,[2] Gieryn's insight spawned a new scholarly agenda devoted to investigating the rhetorical activities that occur at disciplinary margins. As inquiry into boundary work expanded, the demarcation problem became only one context among many. We now understand boundary work to occur at much smaller scales, including disciplinary and subdisciplinary borders. As my readers have already intuited, much of this book will be devoted to questions of boundary work in rhetorical studies. Where does disciplinary inquiry end and a new field begin? Never an easy question to answer.

Part of the reason it is so difficult to grapple with boundary work is that it leaves so few publicly accessible traces. Boundary work largely happens in informal and private spaces that are not documented for all to read. Sheila Jasanoff (1987) draws our attention to this in her studies of boundary work in science:

> Other scholars have called attention to the restrictive processes of entry into science, which involve not only an esoteric professional training but screening by numerous "gatekeepers," such as senior academic colleagues or editors of professional journals. Cohesion within science is also fostered by "invisible colleges," "research circles" or other informal networks that control the diffusion of scientific knowledge... Finally [is] the process of peer review, devised by scientists to validate each other's discoveries... (p. 196)

---

2. The long-standing philosophical debate over how to distinguish science from nonscience.

Graduate student–mentor meetings, desk rejections, peer review, conference Q&A: these are the principal loci of boundary work.

Published scholarship, in contrast, is readily available precisely because it has already survived the trials of boundary work. Very little of it will directly address the issue of proper disciplinary boundaries because it does not need to. The rhetorical manifestation of boundary work can be best understood using either Foucault's notion of discursive rarefaction or Toulmin's theory of argumentative warrants. Under either theoretical rubric, discourse is disciplined through reference to context-specific rules and regulations. However, for both approaches, those rules and regulations are seldom manifest in extant discourse. As I have elaborated previously:

> Finally, there is one additional key parallel among principles of rarefaction, warrants, and the deployment of certain special *topoi*—their typical obfuscation. Speaking of the will-to-truth, Foucault (1972) suggests that focus on true facts engendered by the will to truth cannot help but to "mask" that will (p. 219). Furthermore he argues that "we are unaware of the prodigious machinery of the will-to-truth" (p. 220). Generally speaking, principles of rarefaction are self-effacing. They are constant background features exercising considerable control over discourse. . . . Indeed, principles of rarefaction are generally tacit unless they must be used explicitly in order to rarefy—to exorcise the aberrant discourse. (Graham, 2015, p. 151)

Only when discourse violates a principle of rarefaction will that principle be named. And, thus, most discourse that violates those principles remains unpublished because of its violation, and the naming of the offended principle is also unpublished per the confidentiality of peer review.

I draw our attention to the loci of boundary work to point out the difficultly inherent in the tasks of this introduction. So much of what I want to write about here involves rhetorical boundary work. Are RNM and CR legitimately part of the broader rhetorical project? This is a debate that occurs in informal spaces at the margins of the discipline. Accordingly, to address the arguments directly, I will have to draw on an atypically broad review of the literature. *Literature*—that term itself will not suffice because so much of the argument does not exist in the literature for the very reasons just elaborated. Again, these arguments are the stuff of editorial decisions, mentor meetings, reviewer reports, Twitter fights, Facebook conversations, conference Q&A, and so forth. Unfortunately, this presents a real and practical problem. I cannot fully elucidate the shape of the conversation without referring my reader to the unfindable. Ephemeral moments in hallways, archived tweet storms, and private peer reviews contribute powerfully to the discourse at issue. Ultimately, I have no choice but to ask the reader for trust. Wherever possible I will track down the traces of boundary work in our discipline and present them for your evaluation. But in some cases that will not be possible or ethical, and my personal testimony will be all that I can offer.

The "Otherness" of New Materialisms

New materialisms means many things to many people. Indeed, as a term of art, it resists closure. In their edited collection, *New Materialisms*, Diana Coole and Samantha Frost (2010) describe the term as more of a signpost, and I think there's something to this description. For them, recent developments in new materialisms are to be understood as

> signs that the more textual approaches associated with the so-called cultural turn are increasingly being deemed inadequate for understanding contemporary society, particularly in light of some of its most urgent challenges regarding environmental, demographic, geopolitical, and economic change. (pp. 1–2)

In keeping with Coole and Frost, I understand new materialisms to be a broad rubric that includes any theoretical approach which rejects equally the fetishization of substance in modernism and fetishization discourse in postmodernism. This definition is too broad for many. Casey Boyle and I recently debated on Facebook as to whether object-oriented ontologies (OOO) should be included under the rubric of new materialisms. His reasonable contention was that since OOO rejects the political and emancipatory aims espoused by Coole and Frost, it should not qualify. My sense is that it is the diagnostic consensus with respect to modernism and postmodernism that makes new materialism.[3]

Under the diagnostic/signpost interpretation of new materialisms, many identify Donna Haraway's cyborgs and Bruno Latour's actor-network theory (ANT) as the twin birthplaces of the movement. While these approaches may lack the full theoretical maturity of more recent new materialisms like Annemarie Mol's multiple ontologies, they are among the very first widely recognized theorists to simultaneously reject both the modern and the

---

3. We agreed to disagree, as we often do.

postmodern projects. The caveat "widely recognized" is critical here, for as we will see in chapter 2, Bergson rejects both modernism and postmodernism in almost identical fashion as early as 1896; see *Matter and Memory* (1896/1911). Likewise, Alfred North Whitehead's *Process and Reality* (1929) and Kenneth Burke's (1935) *Permanence and Change* each explicitly follow Bergson in making this move. As with any attribution of priority, suggesting that either Latour or Haraway invented new materialisms becomes increasingly fraught under scrutiny. It would be hard to imagine a cyborg theory without Anne Fausto-Sterling, Sandra Harding, or Michel Foucault. It would be likewise difficult to envision an ANT without Gilles Deleuze or John Law.

Regardless of the "true" origin point, the standard narrative is one that places new materialisms' birth fully outside the rhetorical tradition. Nevertheless, RNM has now come into its own. Thomas Rickert's (2013) *Ambient Rhetoric,* Laurie Gries's (2015) *Still Life with Rhetoric,* Christa Teston's (2017) *Bodies in Flux,* Boyle's (2018) *Rhetoric as Posthuman Practice,* Cooper's (2019) *The Animal Who Writes,* and my own *The Politics of Pain Medicine* (2015) all embrace the RNM project. Likewise, we are seeing a burgeoning array of edited collections devoted to RNM, including Scot Barnett and Boyle's (2016) *Rhetoric Through Everyday Things,* Paul Lynch and Nathaniel Rivers's (2015) *Thinking with Bruno Latour in Rhetoric and Composition,* and Chris Mays, Nathaniel A. Rivers, and Kellie Sharp-Hoskins's (2017) *Kenneth Burke + The Posthuman,* to name a few. Nevertheless, as mentioned above, the new materialist turn in rhetorical studies is broadly understood to be a radical departure from traditional approaches to inquiry.

Interestingly, this is a view shared by adherents and critics of RNM alike. The strange/otherness of new materialisms is something Carolyn Miller (Walsh et al., 2017) remarked on in her recent *Rhetoric Society Quarterly* counterpoint contribution to the symposium on rhetoric and Bruno Latour. As she notes:

> For the rhetorician there is also in Latour plenty that is "curious" (Gries, this issue 442) or "strange," specifically his explicit, programmatic focus on "the nonhuman, the nonsymbolic, and the nondiscursive" (Lynch and Rivers 4). But this strangeness, in fact, is the source of much of his appeal to rhetorical scholars who are trying to escape from rhetoric's traditional constraints, its humanist-modernist convictions, by making a materialist turn. Herndl and Graham welcome Latour's efforts because they "offer rhetoric the beginnings of a nonmodern, materialist rhetorical theory" (41). (p. 455)

Generally, this acceptance of "otherness" arises from a few key argumentative moves centered around disciplinary history and disciplinary boundaries. In the first case, advocates of RNM advance their claims based on a rhetoric of paradigm revolution. The old linguistic turn will be supplanted by a new materialist turn. The Young Turks will overthrow the Old Guard. Those more critical of RNM offer boundary arguments rejecting the place of NM in R. In so doing, they typically argue that new materialisms do not belong in rhetorical studies, as the discipline is properly concerned with the study of language, discourse, signs, and/or argument.

The appeal to paradigm revolution is, perhaps, the most visible claim to otherness in RNM. I, myself, offer this account of the new materialist turn in *The Politics of Pain Medicine*:

> Traditional rhetoric of science and [sociology of scientific knowledge /] social constructivist approaches in [science and technology studies] have focused—somewhat myopically—on internal scientific discourse to the exclusion of the institutional and the material. Recognizing this issue, many scholars have called for a reincorporation of materiality into rhetoric and STS. (Graham, 2015, p. 13)

The less critical variant of this move follows on the exigencies outlined by Coole and Frost and suggests that the shift toward a new materialist rhetoric is necessary because of profound changes in the world itself. Lynda Walsh's introduction to the recent *Rhetoric Society Quarterly* symposium on rhetoric and Latour makes this argument quite directly. As she writes:

> We have all sensed a change in the temperature of late-modern argumentation and persuasion. Arguing in the anthropocene is qualitatively and quantitatively different than arguing in the Classical agora. Now, no matter which direction we turn, we find the forum crowded not only with human speakers of all stripes but also with an awesome flotsam of nonhumans: computer models, polar bears, FitBits, genes, Tweets, YouTube videos, viruses, cookbooks, nebulae, and iPhones. (Walsh et al., 2017, p. 403)

Whether occasioned by a simple disciplinary evolution or by the change in circumstances arising from the inevitable passage of time, new materialisms are broadly construed as "other" to rhetoric and no small turn.

Unfortunately, the focus on paradigm revolution among advocates of RNM cedes crucial ground to our detractors. Indeed, if RNM is essentially other, then what place does it have in rhetoric journals? This critical gerrymandering of rhetorical inquiry is one of the most vibrant, yet least visible discourses on RNM. Like most boundary work, the rejection of RNM occurs principally as a part of peer review and informal discussion/debate/diatribes, many occurring on social media or as a part of conference Q&A. However, there are a few places where its traces may be found in published scholarship. For example, the following excerpt is from Walsh's interview with Bruno Latour:

> Well, I probably won't give a good answer for them because I personally don't think rhetoric extends to the growth of this plant. I think of rhetoric as being limited somewhat as you do, to political discourse. But my friends who want to extend rhetoric to the plant are looking toward your work in ontologies, they're talking about attunement and materialism—both in the object-oriented-ontology tradition and the Marxist tradition. Thomas Rickert's *Ambient Rhetoric* and Jane Bennett's *Vibrant Matter* are both important texts. (Walsh et al., 2017, pp. 416–417)

Here Walsh is able to assert her rejection of RNM, precisely because the interview genre and her goal of fairly representing the "other side" to her interlocutor allow the standard prohibitions on naming principles of rarefaction to relax.

But still the bulk of boundary work occurs in more cloistered spaces—chief among them peer review. I recently served as a reviewer on a manuscript where these ideas were so powerfully in dispute, that it took no fewer than five reviewers to settle the issue for the editor. The initial evaluations were diametrically opposed with Reviewer 1 endorsing immediate unrevised publication and Reviewer 2 rejecting the manuscript as utterly unsalvageable and refusing to review another round. Indeed, one only need ask the proponents of RNM about recent experience with peer review and the floodgates will open. One of my RNM colleagues was kind enough to offer the following account of recent peer-review experiences. Of course, it speaks to the power of peer review as boundary work that anonymity was requested.

> A number of editors and reviewers have suggested that my work in postcritique rhetoric was not connected to conversations in the field. I have been directed, for instance, to consult "standard reference works in the history of rhetoric" and to include more references to Aristotle and Isocrates. While many reviewer suggestions have been useful, several review processes have seemed to make clear that the conversation I am trying to have is not

sufficiently "inside" the field. Were my inclusions of noted new materialist theorists including Karen Barad, Jane Bennett, Gilles Deleuze, Donna Haraway, and Anna Tsing somehow canceling out my mentions of rhetorical theorists like Jenny Rice, Thomas Rickert, Debra Hawhee, Nathaniel Rivers, and Scott Graham?

These are not isolated incidents. Indeed, buy Nathaniel Rivers, Caroline Gottschalk Druschke, Casey Boyle, or Laurie Gries a beer when next you see them if you desire further testimony as to the pervasiveness of this kind of boundary work.

Thomas Rickert and Scot Barnett, perhaps, stand out in the rhetorical materialist landscape in that they argue that realism and materialism can be traced back to our disciplinary antecedents in ancient Greece. For example, Rickert (2013) argues that Plato's *chora* showcases a historical materialist orientation. As he writes, "This sensible, active world is not one of simple presence or mundane materiality. The Greeks, like other ancient peoples, had a strong sense of what remains hidden, obscure, and withdrawn in the world" (p. 52). Likewise, the breadth of Barnett's (2016) *Rhetorical Realism* is devoted "to dig[ging] deeper roots for object-oriented rhetoric within the histories of Western rhetorical theory" (p. 12). While I find that each of these works offers compelling historiographies of materialism and realism in rhetorical history, I'm not as certain that they effectively detail the rise of rhetorical *new* materialisms. Although my work in this book is to argue against the "new" in RNM, I think it is a mistake to suggest that all materialisms are new materialisms. As I have written elsewhere (Graham, 2015, 2016), the defining feature of new materialism is the wholesale rejection of epistemology. Yet, as Barnett clearly argues, the long history of rhetorical realism is a history of epistemological vexation. In his words, "Rhetorical realism is a complicated orientation that blends epistemology and ontology into differing configurations depending on the needs and mentalities of a given historical epoch" (p. 13).

My own boundary work aside, ultimately debates over the place of new materialisms in rhetoric tend to center on the objects of our inquiry. Whether supportive or critical, arguments that RNM is other rest on the sense that *rhetoric* is the object of our inquiry. Rhetoricians study human symbolic action, and the extension into materiality is a violation of traditional understandings of our objects of inquiry. And, here, we find ourselves confronting one of the core conflicts in rhetorical studies. Is rhetoric a *what* or a *how*?[4] I

---

4. See Zarefsky's (1998) "Four Senses of Rhetorical History" for another take on these divisions within speech-rhetoric.

have found that this question serves as a pretty effective (maybe 80 percent accurate) litmus test for distinguishing between English and speech rhetoricians. Speech—especially in the public-address tradition—has a long focus on a canon of rhetorical artifacts, and this tends to create a situation where public-address rhetoricians identify rhetoric with the object of study. English rhetoric's lack of an artifact canon tends to shift the focus to rhetoric as a way. Nevertheless, even those who would articulate rhetoric as a way might fall back on the traditional rhetoric as a what in their arguments over the proper place of RNM. Interestingly, this debate over the nature of rhetoric will come to the fore again in deliberation over the place of CR. Whereas the "otherness" of RNM is generally warranted based on presuppositions about the what of rhetoric, the presumed "otherness" of CR is grounded in rhetoric's how.

A Growing Penchant for Computing

Much like RNM, CR is comprised of an expansive array of theories, methods, and approaches. Work done under the rubric of CR has included automated content analysis, topic modeling, machine learning, network mapping, multivariate statistics, and so forth. For the purposes of this book, I will embrace a big-bucket definition of CR. Specifically, I understand CR as any effort that uses computing as a part of rhetorical inquiry.[5] *Computing* is of course the key here. The mere use of computers is not CR. Traditional rhetorical analyses of computational spaces are not CR. Even much in the way of critical code studies is not CR. But, at the same time, CR does not require any specific technological tool. In its most simple iteration, CR is rhetorical scholarship animated by research questions that engage issues of scale and scope. No analysis of a single rhetorical situation will answer the specific questions posed. Instead, CR focuses on objects of inquiry that exceed the investigational capacity of a single humanist researcher. The sheer size of the data set (indexed to the research questions) requires computing for investigation, analysis, or both.

As was the case with RNM, devotees of CR tend to warrant their focus on computing technologies with appeals to novelty. For example, Jim Brown

---

5. As Hodgson and Barnett (2016) articulate, many of the same definitional struggles revolve around the term *digital rhetoric*. I use the term CR to more fully highlight my interest in rhetorical methodologies. That is, it would be hard to argue that traditional rhetorical studies of digital spaces are not *digital rhetoric*, but I will make the claim that such studies are not CR.

Jr.'s (2015) contribution to *Rhetoric and the Digital Humanities*, aptly named "Crossing State Lines," presents James Berlin's focus on textual interpretation as a traditionalist legacy that CR challenges and overcomes. Similarly, CR also frequently invokes popular rhetorics of technology, suggesting that the C in CR makes our work, bigger, faster, better. I myself have used this rhetoric to justify using statistical methodologies for RGS (Graham, Kim, DeVasto, & Keith, 2015). Attempting to tie into the "big data" turn, my collaborators and I have argued that some data sets are so large (in this case >150,000 pages) that they require quantitative methodologies to adequately analyze:

> We would argue that this constitutes big data—at least for technical communication—and as such will require methods that extend beyond the qualitative and inductive technical communication repertoires. Therefore, to tackle this data set, we offer what we dub statistical genre analysis (SGA), a methodology that combines techniques from rhetorical studies, linguistics, and health communication. (Graham et al., p. 71)

Likewise, Kennedy and Long (2015) have argued that quantitative methodologies can provide keen insights into authorial practices, even if those practices are "qualitative processes" (p. 148).

Arguments for more computational methodologies, frequently driven by the appeal to large data sets, also suggest that computing may lead to greater credibility and/or disciplinary prestige. Miles Kimball (2013), for example, has argued that much in the way of design guidance offered in technical communication is the stuff of lore. That is, there is no solid evidentiary foundation for many of the "effective communication" recommendations offered by our field. Extending this argument, I have argued that technical communicators should embark on "a coordinated and collaborative initiative devoted to producing empirical research testing and validating the tacit and craft knowledges of practicing technical communicators" (Graham, 2017, p. 20). Here I suggest that rhetoricians and technical communicators would do well to learn from our own insights about what kinds of knowledge are privileged in academia and beyond.[6]

---

6. Although invocations of scale and authority are dominant, they are not ubiquitous. Rodrick Hart (2015) compellingly criticizes these moves in CR and DH as a "positivistic overreaction" (p. 154). In so doing, he challenges rhetoricians to shift attention away from a myopic focus on quantification and validity to more cartographic metaphors that place quantitative data more richly in context.

Of course, the pervasive denunciation of positivism in our discipline is all too often understood as a wholesale rejection of empiricism writ large. Hence the one-time need for Charney's (1996) "Empiricism Is Not a Four-Letter Word." And while I don't agree with all of Charney's article, it points to an essential challenge for research in rhetoric—viz., when an anti-empirical sentiment is baked into the founding mythos of the discipline, there are severe consequences for our knowledge-making practices. To invoke a more recent Charney (2015) article, for rhetoric the answer to the "How do you know?" question is all too often "No one knows, so who cares?" Once again, however, in making this argument here, I pit myself and my work against a "rhetoric proper," and in so doing commit an act of self-othering. And I am not alone in doing so. To address text at scale or to gain extradisciplinary legitimacy, we must do something other than traditional rhetorical inquiry. In making these arguments, advocates of CR reinforce the boundary work of those who question the role of computing in rhetorical studies.

While computing is often readily accepted as an object of criticism, it can be rather more difficult to gain traction in the humanities broadly or rhetoric specifically *doing* computing. Even though CR has been a recurrent feature of rhetorical inquiry for longer than RNM, the issues are not closed, and boundary actions are still routine. Like all boundary work, efforts to remove computing from humanistic and rhetorical inquiry often occur in less well-documented spaces. I remember well one of my own former graduate professors who once commented on a paper I'd submitted, "This is great. Can you take the numbers out?" Likewise, I and many others have been criticized for the use or overuse of computing by unnamed reviewers. As was the case with RNM, I have seen computing in rhetorical manuscripts catalyze bitter opposition in peer review. It's not terribly uncommon for one reviewer or another to declare, in the face of CR, something along the lines of "This is a rhetoric journal, after all." The message is clear: numbers need not apply. This time I'd send you beer-on-the-offering to any of the founders of or scholars publishing in the fledgling *Journal of Writing Analytics*. I think that asking them why they felt the need to establish a new scholarly venue for their efforts would provide some powerful insights into rhetoric, boundary work, peer review, and CR.

One place that the boundary work against computing in the humanities is more prominent is in the pages of academically oriented media: the *Chronicle of Higher Education, Inside Higher Education,* and the *Los Angeles Review of Books.* While few, if any, of the hundreds of op-eds in these publications address CR specifically, significant attention is paid to CR's cousin, the digital humanities (DH). Here, the boundary work that surrounds CR is often tied up intimately in the identity politics of the humanities and the existential threats that come from the neoliberalization and STEMification of the university. One of the most (in)famous of such comes from the *LA Review of Books* and was colorfully entitled "Neoliberal Tools." In the essay, the authors accuse DHers of failing to meet any of their lofty revolutionary aims and instead of paving the way for the corporatization of the humanities. As they write:

> Yet despite the aggressive promotion of Digital Humanities as a radical insurgency, its institutional success has for the most part involved the displacement of politically progressive humanities scholarship and activism in favor of the manufacture of digital tools and archives. Advocates characterize the development of such tools as revolutionary and claim that other literary scholars fail to see their political import due to fear or ignorance of technology. But the unparalleled level of material support that Digital Humanities has received suggests that its most significant contribution to academic politics may lie in its (perhaps unintentional) facilitation of the neoliberal takeover of the university. (Allington, Brouillette, & Golumbia, 2016)

Serious criticism to be sure—criticism that cuts to the very core of what it means to be a humanist in contemporary academia.

Boundary work around DH and CR also invokes a certain ideal humanistic identity at a smaller scale. This is the more direct "working with numbers" problem, as it were. In one *Chronicle of Higher Education* op-ed, the author savages DH for fetishizing numbers to no real value. Remarking on a text analysis study of literature, he writes:

> The significance of the appearance of the word "whale" (say, 1,700 times) is precisely this: the appearance of the world "whale" 1,700 times. For all its resources, the digital humanities makes a rookie mistake: It confuses more information for more knowledge. DH doesn't know why it thinks it knows what it does not know. And that is an odd place for a science to be. (Brennan, 2017)

Once again, this is more than a simple critique, and the issues herein raised are certainly worth addressing. However, part of what makes them so difficult to address is that the boundary work of DH is highly complex. RNM is much more straightforward, by comparison.

In Hart-Davidson and Ridolfo's (2015) aforementioned collection on rhetoric and DH, we can watch two fascinating competing boundary claims play out. On the one hand, we see appeals to the manifest newness of CR, with respect to rhetorical studies. On the other hand, the collection's authors argue repeatedly that CR has been DH since before DH was DH, even though they do not always claim DH. For example, we are told that

> much of the territory claimed by DHers was inhabited by rhetoric and composition long before DH arrived. . . . Indeed, we have been here for decades, filling our field's top journals and library shelves with research, scholarship, pedagogical tools, and professional guidelines to address the very issues only recently being raised by DHers. (Carter, Jones, & Hamcumpi, 2015, p. 35)

Ultimately, we see a fraught nexus of boundary work surrounding CR. It was both DH before DH was DH and the antidote to an antiquated traditionalist approach. Contested boundaries and the expansive scope of CR make it very difficult to locate. CR is both novel and long-standing. It is both rhetorical and scientific. It straddles long-accepted divides like C. P. Snow's (1959) "two cultures." It is a hybrid, a chimera, a monster. (And these are the advocates *for* CR.)

Intellectual Ecologies and a Unified Field

As mentioned above, I find it quite odd that the boundary work surrounding RNM and CR exposes significant fault lines *within* more traditionalist rhetorical studies. RNM is other because the object of inquiry is not rhetoric. CR is other because the mode of inquiry is not rhetoric. In each case here, *rhetoric* is differentially operationalized as both our object of inquiry and our methodology. This is one of the principle reasons why I think it's so important to put these two boundary exercises in conversation with one another. The contrasts between them expose an underexamined conflict at the very core of our disciplinary identities: is rhetoric a what or a how? It's both, of course, but the further question remains as to how we go about disentangling the complexities of its bothness.

My first answer is to turn to the insights of Robin Jensen's (2015) "An Ecological Turn in Rhetoric of Health Scholarship," which builds on Edbauer's (2005) rhetorical ecologies to compellingly expand our repertoire of methodological approaches for historiography of ideas. Although her suggestions are pitched at a specific subfield (rhetoric of health), they can be applied broadly to any intellectual history. Jensen's rumination on the affordances of the ecological turn prompt her to elucidate to modes of rhetorical historiography in an ecological idiom: circulation and percolation. Per Jensen, the circulation model functions by

> tracing the communication of ideas, assumptions, and arguments along a largely chronological timeline. Guiding questions for this research might concern, for instance, the ways in which one moment's rhetoric constitutes specific aspects of health and flows into and otherwise relates to corresponding depictions, or the means through which scientific "discoveries" and popular vernacular metaphors interrelate over time to situate certain health-related conditions as medical in nature. (p. 523).

In contrast, the percolation model works "by drawing connections between health rhetoric in different, distinct time periods" (p. 524). Channeling Michel Serres, Jensen offers a compelling methodological argument for an approach to the history of ideas that recognizes and embraces how "ideas, assumptions, and arguments of particular historically distinct moments often re-emerge and repeat themselves in vastly different time periods" (p. 524).

At different times throughout this book, *Where's the Rhetoric?* will work in both circulatory and percolative modes. In addressing much of what has been discussed in the introduction, this book will trace the circulation of ideas from Henri Bergson through Burke, Miller, and contemporary new materialisms. The primary goals of these circulatory efforts are (1) to offer rhetorical studies a deeper sense of its own disciplinary history (with particular attention to the influence of the much-neglected Bergson), (2) to highlight the extent to which RNM and more traditional approaches to rhetorical inquiry share unrecognized theoretical foundations, and (3) to establish a theoretical foundation that might support a more unified field.

Chapter 2 will be the primary site of this more circulatory effort. The chapter begins by outlining the unrecognized legacy of Bergson's work in both new materialisms and rhetorical theory. Specifically, the chapter traces two bibliographic lineages: one that links Bergson, Whitehead, Deleuze, and Latour; and a second in American rhetorical studies that follows how Bergson's ideas circulate through the scholarship of Burke, Schütz, and Miller. Using these bibliographic lineages as a foundation, the chapter shifts toward a slightly more percolative mode of inquiry to document the intellectual parallels between Bergson and early Burke, specifically with respect to the simultaneous rejection of both modernist materialism and postmodernist idealism.

This percolative approach continues into subsequent chapters that focus on contrastive readings of Bergson, Burke, Miller, and contemporary RNM. The goal here is to focus attention squarely on an area of rhetorical inquiry little addressed by contemporary RNM: RGS. Rhetorical approaches to genre have long been vexed by efforts (1) to understand the complex relationship between genre and medium, (2) to account for the dialectic between formal constraints and rhetorical innovation, and (3) to overcome the related paradox of rhetorical agency in the face of normalizing communities. A second major thrust of *Where's the Rhetoric?*, then, is to leverage the percolative approach so as to provide new purchase on long-standing theoretical questions, particularly in RGS.

Chapter 3 moves in this direction, putting the Bergsonian lineage to work for RGS. Specifically, the chapter traces the influence of Bergson's thought on early Burke and Miller's "Genre as Social Action." In so doing, the chapter outlines a more new materialist version of genre as social action (GASA) under the name *genre as process* (GAP). Thus, chapter 3 works to demonstrate the utility of GAP for addressing the relationship between genre and medium through a close reading of selected new-media artifacts. Specifically, the chapter explores the tweetorial, an emerging genre of threaded tweets designed to simultaneously instruct and irritate opposing interlocutors.

Chapter 4 builds on the work of chapter 3 to argue that GAP is an inherently new materialist theoretical apparatus designed to better account for reciprocal and emergent agencies in (rhetorical) events. In making this argument, the chapter offers contrastive readings of contemporary RNM alongside the proto-new-materialist thought of Bergson and Burke. In so doing, I argue that despite RNM's commitment to new materialisms, broadly, it still too often leverages a modernist theory of the human. The result exacerbates long-standing debates over the nature of rhetorical agency. Ultimately, I argue that the posthuman approach to rhetorical agency found in Bergson and Burke provides the kind of theoretical foundation that can more reciprocally account for both agency and its barriers.

Chapter 5 attends to the long-standing problem of genre innovation. It begins with an analysis of extant research in RGS and demonstrates that despite the dictates of genre theory, much of RGS scholarship tacitly assumes that fidelity to genre conventions will lead to success while violation of conventions will lead to failure. This presumption renders the possibility of genre innovation almost nil. In contrast, the GAP framework, along with its focus on Bergson's and Burke's posthumanism, centers scholarly attention more firmly on the dynamic interactions within and between rhetorical and situational processes. In so doing, it allows for a new model of rhetorical innovation grounded in "fit forging," a process of configuring the situation itself as part of the response. Ultimately, chapter 5 demonstrates the applicability of the GAP framework to the problem of genre innovation through an ethnography of a practicing new-media designer. The chapter traces the invention of a novel hybrid genre, and in so doing explores the complex interactions of fidelity, violation, success, failure, and innovation.

Chapter 6 leverages the theoretical insights of the prior chapters to make a case for CR in RGS. In so doing, the chapter begins with a percolative reflection on Bergson's methodological recommendations in contrast with contemporary epistemological commitments in rhetoric. Specifically, chapter 6 explores Bergson's recommendations for a hybrid intuitive-abstractive methodology grounded in both philosophical and scientific approaches for inquiry designed to lead to action. The chapter further explores how the intuition-abstraction dialectic is extended in Latour's account of science-in-the-making and uses this epistemology as a foundation for exploring content analysis and interrater reliability in rhetorical studies. Through building on rhetoric's most widely accepted mode of quantitative inquiry, chapter 6 establishes a new practical and epistemological foundation for CR, especially within RGS. This theoretical work provides the foundation for a more complete embrace of Miller's argument that genre evaluation should be understood through the lens of population dynamics. CR methodologies are precisely what makes this kind of inquiry possible and, in so doing, adds a new level of abstraction to traditionally intuitive rhetorical methodologies.

Chapter 7 provides a demonstration of how inductive and abstractive rhetorical methodologies can be used in tandem to advance inquiry. The chapter continues *Where's the Rhetoric?*'s exploration of the dynamics of success, failure, fidelity, and novelty through exploring related cases from the 2016 presidential primary. Specifically, chapter 7 uses dueling intuitive and abstractive analyses of 2016 primary rhetoric to investigate the hypothesis that electioneering discourse has reached a newfound nadir of negativity. The chapter offers a computational sentiment analysis of all primary debates held over the past eight years and presents the findings in dialogue with a close reading of an infamous Marco Rubio stump speech. Ultimately, the chapter demonstrates how intuitive and abstractive accounts can work productively hand-in-glove to advance inquiry. Furthermore, the analyses demonstrate how genre-analytic activity, itself, can become an influential vector in genred discourses.

Chapter 8 closes *Where's the Rhetoric?* with (1) a final reflection on the problems of boundary work in the discipline, (2) an illustrative demonstration of integrated intuitive/abstractive inquiry with respect to the book itself, and (3) a rumination about new horizons of inquiry made possible in a unified field. Chapter 8 argues that the biggest problem with traditional rhetoric, RNM, and CR alike is that they are evangelical. These intellectual initiatives are supported by totalizing theories that often—both tacitly and explicitly—suggest that all rhetorical problems should be subsumed under a single preferred rubric. In so doing, RNM and CR further exacerbate boundary tensions with more traditional approaches. As a corrective, the chapter provides an action-oriented distillation of the key insights of the book. The aim here is to demonstrate that no single rhetorical methodology can be suitable for every problem[7] and that a unified rhetorical field cannot be a homogenous enterprise. Traditional approaches, RNM, and CR must work alongside one another to advance the discipline and effectively engage new horizons of inquiry.

---

7. If all you have is a hammer, everything starts to look like a nail. This is all the more problematic if your hammers are Heideggerian.

CHAPTER 2

THE BERGSON LEGACY

LET ME BEGIN by thanking you for sticking with this until the start of chapter 2. As I mentioned in chapter 1, I know full well that the burden of proof I have assumed in *Where's the Rhetoric?* is quite high. For most readers, my argument will be seen as profoundly incredible (as in *not* credible), if not downright preposterous. To suggest that the origins of RNM trace back to Burke's use of Bergson and were fully realized in Miller's "Genre as Social Action" is anathema to rhetorical traditionalists and new materialists alike. It flies in the face of boundary rhetorics on both sides and constitutes a threat to disciplinary identity for some and a challenge to priority claims for others. Of course, boundary, identity, and priority claims are not the only sources of resistance that will emerge here. My construal of Burke and Miller as new materialists also runs directly contrary to received wisdom about the place of these pivotal thinkers in the history of rhetorical theory. What's more—and please forgive the indelicacy of this statement—Carolyn Miller is alive and well and available to comment on her own place in the field's history. Let me admit right here and upfront that Miller disagrees with my interpretation of her work. She has most graciously read an early, partial version of my argument and was ultimately unpersuaded. Any reasonable scholar, at this point, might be well advised to consider the argument dead on arrival. Apparently, I am no reasonable scholar.

Most hedging and joking aside, I continue to believe that there is real value in (re)reading Bergson-Burke-Miller as a lineage. Doing so has the potential to provide a critical intervention at a time of disciplinary fracture. That is, it becomes possible to excavate a disciplinary foundation for RNM and (eventually) CR. Reinterpreting Burke in the light of his Bergsonian influences and Miller through her Bergsonian-Burkean influences can usefully surface the points of overlap and synergy between traditional rhetorical inquiry and RNM. This reinterpretation is assuredly different from the received wisdom as well as from Miller's own account of her work. Indeed, it's more than possible that this interpretation is flat-out wrong. Nevertheless, I will beg your kind indulgence as I proceed with this ostensibly ill-advised endeavor.

As mentioned previously, there is ample bibliographic and archival evidence to indicate that Henri Bergson was—and in some circles, continues to be—a profoundly influential figure in new materialist thought. The primary aim of this chapter is to make the case that he has also been—and in some circles, continues to be—a profoundly influential figure in rhetorical thought. This latter argument is, of course, much less recognized. As I pursue this line of inquiry, this chapter will proceed in three primary sections: (1) I begin with a brief account of Bergson himself, his place in history, and his place in philosophy. (2) I then transition to a circulatory[1] citation history of Bergson's influence on continental new materialisms and American rhetoric. (3) I devote the next section of the chapter to a percolative analysis of Bergsonian themes in (rhetorical) new materialisms. The principal aim of these efforts is to help describe how Bergsonian thought circulated through the previously described citation networks and to account for where it remains in extant rhetoric and new materialisms. These analyses will provide the intellectual foundation for subsequent chapters that return to genre as a more central concern for rhetorical inquiry.

Henri Himself

The descendent of Polish-Jewish immigrants to France, Henri Bergson was born in Paris in 1859. Intergenerational family wealth provided him access to an excellent education, which culminated in study at the École normale supérieure and the University of Paris. Not long after his graduation with an

---

1. See the discussion of Jensen's two modes (circulation and percolation) of historiography in chapter 1.

agrégation de philosophie in 1881, he was appointed to a series of secondary school teaching posts which ultimately led to a position as Professor of Rhetoric at lycée Henri-Quatre in Paris. Much of Bergson's early career was consumed with his attempts to secure an academic post at a top-tier French university. Along the way, he published *Matter and Memory* (1896/1911), the reception of which eventually helped him to earn the Chair in Ancient Philosophy at the Collège de France in 1900. From this position, Bergson published several important works including his "Introduction to Metaphysics" (1903/1946), *Creative Evolution* (1911), and "Philosophical Intuition" (1911/1946).

Bergson's work was very well known during his life and tremendously respected in certain circles. William James once wrote Bergson to congratulate him on *Matter and Memory*, comparing it favorably to both Berkeley's *Principles of Human Knowledge* and Kant's *Critique of Pure Reason*. In 1912 Bertrand Russell penned an essay in *The Monist* describing Bergson's thought as the ultimate rejection of empiricist, realist, and idealist divisions in philosophy. (This account was not intended to be entirely laudatory.) Indeed, there is some evidence to suggest that it was Whitehead's encounter with Bergson's scholarship that caused Whitehead to part ways with Russell and reject logical positivism.[2] In 1914 Bergson was appointed to the Académie française. Here was, perhaps, where Bergson's life and accomplishments really begin to deviate from what one might expect from even the most successful academic philosophers. In 1917 he became a Special Envoy to the US and met with President Wilson to urge the US's entry into World War I. In 1922 he and Albert Einstein convened a debate over competing views on relativity, and in 1928 he received the Nobel Prize for Literature. All in all, a pretty impressive CV.

Despite this record of extraordinary accomplishments, and the academic fame he enjoyed during his lifetime, Bergson is no longer especially well known or widely read in contemporary philosophical circles. Both Deleuze's (1991) *Bergsonism* and Keith Ansell Pearson and John Ó Maoilearca's (2002) *Henri Bergson: Key Writings* lament this fact and hope the books will help

---

2. As Robinson (2009) notes, Whitehead's thought was profoundly influenced and transformed by Bergson. This shift was so significant that it helped to provoke a sort of feud between Bergson and Bertrand Russell: "If Russell was an important figure in shaping Whitehead's philosophical fortunes this is all the more the case with Bergson, beginning with the now famous Russellian jest that 'intuition is at its best bats, bees and Bergson.' Despite several commentators pointing to various affinities between Russell and Bergson, it appears that his own prejudices prevented him from seeing them. Indeed, some have suggested that Russell almost single-handedly ruined Bergson's reputation in Anglo-American circles, even waging something of a campaign against him." (p. 9)

redress this state of affairs. However, with the advent and increasing popularity of new materialisms, Bergsonian ideas are enjoying something of a resurgence in certain areas. As Pearson and Ó Maoilearca note in their introductory remarks:

> [*Matter & Memory*] is a text that anticipates many of the recent moves made in the philosophy of mind, such as the stress on approaching perception not in terms representational but rather as bound up with the action and movement of a body, and on consciousness as an emergent property of a network or assemblage of components; it is only abstractly that we can separate brain, body, and world. (p. 15)

Certainly, these connections are substantively made in Deleuze's work, most notably in *Difference and Repetition* (1968/1994) and with Felix Guattari in *A Thousand Plateaus* (1987). Indeed, both texts specifically note their indebtedness to Bergson's thought. Additionally, Jane Bennett's (2010) more recent *Vibrant Matter* makes productive use of Bergson's *élan vitale* in the development of her "political ecology of things." Indeed, even within RNM, there are a few significant references to Bergson's thought. Boyle's *Rhetoric as Posthuman Practice* deploys a version of Bergson in the Deleuzian tradition, and Cooper's *The Animal Who Writes* spends some time addressing Bergson within a Whiteheadian idiom. However, neither of these works engages Bergson's oeuvre through the Bergson-Burke-Miller trajectory that will be so important to *Where's the Rhetoric?* (about which more below).

While much of *Where's the Rhetoric?* is devoted to elucidating Bergson's thought, especially with respect to its relationship with RGS, it is appropriate here to make a few comments about Bergson's ideas in their own right. As with any prolific scholar, there are many different, intersecting trajectories in Bergson's oeuvre. In the broadest strokes, he can be characterized as a committed metaphysician with enduring interests in the very nature of time as well as the proper foundation for the methodologies of metaphysical inquiry. As mentioned above, Bergson's work was both integrative and iconoclastic. He strongly rejected the deep divides between what we would now call modernist and postmodern epistemologies. In *Matter and Memory* (1896/1911), he argues that "neither realism nor idealism can succeed, because neither of the two systems of images is implied in the other, and each of them is sufficient to itself" (p. 15). For Bergson, the presumptive divisions meant that neither project was viable, and thus he "sidesteps the frozen essentialism of reductive naturalists as well as the liquid relativism of culturalists" (Pearson & Ó Maoilearca, 2002, p. 47).

Within this antidualistic framework, Bergson was deeply invested in the problem of time. His writing suggests that philosophers and physicists alike commit a fundamental category error when they insist on reading time through the lens of space. That is, whenever it is explored in Western thought, time is mentally plotted on a physical plane—the space between marks on a clock, an arrow of directionality, or as the fourth dimension on a Cartesian coordinate plane. As he argues in *Time and Free Will*:

> It follows from this analysis that space alone is homogeneous, that objects in space form a discrete multiplicity, and that every discrete multiplicity is got by a process of unfolding in space. It also follows that there is neither duration nor even succession in space, if we give to these words the meaning in which consciousness takes them: each of the so-called successive states of the external world exists alone; their multiplicity is real only for a consciousness that can first retain them and then set them side by side by externalizing them in relation to one another. (Bergson, 1910/1960, pp. 120–121)

The notion of duration (*la durée*) was one of Bergson's key contributions to the philosophy of time. While this tricky concept will be discussed somewhat more in chapters 4 and 5, at present it will be sufficient to think of duration as the intersection of time and consciousness. It is the psychological experience of continuity in the face of the disunity of successive events. While the psychological aspects of duration have largely been left aside, both Whitehead and many new materialists take very seriously the notion of the disunity of successive events as a foundational move in new nonmodern metaphysics. Bergson's theory of time and his larger antidualist commitments foster an attunement to process, becoming, multiplicity, and the affective entanglement of humans and nonhumans. The anchors of these moves can be seen in the passage above. In separating time and space, Bergson's theory of time emerges as a function of the complex entanglement of psychology and materiality.

Furthermore, as mentioned above, a second major thrust of Bergson's work is methodological. In an era dominated by the rise of scientific and mathematical reasoning, Bergson felt compelled to develop an authentically and uniquely metaphysical methodology which he dubbed *intuition*. As Deleuze (1966/1991) remarks in *Bergsonism*, "Intuition is the method of Bergsonism. Intuition is neither a feeling, an inspiration, nor a disordered sympathy, but a fully developed method, one of the most fully developed methods in philosophy" (p. 13). Intuition and its appropriation by Whitehead and Burke will become a more central theme of *Where's the Rhetoric?* For now, suffice it to say that intuition is both methodological and metaphysical. Bergson's ideas about the right way to do philosophy emerge from that philosophy itself. The complex psychological-material entanglements of Bergsonian duration are the wellspring of his intuition. More details to follow, but for now, I will return to the proper circulatory and percolative work of this chapter.

Two Bergsonian Lineages

As noted in the introduction, Bergson's thought has circulated through rhetoric and new materialisms through multiple—sometimes subtle, sometimes surprising, sometimes complex—vectors. To help distill this complexity into a more accessible form, I have developed an illustrative citation network analysis of Bergsonian lineages in rhetoric and new materialisms (Figure 2.1). This network map is, as just noted, illustrative and therefore incomplete. The map was generated by identifying explicit citation trajectories that lead from Bergson to two avatars of contemporary new materialisms and RGS (Bruno Latour and Carolyn Miller, respectively). The primary goal here was to provide a snapshot of the two Bergsonian legacies: (1) a more familiar right-branching legacy that passes through Whitehead, Deleuze, and Latour to create mainstream new materialisms as they are widely known; and (2) a less familiar left-branching trajectory involving Burke, Schütz, and Miller.

In reading the map, you will see that each line of articulation denotes an explicit citation. However, insofar as this bibliographic history spans nearly one hundred years and multiple disciplines, the nature of these citations is not always the same. From later works by Miller or Latour, for example, we see what we expect: formal citations in recognized citation styles. Alternatively, the earlier works by Whitehead and Stephen make frequent reference to Bergson and his ideas but do not always cite the exact source from which those citations came. In these cases, I have done my best to intuit the proper source based on the content descriptions provided. There is one case where the line of articulation is not quite a citation history: the trajectory from Julien Benda's *Le Bergsonisme* to Burke's (1935) *Permanence and Change*. I identified this line of influence through exploring Burke's collected papers with the Pennsylvania State University Library. Several citations were elided between drafts of *Attitudes Toward History* (1937/1984) and *Counter-Statement* (1931/1968), even though the ideas that originally referenced Bergson remain in the final drafts. The evidence detailing these connections is below.

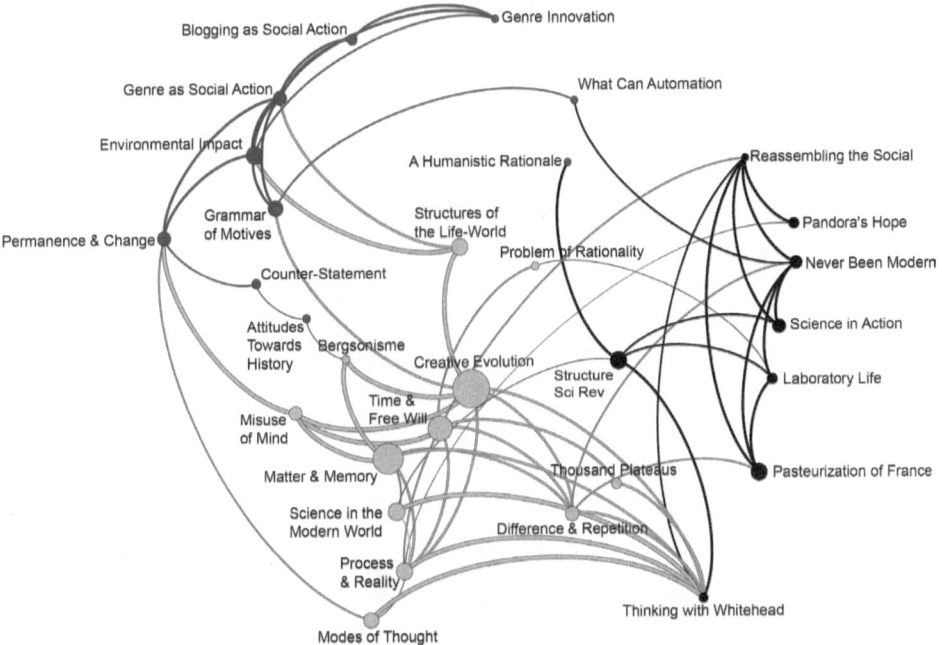

FIGURE 2.1. Bergsonian circulation map. Network diagram of Bergson's rhetorical (left) and new materialist (right) legacies. Note: *Le Bergsonisme* is Benda's (1912) and not Deleuze's later volume. This diagram is read clockwise; so beginning at any given node, follow a curved line clockwise to trace lines of influence. Network data are available in tabular form in the appendix.

Finally, you will note that the nodes representing each scholarly work vary in size. The size of each node is a function of its weighted average out-degree. This is a calculation based on the relative influence of each node in the network. So, if a text is cited by more future texts, its node will be larger. Second-order citations also factor into node size. When a text that cites a prior text is well cited, some of that "weight" will reflect back on the original source text. The weight of each connection is further influenced by values I added to indicate the strength of the attribution. I assigned citation weights on a scale of 1 to 10. So-called drive-by citations received a 1, cases of significant attribution received a 5, and cases where a citation was listed multiple times throughout a work and couched in effusive praise received a 10. Ultimately, from even a hasty perusal of Figure 2.1, it should be clear that Bergson is a powerful contributor to both rhetorical and new materialist networks. The vast majority of the citations represented were not minimal, and the aggregate effect of the weighted average out-degree highlights how impactful *Matter and Memory* and *Creative Evolution* in particular have been on both networks.

First-Order Connections

This circulation map is populated by quite a few figures who both (a) were directly influenced by Bergson and (b) make the attribution explicitly. I shall begin by elaborating these connections before moving on to the second- and third-order Bergsonian influences. Direct and enthusiastic attributions to Bergson's thought span the multiple disciplinary areas that compose our citation network. Bergson's ideas figure prominently in the scholarship of Whitehead, Schütz, Burke, and Deleuze. None of these thinkers are shy about making their connection with Bergson clear. Indeed, their appropriations of Bergson are often peppered with praise.

The lines of articulation along Bergson's right-branching legacy are easily the most well known, even if they have "rarely been studied" (Robinson, 2009, p. 2). The recent edited collection just cited, *Deleuze, Whitehead, Bergson: Rhizomatic Connections*, works to address this gap, and in so doing offers a careful analysis of the many relationships between these three thinkers. However, as the introduction to that work notes:

> The tendency to neglect, distort and marginalize all three philosophers and the relations between them is an outcome of a set of assumptions, attitudes and prejudices toward certain modes and styles of philosophizing that could be said to be characteristic of the divisions and tensions within twentieth-century philosophy. This has not only left each philosopher out of the "mainstream" canons of Anglo-American professional philosophy, it has also hindered a fuller assessment of their approaches to the perennial issues in Western philosophy and obscured the often subterranean connections between them. (Robinson, 2009, p. 3)

Despite this broad erasure it is nevertheless possible to excavate many of these rhizomatic connections from the bibliographic and historiographic record.

In some cases, the work is quite easy. For example, as Robinson (2009) also notes, "Bergson and Whitehead read and admired each other's work and each comment on the other in their published books. In numerous instances Whitehead explicitly links his own key ideas to Bergson, connecting, for example, the very idea of 'process' with what he called Bergsonian 'time'" (p. 2). Indeed, Whitehead's (1929/1978) *Process and Reality* begins with a significant attribution to Bergson (alongside others):

> I am also greatly indebted to Bergson, William James, and John Dewey. One of my preoccupations has been to rescue their type of thought from the charge of anti-intellectualism, which rightly or wrongly has been associated with it. (p. xii)

Bergson's work is referenced favorably throughout *Process & Reality*. One goal of Whitehead's text is to develop a theory of "prehensions," which we might broadly understand as the various modes of entanglement between entities in the processes of becoming (more about this to follow). In so doing, Whitehead essentially presents Bergson's notion of intuition as a special form of prehension, one that requires certain complex assemblages (brains) engaging in certain processes (conceptualization) (p. 33). Furthermore, like Bergson, Whitehead is committed to an epistemology and methodology that is continuous with his metaphysics. Thus, inquiry must be understood as a special case within the broad range of possible modes of material entanglement.

Likewise, Deleuze is also substantively, and quite famously, connected to Bergson's right branch. Bergson's complete works are cited in Deleuze's doctoral dissertation, *Difference and Repetition*. Furthermore, Deleuze has written an entire book on Bergson's metaphysical methodology under the title *Bergsonism*. However, it is important to note here that Deleuze's relationship with Bergson is better described as adaptation and transformation rather than faithful appropriation. Indeed, Deleuze (1966/1991) describes his own use of Bergson's thought as a form of "buggery." Despite this characterization, scholars commenting on the connection between Deleuze and Bergson are often quick to note the significant similarities between Deleuzian assemblages and Bergson's metaphysics. While the fine-grained details of this line of scholarship will not find a primary place in *Where's the Rhetoric?*, Deleuze is, nevertheless, one of the principal vectors by which Bergsonian thought propagated throughout new materialisms. As Robinson (2009) indicates, "Deleuze's own 'Bergsonism' is, in part, responsible for the resurgence of interest in Bergson's work and the 'new' Bergson during the last 15 years or so" (p. 2).

Another powerful Bergsonian pathway helps to establish his left-branching legacy. This connection can be found in the Austrian social philosopher and phenomenologist Alfred Schütz. His early work was devoted to developing a Bergsonian account of social theory. Although the larger trajectory of Schütz's scholarship has been described as a "transition from a Bergsonian to a Husserlian phase" (Schütz, 1996b, p. 3), Schütz never fully abandoned Bergson. Even in his later work, Schütz (1944/1996a) was quite laudatory, noting, for example, in 1944, that "Bergson's philosophy has taught us, in full clarity, the double aspect of movement" (p. 249). Furthermore, in his very last scholarly works, toward the end of his life in 1959, Schütz (1958/1996b) endeavored to blend Bergsonian insights with other philosophical traditions:

> The main topic to be elaborated can be stated in rather simple terms: Philosophers as different as William James, Bergson, Dewey, Husserl and Whitehead agree that the common-sense knowledge of everyday life is the unquestioned but always questionable background within which inquiry starts and within which alone it can be carried out. (p. 71)

Rather than a transition from one phase to the next, the long arc of Schütz's scholarship might better be described as a fusion of Bergsonian intuition with the phenomenological tradition. It is this blending that would ultimately be so impactful in the development of Miller's genre as social action.

Second-Order and Third-Order Connections

Bergson's impact on both contemporary new materialism and RGS proper is predominantly via second-order connections. While Deleuze, Whitehead, Burke, and Schütz were all very directly engaged with Bergson's scholarship, to the best of my knowledge neither Miller nor Latour has substantively cited Bergson's oeuvre despite being deeply connected to it. The importance of Bergson to Deleuze, Whitehead, Burke, and Schütz and the similar importance of Deleuze and (later) Whitehead to Latour and Burke and Schütz to Miller notwithstanding, the Bergsonian legacy is largely lost. No doubt this has a lot to do with the general decline in interest in Bergson in the latter half of the last century. However, another significant reason, no doubt, has to do with Miller and Latour largely receiving Bergson through second- and third-order vectors.

With respect to new materialisms, many of Bergson's ideas were translated through Deleuze and Whitehead. While Deleuze's influence on new materialisms has always been clearly recognized, Whitehead's influence has historically been much less remarked. Nevertheless, the specter of Whitehead arises regularly in new materialist thought. I say "specter" because with the notable exceptions of Isabelle Stengers (and very recently Marylin Cooper), few—if any—new materialists have devoted themselves to substantively and studiously building on Whitehead's insights. Nevertheless, Whitehead has been profoundly influential in the area. Indeed, Whiteheadian insights propagate through trajectories of thought, not always recognized by the authors themselves. As Latour put it in the closing lines from his forward to Stengers's (2011) *Thinking with Whitehead*:

> I have always felt that Whitehead-watching had a lot to do with whale-watching as it is practiced, for instance, on the coast of San Diego in the winter. You stay on a boat for hours, see nothing, and suddenly, "There she blows, she blows!" and, swiftly the whale disappears again. But with Stengers at the helm, the little ship is able to predict with great accuracy where the whale will emerge again, in a few hours. Come on board, prepare your binoculars, and be confident in the captain's watch. (p. xv)

The metaphor is very apropos for my work here. Latour, famously, disavows direct knowledge of Whitehead in his early scholarship. Speaking in a seminar about his early work on irreductions, Latour (2001) remarked:

> Je ne connaissais pas Whitehead ... ce qui m'aurait économisé énormément de temps ... que je suis devenu Whiteheadien depuis grace à [Isabelle] Stengers.
>
> I did not know Whitehead ... [knowing him] would have saved me much time as I have since become Whiteheadian, thanks to [Isabelle] Stengers.

Even though his direct encounter with Whitehead would not come until later in his scholarship, Latour's work was incubated in an intellectual climate that was at least Whiteheadesque if not Whiteheadian. Deleuzian rhizomatics and early actor-network theory (ANT) à la John Law and Michel Callon share a great deal with Whitehead's process philosophy. This connection is, of course, via the Bergsonian lineage.

Indeed, a partial account of early Latourian thought might be described as a reintegration of second-order Bergsonian trajectories. Latour and Woolgar's (1979/2013) *Laboratory Life* is offered as a sociological response to the Popper-Kuhn debates of the era (p. 30). However, rather than engage directly in the philosophical speculations over falsificationist or paradigmatic accounts of scientific inquiry, Latour and Woolgar criticize both approaches for the ignorance of actual scientific practice and proceed to "sidestep these general issues and instead concentrate on specific problems the scientific practitioner and the observer of scientific activity may have in common" (p. 30). Interestingly, toward the end of *Laboratory Life*, the authors make special note of the similarity of their approach and findings with those of Schütz (p. 153). So, one theme of *Laboratory Life* is the rejection of Kuhnian thought in favor of something like Schütz's approach.

Of course, both Kuhn and Schütz figure centrally in our bibliographic map of Bergsonian lineages. Bergson's direct influence on Schütz is detailed above, while his influence on Kuhn is owed to a second-order trajectory. Steve Fuller's (2000) philosophical history of Kuhn excavates this connection and shows how the theory of paradigm revolutions was significantly influenced by Whitehead's (1925/2011) *Science and the Modern World*, "a popularization of process metaphysics" (p. 302) which predated, but covered much the same territory as, *Process & Reality*. Appreciating this history allows us to see how *Laboratory Life* rejected the neoBergsonian Kuhn in favor of something like the neoBergsonian Schütz. What's more, Latour's later oeuvre continues this tradition. As he becomes increasingly dissatisfied with purely sociological explanations for scientific progress, Latour develops a new metaphysics increasingly indebted to neoBergsonian Deleuze and neoBergsonian Whitehead.

Moving to the main artery (if you will) of the left branch, we can also see that one of the most central rhetorical thinkers figures quite prominently in the Bergsonian lineage: Kenneth Burke. The earliest record I could find of Burke's engagement with Bergson is found attached to a March 1921 diary entry that ruminates on the audience's experience of literature. The entry follows a series wherein Burke is working to develop a theory of affective reception. The entire series is remarkably reminiscent of Bergson and centers around a theory of "progression" which he defines as "a sequence of related discoveries . . . each discovery coming as one-step beyond the accumulation of proceeding discoveries" (Burke, 1921, p. 1). An undated fragment after this entry quotes at length from French literary critic Julien Benda's (1912) *Le Bergsonisme ou Une Philosophie de la Mobilité*. The transcribed passage principally describes the novelty and radical nature of Bergson's intuition detailing how it overturns long-held presuppositions about the nature of intelligence and inquiry.[3] The excerpted passage ends with a brief note by Burke himself celebrating Benda's appropriation of Bergson:

---

3. Il tient d'abord à ce qu'il institue le primat du sentiment sur l'idée, du féminin sur le viril, du trouble sur le sévère, du musical sur le plastique. (De ce point de vue la gloire de M. Bergson est le même fait que celle de M. Bataille.) Il tient surtout à ce qu'il proclame la supériorité du vagissement sur la parole, du tâtonnement sur la maîtrise, de

Elsewhere, Benda has pointed out that there is certainly some difference between the "intuition" of a chicken breaking open its egg and the "intuition" of a geometer discovering the relations of a surface. The latter is simply open to the activities of the intelligence; the former is a true intuition, to such an extent that it does not "know itself." That peculiar mixture of dialectic and rhetoric which makes Benda so formidable. For he has met his opponents on logical grounds, and then, since they are professional deniers of logic, he has met them on literary grounds; which is to say; he has slain them with a wicked tongue. The parallels he brings up with the Alexandrians. The peculiarly deadline parallel between Bergson's reasoning by means of loose images, metaphors, analogies, and the Alexandrian weakness for allegorism. (Burke, n.d.-b, p. 1)

The ideas in this early essay find their final form in *Attitudes Toward History* and *Counter-Statement*. Burke had clearly found much to admire in Bergson and neoBergsonian ideas. Indeed, these ideas significantly animate *Permanence and Change*.

Permanence and Change (1935) actually opens with an epigraph from Whitehead's *Modes of Thought*: "Sharp-cut scientific classifications are essential for scientific method, but they are dangerous for philosophy. Such classification hides the truth that the different modes of natural existence shade off into each other" (p. 3). While it may not be immediately clear how much this passage is indebted to the Bergsonian tradition, philosopher F. Bradford Wallack's (1980) analysis of this exact passage highlights its connection to what would become known as new materialisms. As he writes:

This passage affords a number of examples of actual entities: moments in the life-histories of animals; moments in the life-histories of vegetables;

---

l'esprit qui se cherche sur l'esprit qui se possède : on conçoit que des docteurs brouillons, des bardes embourbés, des poétesses mobiles, que tous les incapables d'une pensée possédée se soient rués au triomphe d'une philosophie qui érige leur inquiétude en sommet esthétique et leur jette en pâture l'esprit maître de lui. Tous ces gens-là n'avaient pour eux que des pontifes de ruelle ou des archontes d'estaminet. Ils ont maintenant un "philosophe" ! Ils n'ont jamais été à pareille fête. . . . Il est clair que si on appelle Intuition ce que nous appelons Intelligence et Intelligence ce que nous appelons sottise, le cas de l'Intelligence est mauvais . . . On nous dit que c'est ce fonctionnement bureaucratique de l'esprit ce que les " sociologues " appellent l'Intelligence . . . Mais alors qu'on dise : M. Bergson a ruiné ce que les sociologues appellent l'Intelligence. Qu'on ne dise pas : il a ruiné l'Intelligence. On conviendra que c'est moins grave (Benda, as quoted in Burke, n.d.-b).

moments in the life-histories of cells; moments in the life-histories of large-scale inorganic enduring objects; infra-molecular moments. (p. 28)

Burke's more direct use of Bergson in *Permanence and Change* is also mediated through secondary literature. Specifically, he draws on Karin Stephen's (1922) *Misuse of Mind,* an English-language popularization of Bergson's ideas. Significantly, Burke devotes an entire section of his famous chapter on perspective by incongruity to describing the importance of Bergson's thought for his own. At the outset of this section he identifies Bergson's metaphysical method as the closest antecedent to perspective by incongruity:

> The formulations of the philosopher Henri Bergson came nearest to a central statement of incongruity as a *system*. Nietzsche *exemplified* the procedure consistently enough—but he did not, to my knowledge, give us a specific rationalization of it. The rationalization is to be found at its clearest I believe, in a volume entitled *The Misuse of Mind* (a work by Mrs. Karin Stephen), in which Bergson's doctrine is concisely rephrased. (Burke, 1935, p. 122)

What's more—Burke's interest in Bergson was no mere fleeting moment. By *A Grammar of Motives* (1945/1969), Burke is citing the original *Creative Evolution* and describing his project as, in part, an effort to "make [*Creative Evolution*] over dramatistically" (p. 295).

Finally, we reach the provisional terminus of the left branch (in Miller), where something remarkably similar to the Latourian neoBergsonian fusion happens in the development of GASA. Dissatisfied with extant theories of the rhetorical situation and rhetorical genre, Miller develops a radical new approach to genre that builds on an innovative fusion of Burke and Schütz. The influence of Burke on Miller's thought is, of course, quite well known. Her famous 1984 article cites and makes extensive use of *Permanence and Change* and *Grammar of Motives*. However, her indebtedness to Schütz is much less recognized. This is most likely due to an unfortunate, yet enduring, lack of interest in Schütz among rhetoricians. An early version of "Genre as Social Action" that appears in Miller's (1980) dissertation shows the centrality of Schütz's ideas to genre as social action. Specifically, Miller uses his work to introduce two central concepts into her developing theory. In the first case, she uses Schütz to redefine the rhetorical situation, itself:

> The sociologist Alfred Schütz provides an understanding of situation that is both helpful and appropriate to rhetorical inquiry. It is appropriate because

it is based on "a phenomenological account of knowledge as basically social" and thus necessarily based on communication. (Miller, 1980, p. 36)

Shortly thereafter, Miller (1980) further leverages Schütz's scholarship to hone her notion of typification:

> We typify, according to Schütz, that which is "relevant" (p. 234), that which has an effect beyond itself, that which has meaning. Typification, in turn, creates further relevance by assigning meaning to new experience. (p. 48)

Schütz's theories of situations and typification can both be traced back to Bergsonian theory. Since these concepts are much more central to the larger project of this book, the full details will be elucidated in the chapters to come.

Unfortunately, as mentioned above, even though the ideas persisted, references to Schütz were significantly minimized in the revision of the dissertation chapter into an article. As Miller notes in an interview on the emergence of GASA, one of the *QJS* readers "among other things, did not like my use of Alfred Schütz, suggested that I drop the sections on literary genres, drop the Halliday paragraphs, and said the exigence section was 'irrelevant to genre and you need evidence and examples'" (Dryer, 2015). Indeed, here we see a textbook example of the kinds of occluded boundary work discussed in chapter 1. Only by virtue of the retrospective interview do we learn how influential the presumptively "non-rhetorical" Schütz was on Miller's thought. While some of these references do survive to the final article, it's clear that the treatment of Schütz in Miller's germinal article is much diminished compared with her dissertation. Regardless of this minimization, once again we have a case where neoBergsonian meets neoBergsonian—this time in the crucible of Miller's early work on genre. The ultimate result is a theory of genre that is remarkably Bergsonian, and therefore, remarkably new materialist in its cast and orientation.

(Rhetorical) New Materialisms

For the last chapter and a half, I've been making a whole heck of a lot of claims about X or Y being new materialist or, at the very least, new-materialist-*ish*. While new materialisms, themselves, were discussed briefly in the introduction, I have yet to really substantively engage this body of work. Here marks the pivot in this chapter to a more percolative mode of intellectual historiography. Rather than attempt to account for the ways in which specific lines of thought emanated from Bergson and circulated through subsequent theorists, I will focus on the many resonances between Bergson's ideas and extant (rhetorical) new materialisms. However, before I embark on this more percolative mode of inquiry, it seems appropriate to explain precisely what I mean by new materialisms. (As mentioned in the introduction, there are reasonable disagreements over the term.) This will be a tricky undertaking, because one thing new materialists really have in common is their love of neologisms. Some of this is, quite honestly, academic branding. Broadly speaking, new materialisms are built on a shared diagnostic move—the identification of certain theoretical "errors" in the history of Western thought. Unfortunately, these errors are often so long-standing that sometimes new language is required to break our theoretical presumptions and habits of mind. Let's begin with some key terms:[4]

> **New Materialisms:** A loosely related body of theoretical initiatives bound together by a diagnostic consensus that (1) Western thought has been inappropriately dominated by certain problematic dualistic ways of thinking; (2) these ways of thinking inappropriately focus attention on the relationship between "humans" and "nonhumans," as discrete ontological categories; and (3) these ways of thinking lead to unethical and oppressive ways of approaching the world and its inhabitants. Proposed solutions to the diagnostic consensus frequently involve replacing dualistic metaphysics with a relational model.
> **Dualistic Metaphysics:** The universe is made up of more-or-less discrete entities that can be classified according to certain pre-existing types that exist in opposition with other pre-existing types, for example, mind/body, nature/culture, science/society, humans/nonhumans.
> **Relational Metaphysics:** The universe is not, as is so often assumed, made up of discrete objects that can be classified according to certain pre-existing types. Instead, all "entities" are complex systems of interrelated parts, nested in larger complex systems of interrelated parts, that cohere through active processes of becoming.

---

4. A complete citation history of new materialist thought is beyond the scope of this book. However, for those interested in exploring recent contributions to these ideas more fully, I would recommend Coole and Frost's edited collection *New Materialisms*. The introduction, in particular, provides a thoughtful and concise overview of the project. Additionally, for those interested in further exploring the diagnostic consensus and/or its relationship with postmodernism's similar aims, I recommend Latour's *We Have Never Been Modern*, Mol's *The Body Multiple*, and my own "Object-Oriented Ontology's Binary Duplication" (Graham, 2016).

Processes of Becoming: The complex systems that make up the universe do not persist in a stable state, more or less as they always were. Rather, complex systems are perpetually active, making and remaking themselves as subordinate and superordinate systems change around them.

Situated Action: Following the move from dualistic to relational metaphysics and the corresponding emphasis on processes of becoming, new materialists often make a subsequent move from representation or epistemology to situated action. Under a dualist metaphysics, the driving questions about how humans interact with an ontological separate world center around issues of how humans use language to represent the world and thus how humans "know" the world. Under a relational metaphysics, attention to humans centers on how humans-as-complex-systems participate in the processes of becoming at specific sites of activity.

At first blush, the landscape of theoretical constructs that make up (R)NM appears so vast and disarticulated that it can be difficult to identify any commonalities. A brief (and incomplete) accounting of the rhetorical and nonrhetorical varieties of new materialisms would include the following constructs:

NMs: Cyborg ontology, actor-network theory (ANT), the mangle of practice, companion species, multiple ontologies, agential realism, intra-activity, biocultural creatures.

RNMs: Ambient rhetoric, rhetorical-ontological inquiry, posthuman practice, enchantment ontology.

Despite the dizzying list of neologisms, all of the above listed initiatives are united by a similar founding theoretical commitment—viz., the rejection of dualist metaphysics. The most common stories we tell ourselves about the world position human actors at center stage. Humans, technology, and the world each have their assigned roles, and the human is (almost) always the hero. Long-standing intellectual conceits about the very nature of people, technology, and the world ground this narrative. It is these long-standing conceits that new materialisms reject. Instead, the project calls analysts to eschew preconceived notions about who or what does the doing in the world. For many working in this tradition, the basic methodological stance is that reality is an undifferentiated hot mess. It is the analyst's account that cuts it up into bits and pieces, determines the borders of the whos and the whats, and identifies the doers and the doings.

For example, Donna Haraway's cyborg anthropology rejects preconceived notions about hard dividing lines between humans and technology. Her pervasive rejection of binaries in *Modest_Witness* is clear. Accordingly, her focus is on an approach that "extravagantly exceeds the distinction between science and technology as well as those between nature and society, subjects and objects, and the natural and the artifactual that structured the imaginary time called modernity" (Haraway, 1997, p. 3). Of course, this very same commitment finds its way into RNM. Indeed, it is the founding move of Rickert's (2013) *Ambient Rhetoric*:

> This project suggests we take as provisional starting points the dissolution of the subject-object relation, the abandonment of representationalist theories of language, an appreciation of nonlinear dynamics and the processes of emergence, and the incorporation of the material world as integral to human action and interaction, including rhetorical arts. (p. xii)

With the rejection of metaphysical dualism at their core, new materialist theories focus on relational metaphysics and processes of becoming.

That is, if humans, nonhumans, socioeconomic systems, and technology are not located in binary opposition but rather are part of a more-or-less undifferentiated metaphysical hot mess, then questions immediately arise as to how what we might have once called *individual entities* come to be and interact with one another. The answers to these questions are as numerous as individual new materialists. Karen Barad's work is among the most instructive here. Her germinal *Meeting the Universe Halfway* leverages Niels Bohr's notion of quantum entanglement to provide an account of new materialisms that highlights its commitments to relational metaphysics and processes of becoming. As she writes:

> Bohr rejects the atomistic metaphysics that takes "things" as ontologically basic entities. For Bohr, things do not have inherently determinate boundaries or properties, and words do not have inherently determinate meanings. Bohr also calls into question the related Cartesian belief in the inherent distinction between subject and object, and knower and known. (Barad, 2007, p. 138)

With Bohr's rejection of atomistic metaphysics as a foundation, essential attributes or identities are not central to Barad's analyses. Rather, attributes and identities only exist as emergent properties of "intra-activity."

Barad's rejection of the more common *inter*activity is key here. Interactivity presupposes pre-existing relata that assemble. *Intra*-activity, in contrast, attunes us to the emergence as the foundation of materialization. Additionally, intra-activity attunes analysts to the unending processes of becoming inherent in materialization. Individual entities do not entangle and then become things. This would violate the rejection of atomism that grounds Barad's work. Rather,

> intra-actions are nonarbitrary, nondeterministic causal enactments through which matter-in-the-process-of-becoming is iteratively enfolded into its ongoing differential materialization. Such a dynamics is not marked by an exterior parameter called time, nor does it take place in a container called space. Rather, iterative intra-actions are the dynamics through which temporality and spatiality are produced and iteratively reconfigured in the materialization of phenomena and the (re)making of material-discursive boundaries and their constitutive exclusions. (Barad, 2007, p. 179)

This approach can, of course, be difficult to fully embrace. While it is fundamental to certain areas of physics, intra-activity flies in the face of many of our cultural preconceptions about matter, time, and space. Intra-activity is a powerful rejection of long-standing habits of thought and a radical attempt to ground inquiry in a new framework indebted to relationality and process. Nevertheless, Barad's agential realism substantive animates many of the rhetorical variants of new materialisms.

For example, Cooper's (2019) *Animal Who Writes* is built on a fusion of Baradian and Whiteheadian theory cantered on relational metaphysics and process of becoming. As she describes it:

> Enchantment ontology inspires a focus on how all writing begins in intra-action and is realized through accountability for what comes to be in the process. It is an ontology that requires a major shift in how we understand reality and ourselves. Instead of a world made up of individual entities, enchantment ontology envisions individuals as entangled in intra-active phenomena from which they co-emerge contingently in an ongoing process of becoming. (p. 9)

And here, of course, is where we will find some of the most powerful affinities between contemporary new materialisms, Bergson, and his early followers. In capitalizing on Whitehead's process philosophy, Cooper enlists the Bergsonian legacy for her project, albeit primarily through a second-order connection. The stakes for rhetoric, here, are significant. Indeed, a full embrace of relational metaphysics and process philosophy may well require attendant redefinitions of rhetoric itself. Both Laurie Gries and Christa Teston make this move explicitly, redefining our field in terms of intra-active processes of becoming:

> Rhetoric here, then, is conceived as a virtual-actual event that unfolds with time and space as things—whether they be images, pictures, books, movies, rocks, trees, or animals—enter into material relations with humans, technologies, and other entities. (Gries, 2015, p. 11)

> An ecological model of rhetoric characterizes "rhetoric" as a verb. A performance. A constant process of unpredictable unfolding. To study rhetoric, therefore, is to study flux and flow. To study rhetoric is to explore processes of becoming (Bohm 1981). (Teston, 2017, p. 2)

Finally, as mentioned above and invoked in the preceding passages, the new materialist embrace of relational metaphysics and processes of becoming usually leads to a focus on action over representation. Annemarie Mol's work on ontological politics and biomedical practices is instructive here. Humans *qua* systems act within multiple complex and localized systems, and these actions are part of the processes of becoming that shape local realities. The plural is key here, as Mol (1999) argues: "*Ontologies*: note that. Now the word needs to go in the plural. For, and this is the crucial move, if reality is *done*, and if it is historically, culturally and materially *located*, then it is also multiple. Realities have become *multiple*" (p. 75). If our default position is that reality is a function of complex systems engaged in processes of becoming, then the local instantiation of those complex systems gives rise to the local reality.

Perhaps no work in RNM so well exemplifies this tradition as the one that embraces "practice" in its title: Boyle's *Rhetoric as a Posthuman Practice*. In the book, Boyle responds to a series of theoretical questions that emerge from placing long-standing accounts of rhetorical practice in dialogue with the new materialist and posthuman turn. The book addresses these questions by substantially reimagining the nature of practice in a relational and processual idiom. Thus, Boyle (2018) redefines practice, itself, as "exercise of tendencies to activate greater capacities" (p. 5). As he further elaborates:

All bodies—a human body, a social network, pollination process, a communication infrastructure—become bodies by establishing sets of tendencies. These tendencies—be they commonplaces, networked protocols, cross speciated activity, hardware and software processes—can be exercised to create new capacities of interacting with and mediating other bodies. (p. 5)

While Boyle is more indebted to Deleuze and Simondon than to Mol, he nevertheless makes very similar intellectual moves in the development of his version of RNM.

This indebtedness is a key issue for *Where's the Rhetoric?*, and not just with respect to *Rhetoric as a Posthuman Practice*. The works of Rickert, Barnett, Gries, Teston, Boyle, and Cooper are broadly representative of the leading edge of RNM. They are the forefront of this intellectual initiative. Yet, they all replicate the logics of otherness described in the introduction. (So does my work, for that matter, in *The Politics of Pain Medicine*.) With the notable exception of Rickert's Heideggerian approach and Barnett's engagement with the classical tradition, theoretical innovation in RNM is largely driven by the importation of insights from the right branch of Bergson's legacy: Deleuze (Gries, Boyle, Cooper), Whitehead (Gries, Cooper), Latour (too many to name, but also me), Barad (Gries, Teston, Boyle, Cooper), and so forth. This is one of the most significant reasons why so much of RNM feels so strange. As I have argued elsewhere (Graham, 2015, 2016), the right-hand branch of Bergson's legacy is dominated by a deep rejection of rhetoric. That is, the new materialist turn in Latour, Mol, Barad, Coole, Frost, and others is explicitly positioned as an overturning of the previous turn, of the rhetorical turn. As a result, an RNM that embraces the right branch of Bergson's legacy must reverse-engineer a place for rhetoric in a tradition that fundamentally rejects the principle insights of our discipline.

And, of course, this is why excavating the left-hand branch is so important. As I have been arguing over the last chapter and a half, there already exists a continuous and contiguous *rhetorical* new materialist tradition that can be used to make the same theoretical moves but without the critical need to re-engineer rhetoric. Bergson's left-hand trajectory provides scholars in rhetoric broadly, and RNM specifically, a version of new materialisms that's already engineered to further rhetorical inquiry. Indeed, exploring this rich body of theoretical material is the primary work of this book. However, some preparatory work remains. While I have documented the existence of a robust citation history along Bergson's left branch, this is insufficient to prove that Bergson's new materialist insights survived through successive appropriation of his ideas. So, in what follows, I begin with an account of why it is so easy to misread an absence of new materialism in the left branch and then proceed to a more percolative account of the new materials insights within that branch.

Totalizing Postmodernisms

There's a famous story about Thomas Kuhn among historians of science. Apparently, he was attending a national conference in the discipline, and joined the audience for a panel on "Kuhnian thought." As it turns out, he was so enraged by the content and portrayal of his ideas that he shouted angrily "I am not a Kuhnian!" (Dyson, 1999, p. 16) and stormed out of the session. Recent and careful analyses of Kuhn's work support the veracity of this story. There is ample evidence to indicate that Kuhn was much more committed to materiality than his popular postmodern reception would indicate (Harris, 2010). Despite Kuhn's enthusiastic appropriation by postmodern social constructionists, this was never a project he supported. Even though Kuhn's theory of paradigm revolutions was partially indebted to Bergson through Whitehead, he was never quite new materialist either. All the same, this vignette is important because it helps to provide context for the postmodern era and the so-called linguistic turn. For a time, in humanities and social science academia, it didn't matter who you were or what you thought; you would largely be read as either postmodern or heretical. As a result, Bergsonian and neoBergsonian ideas were forcibly reread into a postmodern idiom.

One place where this happens most directly is in the work of Schütz. As mentioned previously, despite being initially devoted to developing a purely Bergsonian social philosophy, Schütz eventually became committed to integrating Bergson's ideas with phenomenology. A product of his era, Schütz thus postmodernized Bergson and, in part, denuded him of his new materialist commitments. This postmodern/linguistic focus becomes most clear in *The Structures of the Life-World* where he retreats from materialisms:

> It is important above all to stress that the orders of reality do not become constituted through the ontological structure of their Objects, but rather through the meaning of our experience. For this reason we prefer to speak not (as does James) of subuniverses of reality, but rather of finite provinces of meaning, upon each of which we could confer the aspect of reality. (Schütz & Luckmann, 1973, p. 23)

Although his commitments to Bergson's intuition, duration, and structuration persist, Schütz lifts these theoretical apparatuses off of Bergson's metaphysical foundation and, in so doing, ultimately rejects relational metaphysics and psychologizes processes of becoming. This postmodernist transformation will, of course, impact Miller's use of *The Structures of the Life-World* in her development of genre as social action. (About which, more below.) Nevertheless, Schütz's postmodern version of Bergsonian thought maintains the commitment to situated action which is a key area of connection across nearly all moments in our Bergsonian/neoBergsonian history. In the passage below, from *The Structures of the Life-World*, Schütz describes the centrality of situated action in his account of social behavior:

> In the natural attitude the lifeworldly stock of knowledge serves above all the purpose of determining and mastering actual situations. As the analysis of the relevance structures which determine the constitution and structure of the stock of knowledge has shown, this involves either the routine employment of habitual knowledge sedimented from past experiences or the explication and re-explication of past experiences and situations. The current stock of knowledge consequently operates either as an "automatic" pattern of conduct or as an explicit interpretational schema. (Schütz & Luckmann, p. 108)

As is the case with the more new materialist variants of neoBergsonian philosophy, here too we find the shift to situated action to be a result of construing human behavior as a function of mutually interpenetrating complex systems. For Schütz these systems are primarily linguistic, cultural, sociological, and psychological; nevertheless, there are clear parallels with the original Bergsonian formulation.

The postscript to the second edition of Latour and Woolgar's *Laboratory Life* helps underscore the pervasiveness of postmodern linguistic-turn commitments at the time. As many of my readers may recall, the subtitle of the first edition of *Laboratory Life* was *The Social Construction of Facts*. The "Social" was dropped in the second edition, in part, because Latour and Woolgar objected to the postmodern interpretation of their ideas in much the same way as did Kuhn. In a subsection entitled "The Demise of the 'Social,'" Latour and Woolgar (2013) write:

> A misunderstanding which has been more consequential with the expansion of social studies of science, concerns the use of the word "social." . . . So what does it mean to talk about "social" construction? There is no shame

in admitting that the term no longer has any meaning. "Social" retained meaning when used by Mertonians to define a realm of study which excluded considerations of "scientific" content. It also had meaning in the Edinburgh school's attempt to explain the technical content of science (by contrast with internalist explanations of technical content). In all such uses "social" was primarily a term of antagonism, one part of a binary opposition. But how useful is it once we accept that all interactions are social? What does the term "social" convey when it refers to a pen's inscription on graph paper, to the construction of a text and to the gradual elaboration of an amino-cadi chain? Not a lot. By demonstrating its pervasive applicability, the social study of science has rendered "social" devoid of any meaning (cf Latour 1986a and b). (p. 281)

By the time the second edition of *Laboratory Life* was published, Latour was committed to a more complete rejection of dualist metaphysics, and thus it was an important part of his project to reject postmodern dualisms alongside modernist dualisms.

It would be 1993 before Latour taught the anglophone world that "postmodernism is a symptom [of modernism], not a fresh solution" (p. 46). In *We Have Never Been Modern*, we find a compelling account of the birth of modernism and its twin projects of purification and hybridization. In providing this account, Latour (1993b) details how the modernist project enacts certain epistemological and ontological guarantees, under what he calls the "modern Constitution." These guarantees provided powerful theoretical constraints for postmodernism, despite that later project's avowed desire to overcome the limits of modernism. As Latour (1993b) describes it, postmodernism "lives under the modern Constitution, but it no longer believes in the guarantees the Constitution offers" (p. 46).

The modernist work of purification and its attendant constitutional guarantees are what concern my analysis here most directly. The work of purification is most evident in the establishment of the manifold modernist binaries: nature/culture; subject/object; mind/body; and so forth. As I have elaborated (Graham, 2016), these binaries end up being replicated in the supposed theoretical divide: modernism/postmodernism. Despite postmodernism's claims to reject binaries, the postmodern project, by-and-large, accepted those binaries and privileged "the other side" (Graham, 2016, p. 110). So, while modernism's driving theoretical heuristic is nature over culture and body over mind, postmodernism's heuristic is culture over nature and mind over body. Here we see what Latour (1993b) dubs the "third misunderstanding" of (post)modernism: "But if you are not talking about things-in-themselves or about humans-among-themselves, then you must be talking about discourse, representation, language, texts, rhetoric" (p. 5).

Bergson's Left-Branch Legacy

Even in the advent of new materialisms and RNM, it is profoundly difficult to read scholarship outside these (post)modern frameworks. The long-standing endurance of the modern Constitution compels us to read things-in-themselves or humans-among-themselves in all accounts of the world, but not an admixture of the two. The challenge of reading hybrids is made all the more problematic by knowledge of a scholar's "time" and a received hermeneutic tradition based on contemporaneous and near-contemporaneous exegesis. That is to say, we are substantively primed to read Kuhn as postmodern because we know him to have been active during the height of postmodern thought and we have been told he was a postmodern. Likewise, we were primed to read Latour and Woolgar as social constructivist because they were part of the (postmodern) Kuhnian conversation in science studies. The difficult ask I have of you now is to set that aside as we reread Bergson's left-branching legacy.

Bergson and Whitehead: The First New Materialists

As mentioned above, Bergson was committed to many of the ideas that now make up the core of new materialist thought. Certainly, the rejection of dualistic metaphysics is one of the central aims of *Matter & Memory*. Furthermore, his particular rejection of long-standing dualisms is worth citing at length, as it showcases how deeply he was opposed to these habits of thought.

> But in this deduction neither realism nor idealism can succeed, because neither of the two systems of images is implied in the other, and each of them is sufficient to itself. If you posit the system of images which has no centre, and in which each element possesses its absolution dimensions and value, I see no reason why to this system should accrue a second, in which each image has an undetermined value, subject to the vicissitudes of a central image. You must, then, to engender perception, conjure up some *deus ex machina,* such as the materialistic hypothesis of the epiphenomenal consciousness, whereby you choose among all the images that vary absolutely and that you posited to begin, the one which we term our brain—confer-

ring on the internal states of this image the singular and inexplicable privilege of adding to itself a reproduction, this time relative and variable, of all the others. It is true that you afterwards pretend to attach no importance to this representation, to see in it a mere phosphorescence which the cerebral vibrations leave behind them . . . But, inversely, if you posit a system of unstable images disposed about a privileged centre, and profoundly modified by trifling displacements of this centre, you begin by excluding the order of nature, that order which is indifferent to the point at which we take our stand and to the particular end from which we begin. You will have to bring back this order by conjuring in your turn a *deux ex machina*; I mean that you will have to assume, by an arbitrary hypothesis, some sort of pre-established harmony between things and mind. (Bergson, 1896/1911, pp. 15–16)

As Bergson is keen to elucidate, the basic ontological presumptions that underlie dualistic metaphysics have immediate, powerful, and ultimately problematic epistemological correlates. When reality is divided up, a priori, into humans and nonhumans, the division provokes significant problems with respect to our relationship with the world around us. In making this claim, Bergson prefigures the new materialist diagnoses exactly.

Ultimately, these diagnoses lead Bergson to the same conclusion as has been found more recently in new materialist thought: relational metaphysics and process philosophy. The following passage from "Introduction to Metaphysics" effectively articulates Bergson's (1903/1946) final arrival here.

This reality is mobility. There do not exist things made, but only things in the making, not states that remain fixed, but only states in the process of change. Rest is never anything but apparent, or rather, relative. The consciousness we have of our own person in its continual following, introduces us to the interior reality on whose mode we must imagine the others. All reality is, therefore, tendency, if we agree to call tendency a nascent change of direction. (p. 222)

Once again, we will find that Bergson makes the same move that he helped to inspire in more contemporary new materialists. This focus on relational metaphysics and processes of becoming, when attention is turned to humans, becomes a focus on situated action. Bergson's commitment to understanding human engagement with complex systems as a function of action rather than representation or epistemology is clear from his analysis in *Matter and Memory*. As he writes:

> My body is, then, in the aggregate of the material world, an image which acts like other images, receiving and giving back movement, with, perhaps, this difference only, that my body appears to choose, within certain limits, the manner in which it shall restore what it receives. . . . My body, an object destined to move other objects, is, then, a centre of action; it cannot give birth to a representation. (Bergson, 1896/1911, pp. 4–5)

Of course, the case I have been making throughout this chapter is that these are no accidental resemblances. The citation history above makes it clear that Bergson had a direct impact on a number of key thinkers who are more routinely cited in contemporary new materialisms.

In *Process and Reality*, Whitehead categorically rejects the classical notion of metaphysical substance as offered by Aristotle and related metaphysical dualisms. Instead, he provides an extension of Bergson's relational process metaphysics grounded in "events" and "concrescence"—also known as "the site of the process of convergence" (Stengers, 2011, p. 308). For Whitehead, there are no inert objects. There is no docile substance with attributes and accidents, but rather a vibrant materiality which emerges from the processes and practices of constituent (human and nonhuman) parts. For Whitehead (1929/1978), "'Actual entities'—also termed 'actual occasions'—are the final real things of which the world is made up" (p. 18). Actual entities or actual occasions are formed in the mutual coming together of constituent parts: "the coherence, which the system seeks to preserve, is the discovery that the process, or *concrescence*, of any one actual entity involves the other actual entities among its components" (Whitehead, 1929/1978, p. 7; emphasis added).

Three Burkes and Counting

Accusations of inconsistency or hypocrisy on social media are increasingly met with the reply "I contain multitudes." For just a moment here, I want to take this playful retort quite seriously. As mentioned above, one of the primary aims of posthumanism and new materialisms is to reject atomism and essentialisms, not just for things in the world but for humans as well. As I will discuss in more detail in chapter 4, a primary commitment of many left-branch thinkers is that humans themselves are processes of becoming rather than discrete stable entities. One place where this idea is perhaps most readily appreciated is within a scholarly trajectory. Indeed, we can probably all think of a paragraph or even a whole article we'd just as soon disavow. I can't imagine Burke was any different. He was nothing if not prolific, and his oeuvre is marked by a conscious and continuous effort at intellectual development. The Burke of *Permanence and Change* (1935) is not the Burke of *A Grammar of Motives* or of *A Rhetoric of Motive*, or even of *Permanence and Change* (1984).

In a phrase, Burke contains multitudes. The present tense is critically important here. Early Burke and Late Burke endure alongside Burke-Received in the scholarly imaginaries that engage his oeuvre. However, Burke-Received is not far removed from Late Burke, almost to the extent that they are coextensive. Burke (without modifier) is largely understood to be invested in better understanding "man [sic], the symbol using animal" and differentiating between motion and action (Burke, 1945/1969). Of course, neither of these intellectual initiatives is particularly new materialist. As it turns out, the effects of the modern Constitution and its extension into postmodernism were not limited to the initial reception of Kuhn or Latour and Woolgar. There's ample evidence to suggest that at least one version of Burke, too, has been subjected to an overly postmodern reading—in other words, that his ideas were rendered more fully linguistic than they were ever intended to be. Debra Hawhee's *Moving Bodies* (2009) carefully outlines these issues through diligent archival research. As she notes regarding her book's purpose, "I want to make a case for a less dramatic transition from aesthetics to rhetoric by emphasizing Burke's early commitments to phenomenology and materiality" (p. 14). She further argues that

> Burke then reveals his own preference for action or participation, cooperation and communication ultimately equating the entire cluster of preferred terms with life: "Life, activity, cooperation, communication—they are identical" (236). His emphasis on life as activity and not just passive existence helps to situate his strong preference for keeping biology in the mix, and his preference for posing the related questions of bodies and motives as comprehensively as possible. (p. 93)

Despite Burke's enduring interest in embodied communication and the material conditions of human action, his work was never properly received in this manner, something Hawhee also laments (p. 167). Her analysis as to why overlaps substantively with Latour and Woolgar's account of their own overly constructivist reception:

> The linguistic turn depends on a body/mind polarity in this way: when theorized from a basic polarity of body/mind, language becomes an epistemological too—if not the epistemological tool. Just as language in psycho-

analysis is the means of producing self-understanding (and understanding of other), theories of discursive construction, too, tend to emphasize language's role in knowledge-production; as Foucault taught us, articulation is itself a form of knowing. The relatively recent "linguistic turn" in the humanities and social sciences cinched language's centrality. What is more, when a theory of bodies is folded into an epistemological view of language, there is a tendency for bodies to become secondary to language, as evidenced by the theoretical perspectives that view bodies as discursively constructed or made legible through language, or those that stall at discussions of bodily representation. (p. 166)

Postmodern theory and the linguistic turn enjoyed a tremendously powerful gravitational pull, from which it was quite difficult to escape for some time. Even today, it persists as a strong force in humanistic and social scientific academia, precisely because it is so powerfully enfranchising. The linguistic turn generates unchecked authority for experts in language including rhetoricians. As such, it is hard to let go of.

While, to the best of my knowledge, Burke had no similar Kuhnian outburst with respect to his reception, it is clear that he (or at least his publisher) was concerned that his scholarship might be read with an overly narrow focus on language and communication. In a sort of advertisement for *Permanence and Change* at the end of *Counter-Statement*, the revision history of the later book's title is offered so as to underscore the more expansive aims of the work:

He now widened his speculations to include a concern with problems of motivation in general. . . . The first completed manuscript of this material he called "Treatise on Communication." In its final, published form, it was called *Permanence and Change: An Anatomy of Purpose*, the publisher having objected to the earlier title on the grounds that it made the work sound like a text book on telegraphy. Communication, interpretation, orientation, integration, cooperation, transformation, simplification—such are its concerns. (Burke, 1931/1968, p. 214)

The Bergsonian influence on Burke, especially in his early writings, is quite faithful. Burke himself recapitulates many of the same intellectual moves, found first in Bergson, that would eventually become the hallmarks of new materialist thought. In short, there is a clear and substantial difference between Late Burke, Burke-Received, and the Early Burke, whom I will now call the Original Bergsonian Burke (OBB). I use this terminology here not to suggest that this Burke was any more authentic than any other Burke but rather to indicate that there was, at one time, a Burke who was deeply connected to Bergson's left branch, and this Burke is not well remembered alongside Burke-Received.

OBB shows a central concern with how language and human action are embedded in relational structures. This concern manifests itself in two important ways: (1) Burke's interest in the economic conditions of symbolic action, and (2) his exploration of the embodied nature of situated action. The first edition of *Permanence and Change*, for example, is famous for including a lengthy discourse on the economic conditions of production as read through Karl Marx. One particular paragraph cut from the initial conclusion shows much in common with the critical Marxist variety of new materialisms identified by Coole and Frost:[5]

> Communism is a cooperative rationalization, or perspective, which fulfills the requirements suggested by the poetic metaphor. It is fundamentally humanistic, as poetry is. Its ethics is referable to the sociobiologic genius of man (the economic conquest of the machine being conceived within such a frame). Its underlying concept of vocation is radical—for it does not permit our sense of duty to arise simply from the contingencies which our ways of production and distribution force upon us, but offers a point of view from which these contingencies themselves may be criticized. Under capitalism, man must accommodate his efforts to the genius of machinery—under Communism he may accommodate machinery to the genius of his fundamental needs as an active and communicating organism. (Burke, 1935, pp. 344–345)

Burke's account of the benefits of communism inherently rejects the metaphysical dualisms common to Western thought. His account integrates social, biological, technological, and ideological systems into an integrated portrayal of the current (capitalistic) and preferred (communist) states of affairs.

---

5. Diana Coole and Samantha Frost (2010) describe a "new critical" wing of new materialisms that has great potential for rhetorical inquiry but is somehow far less discussed in our field. As they describe it, "In other words, new critical materialists, including those working with new forms of open Marxism, envisage a dense, inexhaustible field that resists theoretical totalization even as they investigate complex material structures, trajectories, and reversible causalities. This renewed attention to structures of political economy complements new materialist sensitivities to the resilience of matter in the face of its reconstruction, the agency of nonsubjective structures, the importance of bodily experience, and the myriad interrelated material systems needed to sustain citizens before they can vote or deliberate" (p. 29).

Likewise, OBB's work is centrally concerned with complex systems as the sites of embodied action. As Hawhee has documented extensively, OBB's theory of the intersections between communication and affect are deeply influenced by his long-standing interest in endocrinology. *Moving Bodies* makes this case quite thoroughly and compellingly, so I'll add little to Hawhee's account save the following passage found in Burke's archives.

> Our discussion of the relationship between meaning and affect would not be complete unless it considers at great length the kinds of mental and physical parallelism suggested by endocrinology. Fear, for instance, may set up in the mimities [sic] of the body's glandular constellation that makes for wakefulness; and the exhaustion caused by this wakefulness may in turn reinforce the fear. (Burke, n.d.-a, "Perspective," p. 97, Reel 3, Slide 0310)

This footnote was added to an early typeset manuscript, yet it does not appear to have survived to the final publication. I cannot say whether Burke himself edited it out or whether the addition was missed in transcription. Nevertheless, it clearly indicates the importance of one Burke's interest in physiological processes as a function of motive.

OBB's commitments to what would come to be called critical Marxist new materialisms and embodiment theory are grounded in the same larger philosophical/metaphysical moves invoked by Bergson, Whitehead, and contemporary new materialists. For example, early in *Permanence and Change*, Burke articulates the historic problems of dualist metaphysics as an antecedent to its inquiry:

> Metaphysicians at one time began their works with a *philosophia prima*, which had to do with the structure of the universe in general. From this they proceeded to deduce their laws of history and psychology, of the good and the beautiful, their anthropology. Subsequent thinkers, noticing the influence of the anthropological in shaping our ideas as to the nature of the universe, reversed this way of proceeding from the cosmos to man. They began with the study of purely human processes and interpreted our views of the universe as an outcome of our psychological, physiological, ethnological, or historical responses. (Burke, 1935, p. 39)

Building on this rejection of metaphysical dualism and glossing Bergson (via Stephen), Burke argues for a more relational metaphysics grounded in processes of becoming:

> The events of actual life are continuous, any isolated aspect of reality really merging into all the rest. As a practical convenience, we do make distinctions between various parts of reality, and by such processes of abstraction, we can even treat certain events as though they recurred, simply because there are other events more or less like them. Each temporal event is new, and cannot recur. We find our way through this everchanging universe by certain blunt schemes of generalization, conceptualization, or verbalization—but words have a limited validity. (pp. 122–123)

Echoing Bergson and anticipating contemporary new materialisms, OBB rejects dualist metaphysics and embraces a relational approach grounded in processes of becoming. What's more, he further shifts attention away from issues of representation as such and toward situated action. Reflecting on his theory of "orientations"—conceptual schemata he described them as similar to Kuhnian paradigms in the afterword to the third edition of *Permanence and Change* (Burke, 1984, p. 313). More importantly, however, OBB (1935) explicitly links human action to his developing relational metaphysics: "Orientation is thus a bundle of judgements as to how things were, how things are, and how they may be. The act of response, as implicated in the character which an event has for us, shows clearly the integral relationship between our metaphysics and our conduct" (p. 24).

In these passages, and many more to be explored throughout this book, we will see that OBB occupies a more-or-less seamless transitory position between Bergson and contemporary new materialisms. To be sure, his reception has been largely read through postmodern linguistic commitments, but that does not make reading him in this way particularly accurate. I am not the first to note the powerful similarities between Burke's thought and new materialisms. Hawhee's aforementioned *Moving Bodies* compares Burke's thought to Bennett's *Vibrant Matter,* another work directly inspired by Bergson. Additionally, a recent edited collection, *Kenneth Burke + The Posthuman* (Mays et al., 2017), offers ten chapters outlining how different tendrils of posthumanist / new materialist thought can be read productively alongside Burke. While Hawhee (2009) offers a limited claim that "Burke did not 'get over' bodies, but it was not for lack of trying. Try as he might, he could never shake the point that language always involved the body" (p. 106), Mayes et al. categorically reject the notion that Burke was posthumanist or new materialist. As they write, "In brief, we argue that Burke is compatible with posthumanism. Not prescient. Not anticipatory. Not nascent. We are decidedly not arguing Burke was a posthumanist: he certainly wasn't" (pp. 3–4). While I appreciate the care that each text takes in hedging their claims about Burke, I cannot agree. One of the central arguments of this book will be that one Burke among the multitude of Burkes (OBB) was inarguably prescient and anticipatory despite our popular understanding of him (Burke-Received). Of course, what allows me to make this argument is the heretofore unrecognized Bergsonian connection.

Materiality, Modernity, and Miller

This history in mind, we now have a new frame of reference with which to begin our reinterpretation of "Genre as Social Action." In 1984 the theoretical landscape accepted the guarantees of the modern Constitution and the hard dividing line between modernism and postmodernism. Modernism was, thus, essentially identical to materialism (nature over culture). Any interest in the discursive or the semiotic required a postmodern approach and the attendant rejection of materiality and materialism. So, what I am arguing here is that Miller had no choice but to reject materiality in that she rejected modernism. In 1984 one must be understood as identical to the other. However, under a different conception of the theoretical landscape—one that does not identify materialism as identical with modernism—other theoretical moves are possible. Now, let me be clear here: this is not just a wishful reconstructionist reading of Miller. A careful analysis of the longer intellectual tradition in which "Genre as Social Action" participates will show a consistent affinity for what would come to be known as new materialisms. In capitalizing on this tradition and rejecting modernist materialism, Miller inadvertently invents RNM.

Given how well known Miller's article is and the rhetorical traditions to which it is typically thought to belong, I imagine most readers will be taken aback somewhat by my description of that particular article as the origin point for RNM. Certainly, it would be more than fair to question this assertion. I can advance my argument here no further without addressing the very significant challenge that "Genre as Social Action" explicitly rejects inquiry into materiality. On this point, it might be reasonable to assume that my argument is dead on arrival; nevertheless, there is evidence to indicate that Miller's rejection of materiality does not necessarily entail a rejection of new materialisms. Furthermore, as I will elucidate in the following section, Miller's notion of genre is indebted to a scholarly tradition that can be traced from Bergson through multiple intellectual trajectories. However, these trajectories of influence are often obscured as a result of the dominant intellectual commitments of the time.

Redefining genre as social action was a strategic response to then current theoretical efforts in rhetorical studies to understand not only genre but also the very nature of the rhetorical situation. As Miller was keenly aware and "Genre as Social Action" clearly described, there was a vibrant extant materialist rhetorical tradition to which the article responded. In order for Miller to develop a new theory of genre as social action, a theory grounded in the notion of recurrent rhetorical situations, it was necessary to grapple with competing theories of rhetorical situations, as such.

Addressing this issue, Miller engaged the debate over the materiality of the rhetorical situation. (And, of course, she eventually comes down in favor of the antimaterialist position.) Glossing competing theories of the rhetorical situation espoused by Burke and Bitzer, Miller (1984) rejects Bitzer, Brinton, and Patton's understanding of "[rhetorical] situations as real, objective, historical events" (p. 156). Ultimately, Miller eschews materiality for two primary reasons. She understands materialism (1) to inappropriately circumscribe the possibility of human agency, and (2) to obviate the possibility of situational recurrence. Echoing Burke, Miller (1984) argues that under a materialist rubric:

> An account of the relationship between rhetoric and situation that thus empowers external, objective elements of situation is a theory that, in Kenneth Burke's terms, features scene above any other source of motive. Such a theory he characterized as "materialist" in a prophetic passage in *The Grammar of Motives*: "with materialism," says Burke, "the circumference of scene is so narrowed as to involve the reduction of action to motion." (p. 156)

Likewise, Miller (1984) rejects materialism for its inability to support a theory of situational recurrence. As she wrote:

> What is particularly important about rhetorical situations for a theory of genres is that they recur, as Bitzer originally noted, but in order to understand recurrence, it is necessary to reject the materialist tendencies in situational theory.... What recurs cannot be a material configuration of objects, events, and people, nor can it be a subjective configuration, a "perception," for these, too, are unique from moment to moment and person to person. Recurrence is an intersubjective phenomenon, a social occurrence, and cannot be understood on materialist terms. (p. 156)

In each case here, we have powerful rejections of materialism. So how do I say that "Genre as Social Action" is the origin of RNM?

For many new materialists, the principle value of the intellectual project lies in its ability to actually meet the aims of postmodernism, with respect to modernism. While postmodernism attempted to reject modernism's project of purification and the attendant binaries, it still ultimately accepted and reified those binaries. Under the modern Constitution, nature and society/materiality and culture remain inviolably separate. This metaphysics entails significant ramifications for inquiry in that it ultimately operationalizes a perspectival epistemology. That is, under the modern Constitution, we must understand inquiry as a function of agentive knowing subjects interpreting an inert material reality. The subject/object dichotomy maps directly onto the society/nature dichotomy, and the two mutually reinforce each other.

Governed by, albeit disenchanted with, the modern Constitution, Miller soundly rejects the materiality of the rhetorical situation for its inertness and lack of impact on genre and rhetorical action. As she notes in her criticism of materialist situationists, "For them, situation serves primarily to locate a genre; it does not contribute to its character as rhetorical action" (Miller, 1984, p. 153). The materiality of the situation is little more than a backdrop for rhetorical action. It is the inactive stage that supports, but does not contribute to, the scene. As she further critiques, materialist situationists "regard the first term as fundamental, as the real part of situation, and the second as a perceptual screen" (Miller, 1984, p. 156). The hard dividing line between subject and object renders the material limp and inagentive. Invoking OBB, Miller (1984) instructs us "that substance is drawn from our 'acting-together,' which gives us 'common sensations, concepts, images, ideas, attitude'" (p. 159).

The more expansive treatment of the situation in Miller's dissertation also offers us important insights into her approach to materiality. It's particularly noteworthy that Miller's rumination on the situation picks up on one of those few moments in Schütz that betrays a greater sense of material-semiotic symmetry. As she writes:

> In Schütz's thought, the "experiencing subject" exists in a "lifeworld," the taken-for-granted structure of reality, which includes not only "material objects and events which I encounter in my environment" but also "the meaning-strata which transform natural things into cultural Objects, human bodies into fellow-men, and the movements of fellow-men into acts, gestures, and communications" (p. 5). The "stock of knowledge" that a person acquires about this lifeworld is what he uses to interpret further experience. The role of situation in this process is instructive. (Miller, 1980, p. 37)

Despite Miller's rejection of materiality and nonhuman agency, we actually see significant vibrancy in her corrective understanding of situation. As I will detail in chapter 3, this sense of material vibrancy becomes even more agentive when Miller turns her attention to the materiality of new media. The rhetorical situation for Miller is not an inert backdrop, but neither is it entirely a social or rhetorical construct. The recurring rhetorical situation arises from the simultaneity of human and nonhuman actants in co-constitutive interaction. Neither the modernist materialist account nor the postmodern subjective account is sufficient to understand the contexts of rhetorical action. Her account in "Genre as Social Action," maintains its sense of human–nonhuman interaction:

> What recurs cannot be a material configuration of objects, events, and people, nor can it be a subjective configuration, a "perception," for these, too, are unique from moment to moment and person to person. Recurrence is an intersubjective phenomenon, a social occurrence, and cannot be understood on materialist terms. (Miller, 1984, p. 156)

Here the parallels between Miller, Bergson, and OBB are quite striking. In her rejection of both postmodern perspectivalism and modern materialism, Miller inadvertently invokes the legacy of Bergson and transforms it into an RNM that prefigures cotemporary new materialisms. For Bergson, OBB, and the later new materialists alike, the backdrop of experience is a vibrant participant in the construction of that experience. Vibrant actants co-articulate and co-construct the concrescence, the assemblage, the actor network, the situation. There are no subjects and objects, so there is no perspective. The human actant is merely a reciprocal part of the event. A human is impacted and constructed by the manifold actants that comprise the society.

Toward a Left-Branch RNM

And finally, we have reached the end of this bizarre exercise in contrastive historiography and authorial hubris. My hope is that following the bibliographic analysis at the outset of this chapter and the subsequent theoretical comparisons across generations, you will find that I am, perhaps, not so crazy after all. I genuinely believe that the collected evidence shows that the philosophy of Henri Bergson has had a real, indelible, and lasting effect on what previously seemed to be quite divergent areas of inquiry. Both contemporary new materialisms and RGS owe a significant debt to Bergson's thought. Furthermore, despite the differences in how and when each area of inquiry engages materiality, certain significant theoretical commonalities persist: (1) a dissatisfaction with binary metaphysics, (2) an enduring interest in complex relational systems, (3) a commitment to understanding those systems as functions of ongoing processes, and (4) a commitment to exploring humanity's place in these systems through the lens of situated action.

As I close this chapter, I will be leaving the historiographic and bibliographic arguments behind. As I say above, I hope you found them persuasive. Whether you did or did not, the remainder of *Where's the Rhetoric?* will now shift to a different warrant for pursuing this line of inquiry: utility. In short, I will argue that greater attention to Bergson's left-branch legacy in rhetoric and a commitment to understanding Miller's "Genre as Social Action" as a critical milestone in the development of new materialist thought will prove to be very useful exercises. Specifically, that utility comes from the left branch's ability to provide us a robust foundation for RNM—one that does not begin with a principled rejection of rhetoric. As such, continued work in RNM that builds on the insights of Bergson's influence through the left branch has great potential not only to further our understanding of new materialisms but also to address long-standing questions in rhetorical theory. Pursuing these insights will be the primary job of the next three chapters. In what follows, I will work to demonstrate how RNM can use the left branch to keep true to the tenets of new materialisms while furthering rhetorical inquiry writ large. Specifically, chapter 3 explores a Burkean foundation for relational metaphysics and the potential that offers for inquiry into genre and medium. Chapter 4 continues with a Bergsonian approach to exploring processes of becoming, one that offers much to rhetorical theories of agency. And to end the first part of this book, chapter 5 leverages insights from Bergson, Burke, and Miller to tackle the problem of innovation and creativity in genred communication.

CHAPTER 3

GENRE AS PROCESS

ATTENTION TO OBJECTS and things abounds in rhetoric and writing studies of late. Through a litany of theoretical apparatuses, we are called to become attuned to vibrant matter, multiple ontologies, object endo-properties, Heideggerian things, and so forth. This massive, unwieldly, and only partially coordinated cross-disciplinary initiative in humanities, philosophy, cultural theory, and media studies has taken root in rhetoric to the extent that it is now possible to explore a new materialist and/or object-oriented rhetoric entirely through scholarship published in our own journals, monographs, and edited collections. For example, see the aforenoted Scot Barnett and Casey Boyle's (2016) *Rhetoric Through Everyday Things*, Laurie Gries's (2015) *Still Life with Rhetoric*, Chris Mays, Nathaniel A. Rivers, and Kellie Sharp-Hoskins's (2017) *Kenneth Burke + The Posthuman*, Thomas Rickert's (2013) *Ambient Rhetoric*, Christa Teston's (2017) *Bodies in Flux, or The Politics of Pain Medicine* (Graham, 2015).

However, as mentioned in chapter 1, when the conversation turns toward RNM, significant questions about the boundaries of the discipline arise. Rhetoric *qua* what collides with rhetoric *qua* how, and fractures radiate across intellectual, institutional, and pedagogical boundaries. As always, in the face of such fractures, boundary work ensues—boundary work, I would argue, that we are better off without. However, unfortunately, once boundary work is engaged, there is no escaping it. Once one declares that such-

and such a project is outside the discipline, counter arguments must be marshaled to (re)locate it inside the field. Even when that boundary work is overcome, the long-standing focus on the right branch of Bergson's legacy means that theoretical insights from mainstream new materialisms must be regained for rhetorical inquiry. In the previous chapter, I endeavored to point toward a productive alternative centered on the left branch of Bergson's legacy.

The devil is, of course, always in the details. Simply because elements of Bergson's new materialisms have found their way into the scholarship of Burke and Miller does not mean that *Permanence and Change* or "Genre as Social Action" will necessarily solve the challenges posed by the emergence of RNM. Thus the aim of this chapter is to provide those details, to showcase percolatively how Bergson's left branch can support a rigorous approach to RNM. And, as it turns out, there is an additional utility here in that a Bergsonian approach to RGS comes from its ability to solve enduring theoretical problems in RGS itself. The relationship between genre and medium, the nature of genre change/adaptation, rhetorical success through conventional violation: each of these areas can be advanced productively through better appreciating the Bergsonism already imbedded in RGS. Indeed, in the previously mentioned 2015 retrospective interview on "Genre as Social Action," Miller herself reflects on the importance of these very issues for the future of RGS. When asked to reflect on "the most pressing unsolved problems for the next 30 years of Genre as Social Action," she replied:

> CRM: I can tell you what *I'm* interested in going forward. The relationship between genre and medium is very intriguing, not very well understood, and pressing in the sense that the new media require us to attend to the question of medium, including the question of old media, which we've ignored because it was invisible to us until we had some alternatives. The whole issue of genre change—the tension between stability and innovation, genres as fundamentally stabilized at least to some extent, but at the same time allowing for change. How does this happen? Does it happen in different ways at different times in different genres in different media? I think there's lots of intriguing empirical examples to look at. Whether we could come up with a grand theory of change, I sort of doubt, but I think we need to understand it better. (Dryer, 2015)

Happy coincidence—a turn to Bergson's left branch allows us to simultaneously tackle the need for a foundational relational metaphysics in RNM and the question of medium in RGS.

In pursuing this coincidence, my position, as indicated in the previous chapter, is that GASA has always already been new materialist in its orientation. Thus, it is already quite well suited to addressing the questions and issues that arise when genre and materiality mix. However, as I also indicated in chapter 2, GASA has primarily been read through the dominant academic ideologies of its time—those of postmodernism and the linguistic turn. Fully appreciating how GASA is already prepared to tackle the question of medium requires more fully appreciating its connection with the left branch of the Bergsonian lineage, including Original Bergsonian Burke (OBB). To that end, this chapter argues that with a focus on OBB (as opposed to one of the myriad other Burkes), you have an ideal foundation to reconstruct GASA as genre as process (GAP). Through exploring Miller's appropriation of OBB and developing interests in the materialities that surround genre, I will demonstrate how genre can be understood as fully imbricated in material systems and how the systems of genre and the systems of medium constitutively compose both the situation and the rhetor's response. To fully elucidate these claims, this chapter will include a GAP analysis of what might be called a new genre, a form of communication recently made possible by material innovations—the tweetorial.

GASA + Medium

Medium presents a significant opportunity and a significant challenge for RGS. With the rapid proliferation of new communication technologies and platforms, we see the common genres of everyday communication made over anew repeatedly. Likewise, the emergence of new digital communication fora has made possible the rise and rapid proliferation of entirely new communication genres. This chapter takes up that challenge and aims to showcase how the history of genre (especially GASA) has a whole heck of a lot more to do with medium than is generally thought. In the meantime, however, it is of course necessary to reflect on prior scholarship at the intersections of GASA and medium. Even though the question of medium is appropriately identified as a central concern for the next thirty years, it is most certainly not a new concern. Given the centrality of RGS and rhetoric of "new media" within contemporary rhetorical studies, it would be astonishing if these two projects had not previously collided.

One of the earliest points of intersection dates back to the 2001 IText Working Group—a loose and temporary association of scholars in rhetoric and technical communication who came together (1) to assess the state of the field with respect to information texts/technologies, and (2) to chart a new program of research that would connect historic expertise in rhetoric and technical communication with then emerging interests in what would come to be called *new media*. The larger IText Working Group's hybrid lit review / provocation (Geisler et al., 2001) outlines multiple new horizons of inquiry with respect to new-media scholarship. These include rhetorical theory, activity theory, literacy theory, usability research, workplace writing, and, of course, genre studies. The authors outline this last potential horizon of inquiry as follows:

> Genre defines the forms in which information enters into people's communicative activity and understanding of the sociosymbolic world. Without the orientation genre provides, people would not know where to look for information or what that information might mean. Archival indexing systems have been aware to some degree of the importance of genre, but the increasing demands on electric archives require a deeper look at this issue. (p. 278)

Note how the initial formulation of this research trajectory maintains and even emphasizes the binary metaphysics that Bergsonian approaches seek to overcome. Genre is offered as a purely sociosymbolic activity that occurs near or in dialogue with certain technical systems. To be sure, there is some sort of interaction worth interrogating, but the social and technical are unambiguously separate phenomena.

One of the earliest and most well-cited analyses of genre and media (Miller & Shepherd, 2004) replicates this tacit acceptance of binary metaphysics. Early in *Into the Blogosphere*, the authors outline the goals of their inquiry. In so doing, they highlight how their analysis will understand blogging as essentially sociosymbolic activity:

> If the blog is an evolutionary product, arising from a dynamic, adaptive relationship between discourse and kairos, then if we wish to understand the rhetorical qualities of the blog as genre, we should examine the late 1990s, when the blog originated, as a cultural moment. This cultural context will illuminate the evolutionary forces operating on existing genres, the opportunities available for innovation, the available social roles and relationships, and the possibilities for social action. Because the decade of the 1990s, like any decade, is globally complex and defies comprehensive summary, we necessarily focus our attention on a few salient issues that will help answer our questions about the rhetorical work of weblogs. (Miller & Shepherd, 2004, p. 3)

For an article that centers on the emergence of what some have described as one of the first authentically new-media genres, media is strikingly nonexistent from this account. Social forces, cultural contexts, rhetorical aims all figure centrally, but the then emerging internet is almost an afterthought.

To be entirely fair, Miller and Shepherd revisit the question of blog genres sometime later and much more directly engage the question of medium. In so doing, they begin to make room for the ways media factor into genre innovation, but it continues to be a factor at one remove. The medium is never as important as the sociosymbolic.

> None of this work, however, has explored the rhetorical relationship between medium and genre, that is, the way that the suasory aspects of affordances "fit" rhetorical form to recurrent exigence. The migration and adaptation of established genres into the new internet medium, as well as the emergence of "native" genres, suggests that affordances are not determining but rather that they interact with exigence, as objectified social need. . . . the medium, in this case, serves a maieutic function for the exigence, coaching—or coaxing—into being a latent social motivation that, when available, is instantly recognizable to large numbers of people. (Miller & Shepherd, 2009, p. 282)

This maieutic function is somehow important but also somehow other than the maieutic effects of genred discourse. To be sure, Miller is far from the only GASA scholar to (re)enforce this separation between genre and medium, even as part of efforts to integrate the two into a single analysis. I myself (Graham & Whalen, 2008) have done precisely the same thing even in the midst of also inadvertently deploying a neoBergsonian analytic framework. My last effort in this area offered the "Mode, Medium, Genre Interaction (MMGI) heuristic" (Graham & Whalen, 2008, p. 88). Despite explicitly and intentionally using a relational metaphysics grounded in Deleuzian and Latourian theory, I still created zones of purification that separated modal, medial, and generic elements—a move I will fully recant in chapter 5.

The recent *Emerging Genres in New Media Environments* (Kelly & Miller, 2017) hints in the direction that I argue GASA should go in this chapter. In the afterword, Mehlenbacher[1] pauses to take stock of the collected chapters and what they might mean for the relationship between genre and medium. As she describes it, "Genre studies in this collection also begin to align with conversations about materiality occurring across media studies, communi-

---

1. Kelly is now Mehlenbacher, and so in an effort to make the continuity of her scholarship more apparent, I refer to her under her current name.

cation, the digital humanities, and rhetoric" (Kelly & Miller, 2017, p. 292). Indeed, Mehlenbacher's summative comments effectively capture the scope of the book and the role the chapters have in "revealing before us complex interactions between materiality, social and cognitive worlds, stability and change, and so on" (p. 293). However, the promise inherent in this book and the collected chapters is somewhat undercut by Miller's introduction, which firmly reinscribes modernist binaries onto emerging new materialist GASA. Ultimately, she rejects the ontological attunement as unnecessary or unhelpful to studies of language and discourse:

> The origins of phenomena such as new species and new languages pose different issues. Their novelty is less radical, being the appearance of new varieties rather than the appearance of a totally new entity. They emerge as unpredictable only in their specific detail, not in the very fact of their existence. They are explainable in and at least partly reducible to the terms of what they emerge from. Thus, when aiming to understand emergence in the world of cultural change, we need to be more concerned with epistemological emergence than with ontological emergence. It's difficult, and possibly fruitless, to focus on ontological emergence in the cultural world because allegedly new entities must be socially constituted in the first place: ontologically, they are conceptual-cultural phenomena, patterns of social meaning. It may be possible to discern in some more-or-less culturally neutral way the existence of new features or patterns of features, but whether these constitute a new genre is a matter that cannot be determined independent of the perceptions and recognitions of the community of use. We are thus necessarily concerned not with ontological but with epistemological emergence, or, perhaps better, phenomenological emergence: the cultural determination that something is new and meaningfully different. This makes cultural emergence less like the birth of a star or the discovery of a new chemical element and more like the dawning of a realization. (Kelly & Miller, 2017, p. 4)

Here again we see the legacy of the modern Constitution at work. The work of purification is laid atop a hybrid assemblage. Contemporary new-media communication is a function of complex entanglements, but those entanglements will, invariably, be read through a binary metaphysics.

Ultimately, I want to argue that the critical importance of the question of medium with respect to genre is driven substantially by the reluctance to fully embrace it as a coequal in the establishment of genred discourse. The question of medium is a big question, precisely as a result of the stubborn insistence that discourse and materiality are ontologically distinct entities. (And not for nothing, the grounding assumption that they are entities at all is also quite problematic.) Accepting the dictates of the modern Constitution and grafting a binary metaphysics onto a relational construct forces GASA to construe the relationship between genre and medium as a daunting and nigh-insurmountable problem. Fortunately, in reframing this question so as to establish a productive foundation for inquiry, we can take inspiration from another neoBergsonian thinker who has already confronted these issues directly.

Latour's (1999) *Pandora's Hope* is fundamentally about the problem of the gap between words and things. The book famously begins with a vignette where an earnest scientist asks Latour, in all seriousness, whether he believes in reality (p. 1). As the book tells the story, Latour is quite shocked to learn that the reception of his scholarship had led someone to ask such a question at all. Thus, *Pandora's Hope* is ultimately an attempt to make sense of an academic environment that can so powerfully pit sociologists and scientists against one another. Fundamentally, Latour argues that it is the very act of grafting a binary metaphysics onto a hybrid reality that creates the situation that allows for such acrimonious discourse between different academic camps. The radical, ontological separation between words and things catalyzes research questions that cut to the very heart of what it means to be an academic. If academics can be said to know things about the world, then there must be some justification for the link between words and things. Subsequently, competing positivist and poststructuralist camps emerge and then conflict ensues. As Latour (1999) describes it, "The old [philosophical] settlement started from a gap between words and the world, and they tried to construct a tiny footbridge over this chasm through a risky correspondence between what were understood to be totally different ontological domains—language and nature" (p. 24).

This is, of course, is exactly the move GASA is now trying to make. GASA accepts the Modern constitution but knows that medium matters. As a result, GASA is desperately working to construct its own sort of tenuous footbridge between what it largely understands to be fundamentally different domains. Let's learn from the epistemologists. Let's not do this. As part of his way out of this problem, Latour traces the work of science-in-the-making to show that the actual gap between words and things is not nearly so large. The second chapter of *Pandora's Hope* offers an ethnographic account of soil scientists working in the Amazon. Latour follows the assemblages that link the dirt of the forest floor with the practices in the lab and finally with scholarly publication. In so doing, he describes many different points of contact between words and things, points of contact that arise through processes of science-in-the-making (processes of becoming) and assembly into complex systems we would eventually call "factishes."[2] The broader scope of this analysis is not needed to illustrate my point here. Rather, we need only look to one of the smaller moments in Latour's ethnographic assemblage: his account of the pedocomparator.

The pedocomparator is a tool that soil scientists use in the field. It's a taxonomic device that helps them classify soil into types. It's a simple instrument—a collection of color swatches that allow researchers to identify which very specific shade of ruddy brown is the very specific shade of the current soil sample. The scientists in Latour's account are very taken with a new model of pedocomparator. The fantastic innovation that's got them excited is that someone had the great idea of drilling holes in the device. Above each color swatch is a tiny hole. The scientist can then press a sample of dirt up through the hole and compare the shades across a gap of less than a centimeter: "The rupture between the handful of dust and the printed number is always there, though it has become infinitesimal because of the holes" (Latour, 1999, p. 60). Latour's point, of course, is that this is not a special case. It's never been

words (over here)

and things (all the way over here).

It has always already been WordThingWordThingWordThingWordThing. And sometimes the space between is about one sixteenth of an inch. Fortunately, GASA already has a theoretical foundation that allows us to sidestep the presumed chasm between words and things or genres and medium. We don't have to go so far as to invent actor-network theory, develop a new relational metaphysics, or import some exotic external theoretical apparatus. We just have to remember our left-branch Bergsonian legacy. We have to be down with OBB.

---

2. *Factishes* are Latour's reinterpretation of *facts* within an anthropological idiom. The neologism combines *facts* with *fetish objects* to highlight how the daily practical and ritualistic activities of science-in-the-making create facts and invest them with the kind of authority that leads to reverence. The term is meant to suggest that facts are made and that the elaborate rituals of experimentation, peer review, and publication invest them with authority, but not that facts are made up or somehow fake.

From GASA to GAP

As mentioned in the previous chapter, scholars who work in the Bergsonian lineage have developed all sorts of clever (and often annoying) neologisms designed to help attune us to the complexities of relational metaphysics and the processes of becoming. Whitehead's *concrescence*, Deleuze's *assemblages*, Latour's *actor network*, and Mol's *multiple ontologies* all provoke us into considering the interrelationship of words and things at local sites of activity. These terms focus our attention on the processes of becoming and modes of action that make up local sites of complex entanglement. OBB, too, had his own special jargon for referring to sites of concrescence or assemblage. He called these loci *situations*. Of course, when speaking of OBB's *situation* in the contemporary rhetorical tradition dominated by Late Burke or Burke-Received, the modifier *rhetorical* has become pervasive. With the adjectivization of *rhetoric* at work, scholars are thrust back into a dualist metaphysics that problematically separates the semiotic from the material. OBB's original formulation of the *situation*, however, comes without adjective or narrow focus on the semiotic.

Developing the theory of "situations" is a key aim of *Permanence and Change*. For OBB (and Burke-Received as well, for that matter) situations are the sites of motive and action. Situations provide the exigencies that motivate action and likewise prescribe the possibilities for response. Situations provide motives and possibilities for response because, as OBB (1935) argues, "motives and situations are one" (p. 282). Motives are a subsystem of subsystems in the supersystem of the situation. Here is OBB's (1935) account:

> Let us make up a motive, even a very tangible one. Let us use an alarm clock as motive. A man, let us say, must arise at a certain hour each morning. This need of arising (based upon such contingencies as office hours, distance of his home from his place of business, time required to dress and have breakfast) is a *situation*. He sets an alarm clock to arouse him at the desired time. The ringing of the clock thus becomes the *motive* of his rising. Yet when it rings, its sound is but a shorthand term for the situation which we have just described. The man acts as he does because the clock has said, in brief translation: "This is the time for you to arise since you live at such-and-such distance from your office, the trip requires so-and-so many minutes" . . . etc. (p. 282)

Here OBB collapses material and semiotic vectors into a single complex situation/motive. The technology of the alarm clock is not merely an external maieutic force. It is the exigence. It is the situation. In describing *situation* thusly, OBB provides an analysis that is remarkably reminiscent of Latour's early reflections on European innkeepers or French speedbumps.[3] The hypothetical actor creates a sociotechnical system, thus enrolling the alarm clock and himself into a specific program of action that was threatened by the potential interruption of his body's tendency to sleep-in. In following OBB, we can define the essential locus of situated action thusly:

> **Situation:** A site of material-semiotic interaction from which motive emerges. Situations are, as the term suggests, the wellspring of situated action.

The material-semiotic symmetry of OBB's situation is not merely metaphorical. It is a recurrent feature of his theory of motive and is built on his understanding of an integrated mind-body as the wellspring of human action and engagement in situations.

As mentioned in the previous chapter and above, the tension between the "situation" and the "rhetorical situation" is never fully resolved in Miller's "Genre as Social Action." While Miller's invocation of Burke-Received and postmodern Schütz pull GASA in the direction of a binary metaphysics, it never fully arrives. This tension is perhaps more clearly evident in the original dissertation version of her germinal article. In the following passage, we see Miller working toward her theory of the situation by integrating insights from Schütz and the communication theorists Thomas Frentz and Thomas Farrell. As she writes:

> It consists of the cultural patterns, both linguistic and nonlinguistic, which give significance to actions, both linguistic and nonlinguistic; it resembles Schütz's conception of a common "lifeworld." Frentz and Farrell distinguish three dimensions in form of life—epistemic, aesthetic, and institutional. The epistemic dimension is the "total conceptual, aesthetic, and

---

3. Here I refer to Latour's "Technology Is Society Made Durable" (1990) and a short vignette from *Pandora's Hope*. In the first case, an innkeeper, frustrated that guests don't return their keys before leaving for the day, creates a sociotechnical assemblage that combines an obnoxious weight on the key, a sign, and a verbal request that, in combination, serve to reduce key loss. Similar, Latour reflects on a humorous French idiom for the speed bump—a "sleeping policeman"—to explore the interpenetration of motive and sociotechnical systems.

cultural knowledge which a society shares and which is recreated and expressed through the overall structure of that society's language" (p. 335). The aesthetic dimension constitutes the patterns and expectations which provide communication with regularity and meaning. And the institutional dimension—found in rituals, ceremonies, procedures of decision making, etc.—regulates and constrains individual acts. (Miller, 1980, p. 59)

While this developing account of the situation does not quite embrace the technological and embodied dimensions present in OBB's account, I would argue that it pushes in that direction. The focus on institutional dimensions provides a connection to material conditions that is never fully erased in GASA.

In this same vein, there is good reason to accept the idea that Miller's situation is ultimately relational and that the binarization of the situation is more a function of the modern Constitution run amok. NeoBergsonians like Whitehead, along with more contemporary new materialists, typically end up adopting a hierarchical account of systematic interaction in assemblages/actor-networks/situations. Different systems in a situation tend to act together, nested inside one another, and it is these hierarchies of interaction that have the potential to stabilize situations despite the vagaries inherent in processes of becoming. Ultimately, Miller's GASA is built on an identical notion of hierarchy and stabilization, even though it tends not to engage the material subsystems within situations.

A brief exploration of hierarchy in Whitehead's fully relational thought will help make this case clear. For Whitehead, it is neither objects nor substances that endure across time but rather the patterns of concrescence in an organized "society." As he describes it, "A 'society,' in the sense in which that term is used here, is a nexus with social order; and an 'enduring object,' or 'enduring creature,' is a society whose social order has taken the special form of 'personal order'" (Whitehead, 1978, p. 34). It is critical, here, to understand that in Whitehead's metaphysics, endurance is not guaranteed. In fact, entropy is a generally accepted condition of the universe, and powerful processes must be at work for a series of actual events to function in (perceived) continuity.

For Whitehead (1978), "the character [of any actual entity is] 'given' for it by the past" (p. 87), but for certain patterns to endure, those patterns must be supported by superordinate structures." "A structured society, as a whole, provides a favourable environment for the subordinate societies which it harbours within itself" (Whitehead, 1978, p. 99). When this is the case, societies may be "stabilized":

> The doctrine that every society requires a wider social environment leads to the distinction that a society may be more or less "stabilized" in reference to certain sorts of changes in that environment. A society is "stabilized" in reference to a species of change when it can persist through an environment whose relevant parts exhibit that sort of change.... By reason of this flexibility of structural pattern, the society can adopt that special pattern adapted to the circumstances of the moment. (Whitehead, 1978, p. 100)

Embracing a relational metaphysics, Whitehead's process philosophy provides us a metaphysical model of acting-togetherness. Concrescence leads to societies, which themselves act together in nexūs (plural of *nexus*, for Whitehead), creating the possibility of stability in what is ultimately a process of becoming.

A similar model is available in OBB's oeuvre. In *Counter-Statement*, OBB details a loose hierarchy of stabilizing systems that emerge out of the base-level interactions between an organism and its environment. As he writes:

> *Modes of experience.* The universal experiences are implicated in specific modes of experience: they arise out of a relationship between the organism and its environment. Frustration and gratification of bodily needs; ethical systems; customs; the whole ideology or code of values among which one is raised—these are involved in modes of experience. (Burke, 1931/1968, p. 150)

Ultimately, it is these systems that serve to stabilize situations or assemblages and thus provide the very possibility of recurrence.

As mentioned above, this dialectic between hierarchy and recurrence is also evident in Miller's fusion of neoBergsonian vectors. Whether we refer to "situations" or "assemblages," stability and recurrence are made possible by hierarchies of acting-together-ness. Miller's genre as social action is built on a hierarchical understanding of multiple levels of substance, form, and action. Miller (1984) describes these successive orders thusly:

> We can think of form, substance, and context as relative, not absolute; they occur at many levels on a hierarchy of meaning. When form and substance are fused at one level, they acquire semantic value which is then subject to formalizing at a higher level. At one level, for example, the semantic values of a string of words and their syntactic relationships in a sentence acquire meaning (pragmatic value as action) when together they serve as substance for the higher-level form of the speech act. (p. 159)

Societies of form, action, and substance are nested in superordinate societies. Drawing on pre-existing hierarchical theories of communication, Miller (1984) ultimately proposes a new hierarchy, far more extensive than prior versions, one that relies substantively on the regulation of superordinate societies which allow rhetorical situations and genres to recur. As she describes it:

> Figure 2 proposes a hierarchy similar to these models but including genre. Genre appears at a level of complete discourse types based on recurrent situations; genres are provided interpretive context by form-of-life patterns and are constituted by intermediate forms or strategies, analogous to the dialogic episode. Because communication must rest on experience, the lowest level must be that in which symbolizing takes place. (p. 161)

Ultimately, hierarchy and complexity are what lead to recurrence. Without sophisticated interactions among societies, there would be no possibility of stabilization.

Hierarchical stabilization is most directly addressed in Miller and Shepherd's (2004) "Blogging as Social Action." In the article, the authors tackle the problem of stabilization and change in the face of shifting contexts and technologies. It is in this further refinement of Miller's original theory that we start to see the centrality of becoming in the metaphysics of genre. As the authors write:

> Schryer's useful formulation, that genres are "stabilized-for-now or stabilized-enough sites of social and ideological action," emphasizes that "genres come from somewhere and are transforming into something else" (pp. 204, 208). In 1984, Miller emphasized that because they are rooted in social practices "genres change, evolve, and decay" (1984, p. 163), and as early as 1973, Jamieson argued that because "genres are evolving phenomena," a Darwinian rather than Platonic perspective should be used in studying them (1973). (p. 2)

A complete rejection of formalism (generic and Platonic) forces a realization that genres simply do not exist as such. They are temporary stabilizing matrices that guide (rhetorical) action in (rhetorical) situations.

Let me say that last bit again: **there's no such thing as genres.** Perhaps an odd commitment in a work that identities itself as part of the RGS tradition. However, the nonexistence of genre is an inescapable conclusion following a rereading of GASA within its left-branch Bersgsonian legacy. Despite considerable attention to the question of when rhetoricians can make genre claims, I would argue that the construal of genres as a discrete, identifiable entity ignores the most powerful and important insights of GASA. Namely, genre is (social) action. Indeed, Miller's dissertation supports this account of the principle insight of GASA where it points toward genre as a phenomenological construct rather than a critical apparatus. As she writes:

> With support from social theory and psychological studies, it becomes credible to assert that in rhetoric, genre can be understood as more than a classifying convenience for the critic; it can be understood as an entity with cognitive existence and social application, a phenomenon that is actually used by rhetors and audiences as they formulate and interpret discourse. (Miller, 1980, p. 45)

To fully reject formalist approaches is to reject genres as (discursive) entities. They are active structuring templates that guide the processes of becoming according to the strictures of currently ascendant hierarchies. Genre is action. Genre is process. Genre is a verb.

I am not alone in making this argument. Although she does not rely intentionally on a Bergsonian theoretical framework, Mehlenbacher makes much the same move in her (2019) *Science Communication Online*. As she writes:

> When Miller and Shepherd (2009) argue that "genre and the medium, the social action and its instrumentality, fit so well that they seemed coterminous" (p. 283), they gesture toward a fundamental distinction that is impossible to uphold in rhetorical accounts of digitally mediated spaces. Infrastructures that establish the basis for particular platforms or blog software, for instance, create a novel space for circulation, limit the nature of visuals and videos that can be shared due to technological constraints, or provide new affordances such as the ability to share original scientific research near-instantaneously around the world from the moment of publication. The social actions we might participate in are dramatically altered by our cyber infrastructures. The rapid proliferation of technologies, and their affordances, means an equally rapid proliferation of genres, or proto-genres—or, better yet, genre-ing activity. (p. 35)

Motivated by the same problematic (GASA + medium), Mehlenbacher makes a similar move to shift her attention from genre as form to genre as activity. My version of this will be the move to GAP, but I will adopt her handy formation and it will become a central term of art in this manuscript:

Genre-ing: The processes of structuring activity that occurs in situational hierarchies and guides situated action.

Lest there be any doubt that this move from GASA to GAP is consistent with the rhetorical side of the neoBergsonian trajectory, let us return once more to OBB. The following passage from *Counter-Statement* makes the case most directly. As OBB argues:

> There is in reality no such general thing as a crescendo. What does exist is a multiplicity of individual art-works each of which may be arranged as a whole, or in some parts, in a manner which we distinguish as climactic. And there is also in the human brain the potentiality for reacting favorably to such a climactic arrangement. Over and over again in the history of art, different material has been arranged to embody the principle of the crescendo; and this must be so because we "think" in a crescendo, because it parallels certain psychological and physical processes which are at the roots of our experience. (Burke, 1931/1968, p. 45)

Here we can begin to see the early tendrils of GAP. There is no such *thing* as a crescendo. Individual artistic works shaped by the structuring templates common to certain musical forms allow audiences to intuit a pattern. Audiences recognize the crescendo as an abstraction made possible through engagement with the processes of becoming in a relational metaphysics. And, as OBB clarifies, intuiting the structuring templates that shape crescendo-ing is made possible because of how similar it is to psychological and physical processes. Again, OBB's situation manifests from a nondualist relational metaphysics. As he argues later in *Counter-Statement*, "Repetitive form allies to all manner of orientation, for we can continue to discuss a subject only by taking up in term various aspects of it" (p. 141). Forms "apply in art, since they apply outside of art. The accelerated motion of a falling body, the cycle of a storm, the gradations of a sunrise, the stages of a cholera epidemic, the preening of crops" (p. 141).

Genres are processes, and the abstracted recognition of them is a function of the long view. In the succession of situations, genre-ing helps give rise to the systems that compose those situations and, in so doing, sets the conditions for situated action (response). But, any actual situation is unique. As Whitehead (1928/1978) puts it, "An actual occasion is a novel entity diverse from any entity in the 'many' which it unifies" (p. 21). So, in the processes of becoming, there is always tension and uncertainty until the moment of *satisfaction*. This is a useful Whiteheadian term:

> **Satisfaction:** The "final phase" of concrescence (Whitehead, 1929/1978, p. 26). It "marks the transition of the present to the past" (Stengers, 2011, p. 297). It is the end of an event, that moment where the situation appears to cohere as complete.

With respect to Burke's example above, the satisfaction is that realization that you have experienced a crescendo.

Although the use of the term is very likely nothing more than a happy accident, OBB himself actually uses *satisfaction* to refer to that moment where the form of a structuring template is recognized by the audience. As he writes in *Counter-Statement*:

> Form is the creation of an appetite in the mind of the auditor, and the adequate satisfying of that appetite. This *satisfaction*—so completed is the human mechanism—at times involves a temporary set of frustrations, but in the end these frustrations prove to be simply a more involved kind of satisfaction and furthermore serve to make the satisfaction of fulfillment more intense. (Burke, 1931/1968, p. 31; emphasis added)

In addition to this accidental assonance, rhetorical theory already had a term of art that shades into the terrain of satisfaction: *kairos*. Indeed, Miller and Shepherd (2004) invoke this theoretical legacy directly in their analysis of blog genres:

> Kairos describes both the sense in which discourse is understood as fitting and timely—the way it observes propriety or decorum—and the way in which it can seize on the unique opportunity of a fleeting moment to create new rhetorical possibility. (p. 2)

There are powerful resonances between rhetorical *kairos* and Whitehead's *satisfaction*. Ultimately, the rhetorical notion of kairos describes a rhetor's attempt to catalyze a satisfaction in the situation. An effective rhetorical response will resolve the tensions of the situation and bring competing vectors of genre-ing, medium, and exigence into satisfaction. And this should not be an altogether strange theory of rhetoric. The more colloquial understanding of *satisfaction* has long been an essential marker of successful rhetorics. Effective rhetors are always satisfying. They satisfy audiences, contexts, and burdens of proof.

Enter the Tweetorial

As mentioned previously, the tweetorial provides an ideal vehicle for exploring my proposed shift from GASA to GAP. Indeed, the tweetorial is a complex concrescence, a *dissoi logoi / multiplex ratio disputandi* assemblage of assertions, counter-assertions, citations, evidence fragments, *stasis* arguments, images, video, and so forth. As such, the tweetorial is governed by multiple complex intersecting structuring structures, including Twitter post limits, tweet-threading technology, multimedia support, standards of evidence, standards of political discourse, and the hybridization of the genre-ing processes of the tutorial and the takedown. The tweetorial is an ideal vehicle for exploring the full interpenetration of genre-ing processes and medium because its emergence is predicated on technological shifts that allowed long-standing exigencies to finally achieve satisfaction. In pursuing these claims, I will begin with a short history of changes in Twitter affordances that made the recent rise of the tweetorial possible. I'll then proceed to an account of the typical moves used to achieve satisfaction in the crucible of the mediated situation, finally reflecting as to how this analysis supports my larger argument about our need to shift from GASA to GAP.

Threads to Tweetorials

On December 12, 2017, with surprising little fanfare, Twitter launched a new feature: threading (Romono, 2017). Following relatively soon after the relaxation of the 140-character limit to 280, this new feature was a major step away from Twitter's generic roots and toward a new potentiality: the long-form tweet (still a short-form microblog post). Certainly, post threads had long predated Twitter's creation of threading as an officially supported option. Users could and would frequently add a bit of inline metadata to the end of each tweet indicating that it was one in a series, in a thread. The simple convention "(1/3)," "(2/3)," and "(3/3)" for subsequent tweets was the most common. However, Twitter being an ideal vehicle for on-the-fly ranting, alternative conventions like "(1/x)" or "(1/n)" were adopted so that thread authors could indicate "I'm not done yet, and I don't know how long I'm going to be."

The utility and readability of user-identified and on-the-fly threading was greatly compromised in 2016 with the introduction of the algorithmic timeline. Prior to 2016 a user's Twitter feed was a simple reverse-chronological aggregation of those accounts they had chosen to follow. Since 2010 these user-curated threads were periodically interrupted by promoted tweets—that is, in-stream advertising content; nevertheless, it was pretty easy to identify and read threads in the order that the author intended. However, with the introduction of the algorithmic timeline, tweets in a user's feed were no longer displayed in reverse-chronological order but rather in a seemingly haphazard order based on the hidden machinations of Twitter's constantly evolving proprietary algorithm. To be sure, it was still technically possible to chase down a thread and view it in its proper order, but it wasn't nearly as easy as before.

Even before 2016, users who were concerned that reverse-chronological was a suboptimal ordering for a thread would leverage Twitter's nested-reply functionality to create threads. Essentially, threads became conversations users had with themselves—each new contribution to the thread was created as a reply to the prior one. This was a partial fix to the problem of threading on Twitter, but it also had the adverse impact of artificially increasing the comment[4] count of any given tweet in a thread. Since comment counts are almost certainly a critically important variable in Twitter's algorithm, leveraging the comment function to create Twitter threads likely was viewed as a threat to the integrity of Twitter's content creation approach. And, thus, threading functionality was born.

Twitter is nothing if not a constantly evolving platform. At the time of this writing, Twitter allows users to create threads using an "add another tweet" button. The affordances of this new approach are huge, and not only for timeline management. One of the most significant benefits of this new threading functionality is that users can now "release" an entire thread simultaneously. Using either the old "(1/n)" or self-reply conventions, thread authors were forced to post thread content one contribution at a time, thus allowing other Twitter users to engage their content before contributions were complete. And certainly, any active Twitter user has been present to witness countless cases where early thread contributions were engaged based on erroneous presuppositions about where the ultimate thread would go. Of course, some users would pre-write their entire threads in another document and rapidly copy-paste-post-lather-rinse-and-repeat as fast as their mouse, keyboards, and personal dexterity would allow. Now with threading support, no such gymnastics are required.

---

4. The @reply is also dead, in case you haven't noticed. Even though that's still the common jargon used with respect to Twitter comments, @reply functionality has been largely deprecated in favor of the new comment system (Meyer, 2016).

Modern Tweetorials

Tweetorials, in their simplest form, are assemblages of threaded tweets with an ostensibly educational purpose. Tweetorialist Juan Lopez-Mattei (2018) defines them in the following tweet: "I am an academic multimodality CV imager. I love doing CV imaging Tweetorials (threads with non-peer-reviewed educational content). Check my Moments in @Twitter. I am an energetic activist for widespread pt access to cardiac CT/MRI #AHA18 #cardiotwitter." Tweetorials are, in many respects, what Mehlenbacher and Miller call a "parascientific genre." In "Intersections: Scientific and Parascientific Communication on the Internet" (Kelly & Miller, 2016), the authors describe this term as follows:

> We will suggest that some of these genres may be characterized as "parascientific," to adopt a notion from Kaplan and Radin (2011). They use the term specifically with reference to the trade journal *Chemical & Engineering News*, which exists "alongside" peer reviewed scientific journals and addresses audiences both within and outside the scientific community, aiming to influence ("deliberately intervene in") scientific practice, particularly through its access to elite audiences in the media and policy arenas (p. 460). The need for such a characterization of an old medium like a trade journal suggests that the binary division of science communication into internal and external has been an over simplification all along. We will use the term in a more general way than Kaplan and Radin do: to refer to a variety of genres that do not fit clearly into the more traditional internal/external binary. (p. 224)

The most popular tweetorials are products of academic research and academic authorship. Researchers in fields from oncology/hematology and microphysics to political history and medical rhetoric (hi!) have used tweetorials to more broadly disseminate research findings and engage in public discussions related to their research area. In practice, however, the majority of popular tweetorials are part lecture, part takedown. They provide an instant onslaught of data annotated with argumentative moves, usually in response to someone else's ill-considered tweet.

Providing great insight into the tweetorial is one of its most prolific practitioners—Vinay Prasad. Prasad is an associate professor of medicine at the Oregon Health and Sciences University. He specializes in oncology and hematology, with particular expertise in the treatment of leukemia. He is also an inexhaustible gadfly. The beneficiary of significant philanthropic funding, he is free to express his disdain for the influence of industry money on biomedical research and practice. A significant portion of his scholarly profile is devoted to publishing on the hazards of cozy industry–medicine relationships, poorly conducted clinical trials in flagship journals, and failures of the US Food and Drug Administration (FDA) to adequately scrutinize new oncology treatments. After receiving some criticism that his tweetorials unethically subverted the scholarly process and that he should, instead, write letters to journal editors, Prasad wrote a now-deleted insightful meta-tweetorial on the benefits of the tweetorial over the letter to the editor (Prasad, 2018, June 10).[5] A few of the key tweets are as follows:

> | | | LENGTH: Tweets are limited by characters, but you can do a lot with THREAD or STRING or TWEETORIAL; In contrast, the NEJM has this moronic policy [image of 175-word limit for *NEJM* letters to the editor] | TIMING: Tweets can correct the scientific record immediately. LTE's rot in journal processes for months, while companies and authors can spread the misleading interpretation of the work. . . . | | | ACCEPTANCE or NOT: You can TWEET out mild, medium, or hot salsa, while NEJM prefers tepid, pandering comments; They tend to reject many many meritorious letters b/c of the bullshit reason of "space" . . . | | |

Here Prasad essentially identifies the tweetorial as a parascientific genre and details how the affordances of tweeting and tweetorials allow researchers to more productively engage with the published literature than letters to the editor.

Tweetorials, however, are not exclusively targeted at academic audiences. Historian Kevin Kruse is a prime example of that wing of tweetorials designed to directly engage the public sphere. Kruse is a professor of history at Princeton. His scholarship is devoted to better understanding conflicts over race and religion in twentieth-century American conservatism. He is the author of numerous books, including *One Nation Under God*, *White Flight*, and *Fog of War*. Kruse's writing effectively targets that audi-

---

5. While the good folks at the American Psychological Association have adopted a citation format for individual tweets, they have yet to adopt one for the tweetorial. Since I shudder at the idea of individually citing each tweet in a thirty-tweet tweetorial, I'm just going to cite the first tweet in each tweetorial. Not to worry—thanks to Twitter's new threading functionality, the link for tweet 1 will take you straight to the entire thread. Additionally, I'm adopting a pipe (|) convention to mark the boundaries between tweets in a tweetorial and the pipe-ellipsis (| | |) to indicate that multiple individual tweets are present in the original.

ence sweet spot between academic readers and those who subscribe to the *New Yorker*. Thus, even his academic press publications have successfully garnered reviews in the *Washington Post* and the *New Republic*. Tweetorials have become a major publicity initiative for Kruse, such that a "Thread of Threads" is pinned to the top of his feed. While he's spent less time talking about his reasons for tweetorializing than has Prasad, it's clear that fact-checking conservative media is a central concern. He credits that orientation as one of the reasons he's recently done so well in attracting Twitter followers. In a recent tweet as part of a requested tweetorial on how to get 200,000 followers as an academic, Kruse had the following to offer:

> Now, my last bit of advice is probably the most important. Dunk on Dinesh D'Souza. I mean, people really do NOT like that guy. I went from 80k to 160k in two weeks just from a few threads on his nonsense. (Kruse, 2018, November 3)

It's hard to argue with these results or, indeed, with the suggestion that D'Souza has been known to inspire enmity.

Tweetorials now come from all over academia, including close to home. Katja Thieme, a scholar in writing studies, genre, and discourse analysis at the University of British Columbia, is creating something of a cult following, putting writing studies insights to work addressing the questionable "scientific" claims advanced by devotees of *Quillette*, Jordan Peterson, and the like. Thieme uses rhetorically informed citation analyses to demonstrate how some claims presented as scientific lack the necessary participation in academic conversations for them to actually be considered so. This unique take on addressing fake news provides a promising alternative to using "facts" as blunt instrument. A similar approach can be found in the tweetorials of Ellie Murray, an assistant professor in epidemiology at Boston University. Murray's tweetorials provide in-depth accounts of the statistics used to generate epidemiological claims and offer advice on how to ensure that the methods used do not lead authors to overstate the significance of their findings.

As I'm writing this sentence, the Johns Hopkins University Coronavirus Resource Center tells me that there are over 2.6 million confirmed and admitted cases of COVID-19 and 181,235 deaths worldwide. As I remain socially distant, I'm supposed to be simply finalizing copyedits for *Where's the Rhetoric?* However, in the face of the coronavirus pandemic, tweetorials have recently proven to be far more important to our national discourse than

I ever could have possibly imagined when I originally drafted this chapter. While I will not be able to discuss COVID-19 tweetorials here in full detail, I would be remiss if I failed to address them entirely.

Like many, I mistakenly assumed that coronavirus public health messaging would come directly from the experts at the Centers for Disease Control and Prevention (CDC). Preferring to shape talking points directly, the White House did not allow this to happen. Taking the lead on nearly all communication, President Trump first acknowledged the novel coronavirus on January 22nd as part of a television interview with CNBC's Joe Kernen. When asked if the administration was concerned about the emerging pandemic, he replied, "No. Not at all. And we have it totally under control. It's one person coming in from China, and we have it under control. It's going to be just fine" (Leonhardt, 2020). As the crisis unfolded, President Trump's public comments did not indicate that his administration was taking the situation seriously until after the World Health Organization declared COVID-19 a global pandemic on March 11. Despite a somewhat more serious approach to the situation, the CDC is still not centrally involved in public communication and most official government messaging comes directly from the White House. Unfortunately, daily press briefings have been filled with questionable information, dubious projections, and outright falsehoods.

Given this situation, many have turned, ironically and not always unproblematically, to social media for answers. One result of this has been that the epidemiology (#EpiTwitter) and medical (#MedTwitter) Twitter communities have found an unexpectedly large public audience. #EpiTwitter and #MedTwitter are informal groups of research scientists, professors (including Ellie Murray), postdocs, graduate students, and in the case of #MedTwitter, physicians who have been leveraging Twitter and the tweetorial to share important insights about medicine, public health, and biomedical research since long before SARS-CoV-2. As a result, #EpiTwitter and #MedTwitter were among the very first to provide the public with scientifically grounded information on the emerging pandemic. In the absence of accurate or useful information from federal authorities, #EpiTwitter and #MedTwitter tweetorials have often taken center stage, alongside Johns Hopkins's Coronavirus Resource Center, in public messaging about the coronavirus.

One of the very first English-language tweetorials came from Scott Gottlieb, former commissioner of the FDA. One day before Trump's famous dismissal of COVID-19 as a nonproblem, he published a short informative thread explaining why the international health community should put more pressure on China to share "samples of the novel #coronovirus [sic]" (Gottlieb, 2020). One of the most popular and widely known COVID-19 tweetorialists is Eric Feigl-Ding. He was an early contributor to online discussions about coronavirus with tweetorials on infectiousness (R0) data from Wuhan on January 24th and January 25th. Unfortunately, this is one of those cases that proves the dangers of Twitter for actionable public health information.

Feigl-Ding is an epidemiologist, but he is not an infectious disease specialist. And while he touts his Harvard connections, he apparently holds an "unpaid visiting-scientist appointment in the nutrition department, not the epidemiology department" (Bartlett, 2020). In a partially deleted countertweetorial, Marc Lipsitch, the director of Harvard's Center for Communicable Disease Dynamics, offers a scathing criticism of Feigl-Ding and his tweetorial effort. Among other things, Lipsitch (2020) argues that Feigl-Ding "gets something spectacularly wrong sufficiently often that you just should find other parts of the firehose of info to drink from, and you will get better water." Indeed, following withering criticism from many in infectious disease epidemiology, Feigl-Ding deleted one of his most popular tweets—the first entry of his January 25th tweetorial which apparently significantly overstated coronavirus R0. Nevertheless, even Liptich (2020) says most of what Feigl-Ding tweets "is not wrong."

For good or ill, Feigl-Ding, Gottlieb, Lipsitch, Murray, and countless others in #EpiTwitter and #MedTwitter have been pouring out content since this all began. They now serve as invaluable (but also problematic) sources of information on the spread of coronavirus, the progression of COVID-19, and emerging possibilities for vaccination and treatment. Without regular and reliable information from official government agencies, it is hard to fault people for turning to Twitter, despite the potential for problems. As the pandemic is still unfolding, I am not ready to make claims about the impact of #EpiTwitter and #MedTwitter tweetorials on our current national discourse or overall safety. I'll need to save that for a future essay, so for now I'll return to a less current events-focused analysis of tweetorials and what they can teach us about GAP.

Tweetorial Satisfaction

Ultimately, the situations that give rise to tweetorials combine multiple intersecting elements. The tweetorial is equally the result of changes in Twitter infrastructure, the proliferation of fake news, the so-called replication crisis and concerns over statistical manipulation in scientific research, and the emergence of a new wave of academic activists devoted to combating misinformation in the public sphere. Each of these vectors is an essential component in the situations that lead to tweetorials. The social, ideological, and technological elements of each situation combine to provide a range of possible pathways to satisfaction. Within the language of GAP, this is how we will understand the "move." Moves are available responses to genred situations. Thus, even within the seemingly strange idioms of GAP (compared with GASA), we can still produce similar analyses of genred situations.

Tweetorials can range widely in length from as few as three or four individual tweets to as long as twenty or more. The typical tweetorial has a three-part structure: (1) an invitational opening that assumes the burden of proof and frequently establishes a *dissoi logoi*, (2) a multitweet data dump, and (3) a closing metacommentary that might generally be one to three tweets long. Additionally, nary a tweetorial goes by without some (shameless?) self-promotion. It is social media, after all. The individual tweets of the tweetorial are subject to their own genre-ing processes. The tweet itself, as a microblog post, has certain media affordances and disaffordances, including—most notably—a maximum length of not more than 280 characters, embedded image and video support, hyperlinking support, and folksonomy (hashtags) support. These affordances allow multiple intersecting genre-ing processes to come to bear on each individual tweet as well as the larger tweetorial. Conventions for microblog subgenres work in combination with meme conventions, hashtag conventions, and the like to provide the structuring templates that lead to satisfaction. The features of the tweetorial are, perhaps, best understood through reviewing them in the wild, as it were. So, let's dive in with each of the above mentioned tweetorial chunks:

The invitational opening: Figure 3.1 shows three invitational openings from Kruse, Thieme, and Murray. "Let's address it." "Here's the thing," and "Pull up a chair" each provide the basic invitational context. However, you will see that these invitations are arrayed across an agonistic range, with the Kruse and Thieme invitations being directed quite clearly at prior discourse the authors find objectionable. In the first case, it's a historical claim by D'Souza, in the latter it's an unnamed (until you click) computer scientist making unsourced claims about "the science of sex differences." Murray's invitation is less overtly adversarial, although it still ties into a pre-existing debate by linking the invitation to a prior poll. Additionally, the tweetorial addresses a hotly contested topic in epidemiology: causal survival analysis. In so doing, it responds to a pervasive concern that much

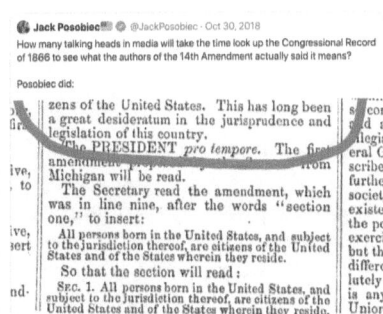

FIGURE 3.1. Opening invitational tweets by Ellie Murray (EpiEllie, 2018), Katja Thieme (Katja_Thieme, 2018), and Kevin Kruse (KevinMKruse, 2018, July 27),

of epidemiological research overstates causal findings. So, while Murray's tweetorial is not a response to a specific objectionable claim, it is a response to many objectionable claims. Finally, Murray's tweetorial comically segues into the data dump with an animated gif showing a character being repeatedly beaten over the head by a book in a library.

The Data Dump: Data dumps are, of course, very much what they sound like. Sometimes quite long series of threaded tweets providing rebuttal evidence against the "other party" in the *dissoi logoi* established by the invitational opening. The total quantity of data dump tweets varies widely. Figure 3.2 offers a bar chart of data-dump lengths (by number of tweets and pixel height) drawn from a hastily assembled sample of convenience.

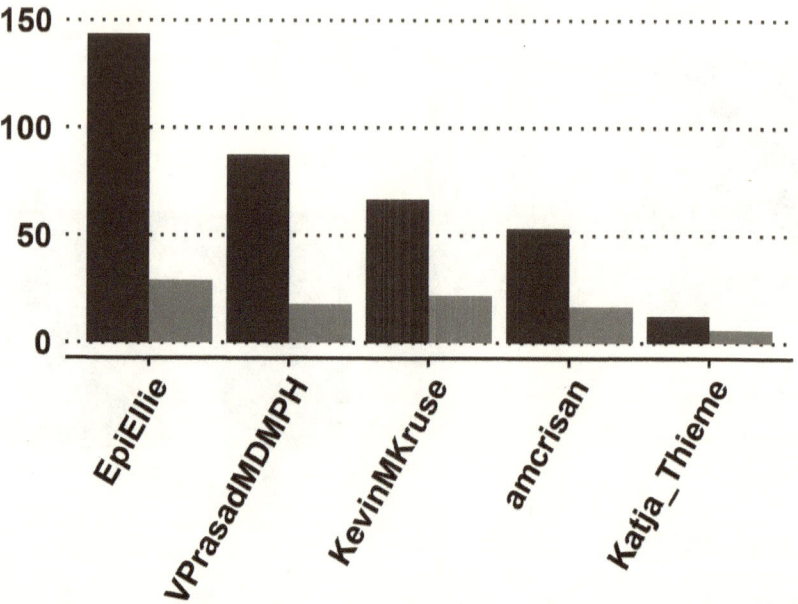

FIGURE 3.2. Height of data dump (units: 100 pixels at 1920x1080) among sample tweetorials. Left-to-right: The results of my #tweetorial poll were pretty clear (@EpiEllie, 2018, November 10); Perverse incentives in FDA policy tweetorial (@VPrasadMDMPH, 2018, May 14); Tweetorial on civil rights support by party affiliation (@KevinMKruse, 2018, July 27); Visualizing genomic epidemiology tweetorial (@amcrisan, 2018); Citation analysis tweetorial of sex difference claims (@Katja_Thieme, 2018).

Regardless of size, within these data dumps, there are also multiple different types of individual tweets, each conforming to their own conventions. Individual tweets that take inspiration from the tutorial ancestral genre can be didactic in orientation, a straightforward attempt to teach audiences about an underlying concept. Murray's tweet, with illustrative sketch-graph (Figure 3.3), is just such a post. It illustrates a basic epidemiological research concept, with a representative sketch of what actual data using this approach might look like. The goal is to disseminate basic background research that feeds into the larger tweetorial narrative. Other individual tweets within a tweetorial may be more overtly adversarial. These posts take the form of rebuttals and may showcase evidence of either the limitations of opposing claims or support of the tweetorial author's larger argument. So, for

FIGURE 3.3. Murray tweet within data dump

example, in rebutting "American internet troll and conspiracy theorist"[6] Jack Posobiec's claims about the origin of the 14th Amendment, Kruse points out that the source Posobiec cites (the *Congressional Record*) didn't exist at the time in question: "| | | First of all, there's no way you really looked up "the Congressional Record for 1866" because the Congressional Record didn't start until 1873 . . . | | |" (Kruse, 2018, October 31). Another example comes from a Thieme tweetorial:

> | | | Let's have a look at who you're citing and upon what recognized peer-reviewed scholarship your discussion relies . . . [list of cited sources]. That's it. | Hate to break it to you, but there's no credible research on gender identity and sexual difference among these sources. None of these people have active research profiles in the fields of gender and sexuality studies. None of these texts are peer-reviewed scholarship. | So, when you—a scholar on #compsci education—have graduate students filing a grievance bout the negative effects that your public comments about women in computer

---

6. That's how Wikipedia describes him, so who am I to quibble.

science had on them and that grievance has been settled—THAT IS IT. ||| (Thieme, 2018)

Here Thieme analyzes citations used to support Jordan Peterson's sexist claims and demonstrates how they fail to amount to a credible evidentiary foundation for his arguments.

Closing Metacommentary: The final tweets in a tweetorial typically offer a brief recitation of key claims and further emphasize the failings of opposing arguments. In short, they are conclusions that follow the typical conventions of conclusions in other genred academic discourse such as research articles. It's often easy to see the impact of these ancestral academic discourses on the tweetorial. For example, the first tweet in Prasad's closing metacommentary on pernicious effects of FDA regulation so faithfully embraces academic registers that it borders on parody: "Ergo, the current regulatory system is SO broken, it would be profitable for drug companies to test useless portfolios of drugs" (Prasad, 2018, June 10). Closing commentaries on the more adversarial end of the spectrum might shift perspective to address opponents directly. Thieme does just this with her penultimate tweet: "Don't delude yourself into thinking you are kicking off a 'discussion of sex differences.' Nope. You are merely stringing together a bunch of tendentious articles & interviews by academics who also don't do research on gender & sexuality. There's no scholarship here" (Thieme, 2018).

Self-Promotion: Certainly, self-promotion is a central feature of social media generally and academic Twitter in particular. The tweetorial is no exception, as evidenced by Kruse's tweetorial on how to maximize followers or Prasad's rumination on the tweetorial as a more effective vehicle for disseminating criticism. Indeed, recognizing the value of the tweetorial for self-promotional success, both Kruse and Prasad have adopted the growing convention of creating threads of threads—Twitter threads where each entry is the first tweet in a tweetorial—and pinning those threads of threads to the top of their Twitter profiles. The self-promotional aspects of tweetorials can take many forms, both subtle and not. Among the more overt acts of self-promotion, Crisan's (2018) genomic epidemiology tweetorial ends with "Finally, let me say that I'm on the job market this year! Learn more about my work here: [url]." (I offer no criticism here. This seems like a potentially effective way to hack the tragically oversupplied academic job market.) Another, more common, mode of self-promotion can be found in any number of Prasad tweetorials, which are essentially distillations of recent article publications. Frequently, Prasad's article tweetorials include screen captures of the data displays in the articles. Interestingly, the photos often provide just enough context to read the entire article regardless of any paywalls that might otherwise end up limiting reader access.

Ultimately, as a result of the nested nature of tweetorials (tweets within threads), it's not possible to conduct a complete genre-ing analysis. Threading technology allows users to assemble multiple individual microblog posts into a cohesive whole. But those individual posts may be attempts to satisfy upwards of twenty different genre-ing structures. Establishing *dissoi logoi*, accepting the burden of proof, providing rebuttal evidence, throwing shade, self-promotion all combine into a complex communicative form that cannot be understood in isolation from the material elements of the media that intersect at the aforementioned exigencies. Threading technology is only the beginning. The previously included tweets are made possible through animated gifs, comics, data displays (actual and representative), previewed hyperlinks, and so forth. The tweetorial does not exist without all the sociosymbolic and material elements combining in reciprocal agitation.

Even within this reciprocal metaphysics, there is still hierarchy, but it not a Miller-style hierarchy with maieutic material at the bottom and discursive genre near the top. In contrast, the hierarchies of GAP are particular to each situation. Figure 3.4 illustrates this by detailing the hierarchy of structuring structures that compose an individual tweetorial. The tweetorial itself, as a single entity, is made possible by the platform affordances of Twitter threading and the exigencies of the situation to which the author responds. However, nested within the larger genred artifact of the tweetorial are the individual moves (data dump pictured here) that respond to their own genre-ing processes and media affordances at tweet and meme levels. Individual posts themselves, too, are genred entities made possible by a certain media infrastructure. Thus, they respond to their own structuring structures nested within the larger structuring structures that establish the data dump and the still larger structures of the tweetorial. Shed of the Modern constitution, the GAP approach does not establish fixed a priori levels in any given hierarchy. It is hierarchization itself that is interesting, and the nature of each hierarchy always emerges within and through the genre-ing processes. Even individual "levels" within the same situated response may have more or fewer sublevels. Again, in Figure 3.4, we can see the difference between an individual dyadic microblog post that is the bottom of its hierarchy and a shade-throwing post that is further entangled in the genre-ing processes of memes.

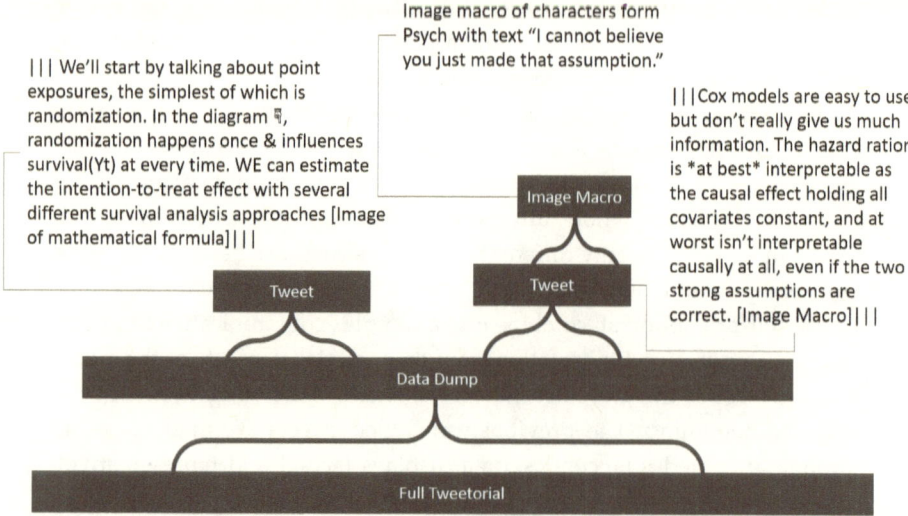

FIGURE 3.4. Hierarchy of genre-ing processes within tweetorials and tweets (Murray, 2018)

Here again, we can best appreciate Latour's insights about the gap between words and things. There is no great chasm. Any gap that exists between words and things exists within the structure of the hierarchy. An individual tweet is words+things. A move is words+things. And the tweetorial itself is words+things. Any attempt to locate words on one side and things on the other will seriously hinder how we understand the tweetorial as an emergent communicative form. But the tweetorial is not special. You don't actually need fancy new technologies to make these kinds of analyses possible. The sociosymbolic and the material mix across a million microgaps in every act of communication. And this is precisely why we must move from GASA to GAP.

As stated above, the GAP approach understands genres as verbs. Genres are orders / templates / patterns of life that comingle vibrantly and frequently agonistically in the processes of becoming. Within the crucible of tweetorial situations, the ordering templates of individual post types, memes, rebuttals, and smack talk intersect with the order templates of media affordances, and from this emerges the possible moves that compose conventional tweetorial response. Here my analysis finds something quite similar to Miller and Shepherd's original account of the emergence of blogs. As they write:

> Blogs appeared, and then multiplied exponentially, when technology made it evolutionarily possible to combine features from a set of antecedent

genres that in other circumstances might never have produced any common progeny: the diary, the clipping service, the broadside, the anthology, the commonplace book, the ship's log. We might see the blog as a complex rhetorical hybrid (or mongrel), with genetic imprints from all these prior genres. (Miller & Shepherd, 2004, p. 14)

The advent of new technologies created a new situation forging together the organizing templates of diaries, clipping services, broadsides, anthologies, and ship's logs into a new recurring stabilized-for-now "genre."

But the GAP framework also reminds us that genre is a process. It is an active unfolding like the contributions to a tweetorial or the assemblage of a crescendo. The phenomenological experience of the process is what demonstrates the sense of genre-ing. Perhaps nowhere is this clearer than in Adam Banks's (2011) rumination on the scratch in DJing. As he writes:

THE SCRATCH IS AN INTERRUPTION. It breaks the linearity of the text, the progressive circularity of the song. It takes the listener or reader back and forth through the song, underneath the apparatus that plays it, either to insert some other song or for the sheer pleasure of the sound of the scratch itself. What was noise, what was seen as the sign of a broken record or stylus, an unwelcome interruption in the continual march of text, groove, history, became a purposeful interruption, became pleasurable, because a way to insert other voices into a text, to redirect one's attention. (pp. 1–2)

Sign, sound, and medium converge into one, but not only into one. There is synthesis and dissonance in this account. Like Burke's crescendo, the DJ's art emerges through the distillation of an experience. That experience can become a satisfaction in dissonance only through the power of the structuring structures that compose the genres of DJ art.

In these analyses, we see emergence from complexity. Different intersecting genre-ing processes are required for the response to achieve satisfaction. However, the material changes to the communicative media are also critical components of the situation. The exigencies that motivated the creation of tweetorials predated proper threading support. No clearer proof of this can be seen than in the efforts to hack threading (e.g., reply threading and tweet numbering) before threads were technologically possible. Users wanted to tweetorial but were prevented from doing so effectively. Likewise, bloggers wanted to diarize publicly but were prevented from doing so effectively. This is why social and rhetorical experiences purified from media and materiality cannot be allowed to exclusively dominate what it means to study genre. The media are not merely maieutic; or, perhaps, media are maieutic in just the same way as social and rhetorical exigencies. Indeed, this is what the tweetorial, the blog, and OBB's alarm clock tell us.

Conclusion

Ultimately, I believe this chapter offers a compelling case for understanding GASA as GAP and Carolyn Miller as, in some ways, the original rhetorical new materialist. GASA has always been a unique and innovative approach to rhetorical inquiry, one that appropriately rejects both modernist materialism and the postmodern fetishization of discourse. Fully appreciating its participation in Bergson's left-branching legacy, especially as mediated through OBB, allows us to see how GASA was really GAP all along. It has always been inherently antidualist and relational. Burke's *situation*, Miller's *hierarchy*, and Whitehead's *kairotic satisfaction* provide an effective rubric for evaluating the intersections of genre-ing processes and media.

Perhaps even more importantly, Bergson's left branch provides rhetorical theory an approach to new materialisms that does not begin with an a priori rejection of rhetoric. Burke's situation is fully material-semiotic. Semiosis does not become a secondary effect to material forces, but neither does the material become epiphenomenal to representation. Miller's careful engagement with the history of materiality in the situation capitalizes on these insights to develop a robust process-focused relational metaphysics. Thus, GAP, understood properly as the origin point of RNM, offers unparalleled insight into the fully reciprocal interactions among signs and objects in situations. Following OBB, GAP understands each situation as a unique event composed of intersecting forces. If there is a gap between that which we might call semiotic and that which we might call material, it is small and dispersed. Actors (rhetorical and otherwise) are called to respond in each situation to which they are party, and an effective actor will quickly assess and identify the salient commonalities among this unique situation and previous situations encountered. In so doing, the actor intuits the crescendo, the genre-ing processes and uses that intuitive abstraction as a resource for action. Thus, we might define **rhetoric,** itself, as the art of attempting to effect a satisfaction.

This redefinition of rhetoric will become more central in my analyses of multimedia design (chapter 5) and electioneering discourse (chapter 7). But first I must address what GAP means for rhetors, or perhaps rather what it means to be a rhetoric in a GAP idiom. The idea of "attempting to effect a satisfaction" has the potential to imply that I subscribe to a more classical or modernist notion of human agency, one where the rhetor can exercise mastery over genre conventions and thus the situation. This is not at all the case, or what I mean to imply. Thus, in chapter 4, I extend GAP's emphasis on relational metaphysics and processes of becoming in order to account for how people, too, are processes. To advance this argument, I begin with more recent moves in agency theory, those that constrain rhetorical agency (almost) to naught. From there, my goal is to move slowly into a more balanced account of reciprocal agency among subsystems within unfolding processes of becoming.

CHAPTER 4

PEOPLE AS PROCESS

SINCE 2011, 4.9 million people (and counting) have marveled as a one-year-old tried to use a glossy print magazine as though it were a tablet. The famous YouTube video (UserExperiencesWorks, n.d.) begins with the child expertly navigating an iPad. She deftly flips through the app menu and selects desired content. Eight seconds and a cut scene later, the same child is shown trying to pinch-zoom an ink-on-paper *Marie Claire* magazine, sadly to no avail. The video continues as the child tries to use several different magazines as tablets. She is clearly attempting to swipe apps left or right and to zoom in on desired content. Although this example is more poignant than most, similar materiality glitches pervade contemporary communication. The politician who tries to whisper a bawdy joke and forgets about the hot mic at the podium, the forgotten hyperlink on the printed page, tiki-torch-wielding neo-Nazis: each of these are instances where expectations about materiality resulted in something other than the desired outcome.

As Casey Boyle reminds us, glitches can amount to a whole lot more than a moment of frustration or a quick chuckle. Indeed, glitches—when properly read—have the potential to be highly instructive. Channeling Olga Goriunova and Alexei Shulgin (2008), Boyle (2018) writes:

> "Glitches," Olga Goriunova and Alexei Shulgin write, are "a short-lived error in a system or machine" (110), and while "a glitch does not reveal the true functionality of the computer, it shows a ghostly conventionality of the forms by which digital spaces are organized" (114). Glitches, for many, help to foreground a conventional background at the moment of its perceived rupture.... Current digital rhetorics along with many traditional rhetorical practices cherish glitch-line events like those mentioned above because they offer a possibility to render apparent that which is transparent by design. When we are positioned to pay attention to in-betweens, especially the mediation work of interfaces and infrastructures, we often come to better understand how those in-betweens help configure our personal, academic, professional, and civic practices. (p. 94)

The figure of the iPad baby and her glitch draw our attention to a very important in-between for rhetoric, RGS, and RNM—the modes of human entanglement with the world. In a few seconds of video, iPad baby forces viewers to confront preconceived notions about how we engage with technology and corresponding questions about the locus of agency.

The power of this glitch to focus our attention on human–world interaction is not only something remarked on by rhetoricians or media studies scholars. Indeed, the high viewership of the video indicates clearly that many find the portrayal compelling. What's more, the online description of the video foregrounds the questions raised by the glitch with respect to human–technology interactions:

> Technology codes our minds, changes our OS. Apple products have done this extensively. The video shows how magazines are now useless and impossible to understand, for digital natives. It shows a real life clip of a 1-year old, growing among touch screens and print. And how the latter becomes irrelevant. Medium is message. Humble tribute to Steve Jobs, by the most important person: a baby. (UserExperiencesWorks, n.d.)

In many respects the video and the accompanying vignette reinforce RGS's typical notions of rhetor–situation interaction in that it shows a novice user/rhetor deploying trained heuristics to respond to the world, and presumably using the negative feedback of the glitch to refine those heuristics.

These synergies notwithstanding, I worry that this model of rhetor–situation interaction presents something of a threat to RGS in general and to GAP in particular. Specifically, a model of rhetor–situation entanglement founded on "coding our minds" doesn't leave a lot of room for the creative agency required to respond dynamically to the local particularities of the situation. That is, if we are coded and conditioned, how do we invent? How do we innovate? These are, of course, not new questions for rhetoric or even for RGS. The dialectic between stability and innovation has long vexed genre theory and will be the principle subject of the next chapter. However, before we can resolve the problem of stability and change, we must first address the baseline presuppositions about rhetor–situation engagement that serve to create this genre paradox.

While little, if any, recent scholarship in the RNM tradition has been pointed directly at the problem of genre, it nevertheless has great potential to help in addressing this paradox. One thing that RNM research has been centrally concerned with is coming to a better understanding of the dynamic mix of agencies involved in human–world entanglement. In this chapter, I argue that RNM accounts of human–world entanglement can be mapped directly onto the problem of rhetor–situation interaction and that doing so provides compelling possible solutions to the paradoxes created by presuppositions that may inadvertently overdetermine the situation and thus entirely circumscribe the possibility of rhetorical agency. However, this work must be done carefully, for RNM too has a tendency to overdetermine the world. As a result of a reasonable desire to overcome the excesses of modernist positions that place humans at the center of all action, advocates of RNM have developed distributed theories of agency that reinforce the vignette of the iPad baby. We have been coded to behave in certain ways, and what we do is more a product of our ambient conditioning than of our human agency.

The solution here, however, is not a retreat from new materialisms but rather a fuller embrace, particularly with respect to Bergson's left branch. My concern is that rhetoricians may move too quickly for the deconstruction of subject/object dichotomies to the reconstruction of human individuals as rhetorical agents. Indeed, one of the primary insights of at least some versions of RNM is ontological de-atomization. But, if we too quickly rebuild the human, the human is never de-atomized along with all the other objects and things of the world. Ironically, in this chapter, I will argue that more fully de-atomizing the human presents less of a threat to rhetorical agency. In pursuing this line of inquiry, I will begin with an exploration of environmental overdeterminism in current approaches to RGS and RNM. Moving forward, I will argue that the left-branch scholarly tradition again provides a compelling solution, specifically in the form of metabiology's de-atomization of the human/rhetor. Through folding the redistributed human back into Burke's material-symbolic situation outlined in the previous chapter, I develop an extended and enhanced GAP framework that avoids the traditional paradox of genre while providing a stronger foundation for a notion of constrained rhetorical agency.

Overdeterminism in RGS and RNM

Addressing the problem of an overdetermined situation begins with the advent of RGS. Miller's (1984) germinal essay on the subject tackles the question most directly through an invocation of Burke's *Grammar of Motives*. As she argues:

> An account of the relationship between rhetoric and situation that thus empowers external, objective elements of situation is a theory that, in Kenneth Burke's terms, features scene above any other source of motive. Such a theory he characterized as "materialist" in a prophetic passage in *The Grammar of Motives*: "with materialism," says Burke, "the circumference of scene is so narrowed as to involve the reduction of action to motion." (p. 156)

From this very first moment in the history of contemporary RGS, the challenges brought forth by the rhetor–situation dialectic become apparent. To render the problem in Burkean terms (following Miller), presenting the rhetor–situation encounter as a dyad runs the very real risk of either overprivileging the scene or overprivileging the agent in any given analytic account. The end result is, quite often, asymmetrical and polarized accounts of agentive conflict. That is, when the scene wins, we are iPad baby, programmed and inagentive. But when the rhetor wins, we are master-orators, champions of our own destiny.

Given the nuanced account in RGS's founding text, genres *ostensibly* have always been understood to occupy an odd nexus between determinism and improvisation. Under Miller's (1984) original theory of genre as social action, rhetorical success is understood to be a medial position between adherence to convention and accommodation to the recurrent rhetorical situation. Catherine Schryer's (2000) pivotal extension of RGS recognizes this most directly in her rearticulation of genres as "constellations of regulated, improvisational strategies triggered by the interaction between individual socialization, or "habitus" (Bourdieu and Wacquant 139), and an organization, or "field" (Bourdieu and Wacquant 17)" (p. 450). However, despite this broad recognition of balance between determination and rhetorical agency, the bulk of RGS tends to focus on the constraining elements of genre. Interestingly, this shift in focus from genre as constraining and enabling to genre as predominantly constraining can be found in Miller's own oeuvre. For example, while Miller (1984) describes genre accommodation as habituated response ("We learn to adopt social motives as ways of satisfying private intentions through rhetorical action"; pp. 161–162), conventions become imperatives in later formulations. When Miller revisits the relationships between genre and community in 1995, she writes:

> The individual *must* reproduce patterned notions of others, institutional or social others, and the institution or society or culture must provide structures by which individuals can do this. The mutual, cultural knowledge that enables individual actors to communicate as competent participants includes structures of interaction, of exigence, of participant roles, and of other rules and resources. (p. 72; emphasis added)

In this passage, we can see two critical moments in the history of rhetorical genre studies: (1) a shift in attention to deterministic constraints, and (2) an increased focus on developing competence.

Ultimately, this shifting emphasis toward determinism tracks RGS's increasing focus on (1) the genres we use, and (2) the genres we teach. In the first case, as GASA turned its attention to academic writing (the genres we use), it found an increasing emphasis on the power of generic constraints to determine rhetorical action. Schryer's (1999) rumination on the conference paper illustrates the newfound focus on constraint and the potential for disciplinary enforcement in the face of conventional violations. As she writes:

> The conference paper is a monologic form of discourse in which the speaker is authorized to speak for a certain period of time in a legitimated location. During that time (unlike other forms of discourse) the listeners know that respectful silence is the norm. However, if the speaker violates his or her time frame, then listeners also know that an authorized representative is permitted to interrupt and call the speech to a conclusion. In "The Problem of Speech Genres," Bakhtin recognized the inherently socializing nature of genres. (p. 83)

Failure to adhere to the generic conventions in a given communication situation will result in punishment. Blame and shame will be leveraged to operationalize the "inherently socializing nature of genres."

RGS's approach to genre is also, of course, significantly inflected by our pedagogical commitments and the genres we teach. Notably, Natasha

Artemeva (2004) suggests that "the development of Rhetorical Genre Studies followed the rise and fall of the product-based and later process-based approaches in composition studies" (p. 4). Irrespective of the reason, RGS has a long-standing focus on the transition from the ignorance of the novice to conventional mastery. Community and professional success is achieved through proper understanding and effective deployment of genre conventions. As Henze (2004) describes it, genres "regulate the social structure of the discourse community by sorting out insiders who know the appropriate genre forms from outsiders or neophytes who do not" (p. 396). Ultimately, our recurrent focus on the professional inculcation of novices leads us to erroneously conflate rhetorical success with adherence to conventions. This tacit conflation continues to occur despite our more sophisticated theory of genre which understands it as a constellation of regulation and improvisation.

RNM has a great deal of potential for providing a more sophisticated understanding of the rhetor–situation dyad, principally in that it offers multiple theoretical frameworks for sidestepping the historic focus on solely the textual or cultural elements and in its potential to reconfigure human–world entanglement as nondyadic. Rickert's (2013) notion of attunement, in particular, is especially helpful for gaining additional purchase on human–world entanglement in the context of GAP. Rickert's attunement draws our attention (it attunes us) to how our entanglement with the world can differentially focus our attention on certain phenomena and possibilities. As he writes:

> While perception remains important to understanding ambience, other important aspects include feeling, mood, intuition, and decision making. This gets us to the issue of attunement. That is, ambience involves more than just the whole person, as it were; ambience is inseparable from the person in the environment that gives rise to ambience. There is no person who can then be tacked onto the environment. Attunement is not additive. Rather, there is a fundamental entanglement, with the individuation of particular facets being an achieved disclosure. Thus, wakefulness to ambience is not a subjective achievement but an ambient occurrence: an attunement. Attunement can, of course, take place at numerous levels, with consciousness being only one. Further, attunement is nothing static. It is always ongoing. (Rickert, 2013, p. 8)

In the above passage, Rickert instructs his readers on attunement while challenging their attunement. By dint of their disciplinary training, rhetoricians and scholars of language tend to be powerfully attuned to language, signs, and discourse. *Ambient Rhetoric* advances a new approach to rhetorical inquiry, one grounded in a form of material-semiotic symmetry. In so doing, it challenges rhetoricians to reattune themselves such that they are more entangled with the material dimensions of our sites of inquiry.

As such, attunement helps us to better understand part of the figure of the iPad baby. She has become attuned through her material-semiotic engagement with iPads. She is awake (perhaps too awake) to the affordances of apps and pinch-zooms. Indeed, Rickert's (2013) rumination on kairos within an ambient rhetorical framework resonates productively with the GAP framework and the dynamic of structuring structures in coordinating situated action. As he writes:

> Kairos is not about mastery but instead concerns attunement to a situation, with attunement understood not as a subjective state of mind or willed comportment but as an ambient catalysis within which is most material and concrete, a gathering that springs forward. Kairos is less about the irrational, then, than about refining what rationality will have meant when it is made again ambient in a worldly sense. (p. 98)

However, despite a broad theoretical commitment to actor–actant symmetry, intra-active agential realism, or the dance of agency, when RNM turns its insights to rhetoric, the rhetor–situation dyad and the corresponding (over) determinism of the scene sometimes return. As the above passage indicates, a central concern of *Ambient Rhetoric* is to correct the overdeterminism of the agent. One of Rickert's primary aims is to disrupt classical rhetorical notions of agency with particular attention to the sense of human mastery therein contained.

With this as a principle aim, Rickert (2013) has no choice but to champion the agency of the scene as the corrective to the presumption of human mastery. To be sure, the new materialism of *Ambient Rhetoric* disrupts the facile dyadic construction of rhetor–world relations. Nevertheless, the denial of mastery results in an enveloping where human actants with delusions of agency are constrained by an agentive scene. This ontology is, perhaps, most clearly articulated in Rickert's rumination on embodiment theory and Burke (as read through Hawhee). As Rickert writes, "As important as embodiment is, however, it cannot be a resting point for rhetoric. A body needs a world" (p. 163). In what immediately follows this passage, Rickert nuances his claim in a direction that almost parallels the aims of GAP in *Where's the Rhetoric?* However, in the final analysis, *Ambient Rhetoric* offers a theory of rhetoric as "attunement to the world," a construct that is not dyadic but still partially oppositional. *Ambient Rhetoric*'s focus on the withdrawal of essence within thing theory disallows full interpenetration of subsystems. This creates a sort of fuzzy atomism where Thing 1 and Thing 2 encounter each other in the world, and entangle, but still retain mutually inaccessible essences. Now let me be clear here. I do not mean to say that Rickert's account is wrong or unhelpful. Indeed, his reinterpretation of the concept in an ambient idiom artfully addresses the principle problems identified in his monograph. *Ambient Rhetoric* is substantively concerned with facile notions of human agency and presumptions of mastery, and thus it provides a useful corrective that escapes these modernist conceits.

However, as compelling as Rickert's ambient rhetoric is, it doesn't help me address the genre paradox. Indeed, in the final analysis, Rickert's theory of ambience powerfully parallels both the figure of the iPad baby and the tacit assumptions of genre theory with respect to the agency of the situation. Nowhere are these parallels clearer than in Rickert's (2013) invocation of Heideggerian dwelling:

> When Heidegger introduces the concept of "dwelling," for instance, he means it to complement being-in-the-world; not only must we already have a world and other beings to show up in the first place, but that world calls us, occasions us, moves us to particular comportments: we are "the conditioned ones" (*PLT* 181). Such conditionings induce attunements. Dwelling, he tells us, is a mode of thriving—knowing, doing, and making—attuned to what an environment affords (*PLT* 147–148). The things of the world take on real agency; we do not gather things but are gathered across them (*IPLT* 152–153). The later Heidegger, then, engages things and technology so as to suggest a profoundly ecological understanding of human flourishing, one that tethers building, doing, and sociality to a dynamic sense of emplaced attunement. This reimagines human agency less as a form of potent mastery than as caretaking, shepherding, sparing, or cultivation (*PLT* 147, 149). Agency emerges as activity both occasioned and conditioned by surrounding land, communities, and forces. (p. 15)

While to be "the conditioned ones" is certainly not identical to brain-as-programmed-OS or, indeed, to poststructuralist agency-denying theories of false consciousness like Althusser's ideological interpellation, it lives on that same spectrum of scenic prioritization. When applied to genre theory, these situational constructs simply do not allow for the possibility of innovative response, and that possibility must be endogenous to our notions of genre and response in order to adequately explain the rhetorical activity we see in the world. As mentioned above, I still see great promise in what RNM has to offer here. But my question is how to keep hold of the explanatory power of attunement without losing out on the distribution of agency that includes rhetors in the world. As mentioned above, my suggested solution involves going all in on the "post" in *post*human.

De-Atomizing the Rhetor

De-atomizing the rhetor is a fraught prospect for several reasons. The lesser concern—which I will address over the next two chapters—is that the rhetor is the presumptive locus of rhetorical agency, and so de-atomizing the rhetor constitutes a potential threat to much of rhetorical theory. The greater concern, which must be addressed immediately, is that de-atomization can often begin to feel like objectification and thus raises serious ethical concerns. There has, inarguably, been a long tradition of dehumanization of marginalized peoples as a part of sexist, racist, and colonialist projects that have brought great suffering to the world. I in no way mean to support these initiatives. Rather, I am inspired by Frost's (2016) arguments that troubling (but not discarding) the category of the human is an essential part of deeply ethical projects. As Frost argues, in rejecting the human exceptionalism endemic to the modern, some new materialists have discarded "human" as a category outright. And, certainly, as a principal referent or index for all thought, this is an appropriate and ethical turn. However, Frost raises a critical concern with respect to the total rejection of the human:

> For a number of scholars have suggested that it's precisely because we have lived and labored under the fantasy of the human that we have wrought such terrible crises on the world (Bennett 2010; Latour 2004; Morton 2012). If this is the case, then a fundamental reconceptualization of what humans are, of what the human might be, could provide useful resources for cogent, creative, and robust engagement with the difficult questions of how we should transform the ways we live. (p. 3)

It's hard to argue with the suggestion here. How, indeed, are we to "address the crises of the day" without, as Frost puts it, "a politically useful category of the human subject that theorists can mobilize?" (p. 1).

In a recent *Rhetoric Review* symposium entitled "Perspectives on Cultural & Posthumanist Rhetorics," Casey Boyle tackles this issue directly, bringing the challenges of posthumanism directly into dialogue with one critically important crisis of the day. Specifically, he challenges readers to reconsider the perception that de-atomization is necessarily dehumanization directly through a rumination on the ethical affordances of posthuman thought for addressing the challenges of translational migration. As he writes:

> I want to propose that the occasion of global migration seen through these images and the response to that occasion by "the west" (as *traditionally* understood) materially manifest the core issues between humanism and posthumanism. Indeed, most responses against humanism are that humanist practices and institutions center one mode of human being as the standard by which all other modes of being human are, at best, but deficient versions of that ideal. At worst, *subhuman*. Building from a generation of feminist-materialist thought, Rosi Braidotti productively interrogates this ideal beginning with the first sentence of her book *The Posthuman*: "Not all of us can say, with any degree of certainty, that we have always been human, or that we are only that." Her second sentence drives the point even further: "Some of us are not even considered fully human now, let alone at previous moments of Western social, political and scientific history" (*The Posthuman*, 3). (Boyle, 2019, p. 378)

Ultimately, Boyle's account of critical posthumanism compellingly argues that "it is in this vein of non-essentialism that posthumanism is already a cultural rhetorics but one that understands its target, liberal humanism of the West, must be undone, unthought, and unwound from within its own machinations" (p. 379). Building a de-atomized-but-not-dehumanized-yet-still-politically-useful category of the human will be no easy task. Nevertheless, for the reasons Frost and Boyle mention, I would argue that it is worth the attempt.

As mentioned in chapter 2, one of the fundamental precepts of most variants of new materialisms (including RNM) is the commitment to de-atomization. That is, RNM is foundationally built on a metaphysics that rejects the notion of essential objects, individual entities, that compose the world. Rather, what we take to be objects (rocks, trees, dogs, atoms) are loci for intersecting processes and subsystems, and it is we who draw the lines around those "objects" and define them as objects. This is Barad's notion of the "agential cut." The kind of relational thinking advocated by RNM does not come easy. We, in Western academe, have a long history of thinking atomistically. Scholarly inquiry, within Western frameworks, has historically been dominated by a drive to identify fundamental units, essential objects, prime movers, and so forth.

As a result, most scholarship in (R)NM has to take care to reattune the reader, to guide them into relational thinking about what they would normally call the "objects" of inquiry. (And, here again, our default language invariably leads us away from (R)NM.) These reattunement efforts generally take the form of pedagogical expositions that begin with some preconceived "object" and guide the reader to reconsider that object in a relational framework. Thus, there are two primary relational reattunement moves: zooming in and zooming out, if you will. Barad begins with the literal atom and *zooms in* to show us that what we had understood as the fundamental unit of matter is, instead, an emergent property of nested forces and subsystems. In so doing, she breaks apart (de-atomizes) the atom, so the reader is reattuned. In contrast, Mol begins with the disease (atherosclerosis) and *zooms out* to the scene of the surgery ward or the pathology clinic. This reattunement shows us that what we once took to be a discrete entity (the disease) is in fact substantially (and differentially) configured by the various sites of practice it inhabits.

And, of course, the rhetorical wing of new materialisms is no stranger to these moves. In *The Politics of Pain Medicine,* I zoom in on neuroimaging technologies to show how they create (rather than uncover) the objects of study. Gries's *Still Life with Rhetoric* zooms out on the Obama Hope image to detail how it was not simply a singular act of rhetorical invention but rather part of a continuous process of reinvention across various complex media landscapes. For the reasons mentioned above, rhetoricians are often reluctant to de-atomize the rhetor. Interestingly, however, within RNM scholarship that is willing to de-atomize the rhetor, it largely only zooms out. This statement may strike my readers as strange, since there's no shortage of work in RNM that discusses certain human subsystems (usually centered around issues of affect). However, a careful reading of the scholarship in question will show that these moments of zooming in are usually deployed as a justification for eventually zooming out, and it is that zooming out which animates the principal scholarly insights.

Let us look at three exemplary works of RNM: Rickert's *Ambient Rhetoric,* Boyle's *Rhetoric as a Posthuman Practice,* and Cooper's *The Animal Who Writes.* As mentioned in chapter 2, the latter two, in particular, are most theoretically consonant with *Where's the Rhetoric?* This is because both are powerfully driven by insights from the (right-branch) Bergsonian tradition—Boyle in his reliance on Deleuze, and Cooper in her appropriation of Whitehead. Regardless of the theoretical pedigree, in each of these works the author's discussion of de-atomizing the rhetor begins with a zoom-in, but ultimately this zoom-in is used to justify a zoom-out. The end result is a version of RNM that de-atomizes the rhetor primarily through focusing on the rhetor's "exterior" entanglements.

In the first case, Rickert's (2013) invocation of Andy Clark's theory of subjectivity is the same kind of zoom-in de-atomization suggested by my theory of GAP, but it almost immediately pivots to a zoom-out focus on humans in sociotechnical systems. The first of these two moves proceeds as follows:

> I am looking for ways to theorize subjectivity ambiently, that is, in terms of embedded and embodied immersion rather than connection, dispersed and interactive flow rather than node, conditions of possibility rather than static presence. Such an ambient subject might be described in Andy Clark's words as "a spatio-temporally extended process not limited to the tenuous envelope of skin and skull" (Being 221). (p. 92)

Here Rickert walks up to the edge of zoom-in de-atomization. By invoking the tenuous permeability of the integument, he hints at an ontology of reciprocally interacting subsystems. However, when *Ambient Rhetoric* moves on to the analysis of human activity in the world, that aforementioned enveloping returns. More-or-less atomistic humans engage with the containing sociotechnical systems—in this case air traffic control.

In what follows, Rickert (2013) offers an engaging account of the human–nonhuman entanglement in air traffic control. In so doing, he highlights the agency of the scene, noting the misnomer of "control," which is especially poignant in light of *Ambient Rhetoric*'s rejection of the mastery analytic.

> The air control center is a series of events in a specific environs, of kairotic moments in a generative place, that form an ambient whole. Elements are individuated in practical activity from this ambient whole while still related to all other elements; this complex, relied-on background of relations constitutes the place as place. The immediate environs radically distribute the activities of the subjectivities working within it, even as particular aspects do emerge through discrete practices. No "subject controls" because there are not discrete subjects absent their relations and connections. However, the environs here are not just a material reality to which we adapt or a material situation that somehow "determines" us. Instead the environments *enable,* but they enable inclusively of human beings insofar as human beings take shape within the environs. (p. 93)

Despite the initial theoretical invocation of the limits of humans *qua* atoms (the limits of the skin), Rickert drives home his version of de-atomization through a zoom-out where humans *qua* humans represent the lowest level of granularity. As soon as *Ambient Rhetoric* turns to a case study, humans-as-systems become humans-in-systems.

We find a strikingly similar approach in Boyle's *Rhetoric as a Posthuman Practice*. Here, the fifth chapter actually begins with an epigraph from Bergson's *Creative Evolution*. The passage could easily find a home in the work of Barad or Mol and is a classic example of zooming in on the human, in a biological register:

> In fact, we do indeed feel that not one of the categories of our thought—unity, multiplicity, mechanical causality, intelligent finality, etc.—applies exactly to the things of life: who can say where individuality begins and ends, whether the living being is one or many, whether it is the cells which associate themselves into the organism or the organism which dissociates itself into cells? (Bergson, as quoted in Boyle, 2018, p. 157)

Despite the inward focusing de-atomizing of this passage, the primary figure of Boyle's chapter is the "homeless hotspot." This concept refers to a new and ethically suspect marketing practice whereby telecommunications companies outfit local members of the homeless population with Wi-Fi hotspots during technology conferences. Ultimately, in an artful example of the zoom-out reattunement, Boyle uses the figure of the homeless hotspot to argue for a transindividualist rhetorical framework grounded in the notion of bodies as one node-type in larger sociotechnical systems.

Similarly, when Cooper is channeling proto-new-materialist scholarship, she embraces zoom-in reattunement. However, her own theory building quickly pivots to zooming out. Specifically, Cooper's developing account of the writing animal is zoom-in de-atomized when she invokes the work of cybernetician Gregory Bateson. The following passage is worth reviewing at length, because it clearly articulates a systemic model of de-atomized human intra-action (to use Barad's term) with the de-atomized environment:

> Bateson ascribes his understanding of mind as a total system as developing from his nascent understanding of feedback in cybernetic systems. . . . He realized that "obviously there are lots of message pathways outside the skin, and these and the messages which they carry must be included as part of the mental system whenever they are relevant" (458). The mental system operates through feedback from outside the nervous system; for example,

when a man is cutting a tree with an axe, "Each stroke of the axe is modified or corrected, according to the shape of the cut face of the tree left by the previous stroke. This self-corrective (*i.e.*, mental) process is brought about by a total system, tree-eyes-brain-muscles-ax-stroke-tree; and it is this total system that has the characteristics of imminent mind" (317). (Cooper, 2019, p. 62)

In this passage, there is great potential with respect to solving the genre paradox and building up a more robust model of GAP. By treating the individual rhetor as a complex set of nested peopling processes—each entangled with the manifold systems and subsystems of the environment—we become quite close to having a model of human–world entanglement that appreciates the insight of Rickert's attunement without overdetermining the scene.

Ultimately, however, Cooper (2019) backs away from the zoom-in de-atomizing moves of Barad and Bateson. In the end, she is quite interested in "putting the agent back into agency" (p. 129). Her writing animal (who is admittedly imbricated in the complex systems of a material world) creatively invents/innovates. In bringing the agent back to agency, Cooper commits to zoom-out de-atomization and leaves the potentialities of zoom-in de-atomization aside, at least for the category of the writing animal. To be 100 percent clear, my goal here is not to say that Boyle or Cooper are wrong. Zoom-out de-atomization of the rhetor has strong affordances for rhetorical theory, as each author demonstrates through compelling accounts of rhetoric in practice. However, addressing the particular challenges of the genre paradox will require zoom-in de-atomization alongside zoom-out de-atomization.

Subsequently, and in keeping with the work of the previous chapters, I argue that a return to the left branch of Bergson's legacy can help us effectively address the twin challenges of the genre paradox and the distribution of agency in RNM. Furthermore, both Bergson and Burke provide us useful accounts of zoom-in de-atomization that can be developed and extended as part of the GAP framework put forward in *Where's the Rhetoric?* As mentioned above, Miller has already pointed out that the Burke of *Grammar of Motives* was troubled by accounts that overdetermine the scene. As it turns out, Burke's rejection of scene-dominant thinking was long-standing. One place he makes this particularly clear is in his rumination on metabiology in *Permanence and Change*. Capitalizing on the Bergsonian tradition and provocatively prefiguring several lines of thought in contemporary new materialisms, Burke argues for a de-atomized account of the human as a corrective to environmental overdetermination. Burke's argument, in this case, is twofold.

He begins by rejecting the human–environment dyad and then proceeds to redefine the human along metabiological terms.

In the first case, Burke (1935) is quite clear in his articulation of the overdetermination. As he writes:

> The keystone of *vis a tergo* causality, when applied to the biological, anthropological, and sociological spheres, was an evolutionary relationship between organism and environment. In true individualistic fashion, the organism was considered a separate unit more or less at odds with its environmental context—and to this context it sought with varying degrees of success to adapt itself. By this schema, the environment was causally prior. (pp. 296–297)

This is an interesting moment for rhetorical theory, which, of course, tends to be centered on context as deterministic of fit. However, in focusing on the more biological part of metabiology, Burke helps to show the problems that arise in this framework.

In so doing, Burke points to the problem of ontological gerrymandering (to use Woolgar's term). The traditional boundaries of organism and environment immediately begin to erode when considered from a biological perspective. And, indeed, Burke draws our attention to this in his rumination on and eventual redefinition of the organism:

> Is oxygen environmental or internal? Are the microscopic creatures in our blood stream separate from us or a part of us? They are members of a "civic corporation" which we call the organism. Who knows?—perhaps they were originally invaders which the body, in learning to tolerate, eventually naturalized as an integral part of its economy . . . All told, it seems hard to understand how we can select the environmental as the distinctly prior factor. (Burke, 1935, p. 298)

This is one of those moments where I deeply suspect, but cannot outright prove, that Burke was being influenced by the Bergsonian tradition, specifically via Whitehead. Burke's account of metabiology parallels several arguments in *Process and Reality*, and those parallels are all the more powerful when one focuses on Whitehead's account of the philosophy of organism. Indeed, the opening passages in Burke's (1935) section on organism and environment begin with the above caution regarding environmental overdeterminism and move quickly to the assertion that "an environment gets its quality, nature, or meaning from the demands which a particular organism makes of it" (p. 232). These moves are strikingly similar to the opening passages of Whitehead's (1929/1978) chapter "Organism and Environment," which includes the following: "It follows from this doctrine that the character of an organism depends on that of its environment. But the character of an environment is the sum of the characters of the various societies of actual entities which jointly constitute that environment" (p. 110).

Regardless of the pedigree of the argument, both Burke and Whitehead argue for a model of the organism (including the human) that is consistent with their broader proto-new-materialist metaphysical positions. Neither understands the human to be an atomic entity situated in an environment. Instead, the human must be understood as, itself, structuring structures engaged in reciprocal structuring processes with the other (nonhuman) structuring structures of the "environment." Andrew Pickering (2010) calls this the "dance of agency," while Ingold (2013) discusses the "dance of animacy." Either way, the reciprocality is key, but the reciprocality is predicated on both modes (in and out) of de-atomization.

Additionally, in the afterword to the third edition of *Attitudes Toward History* (1984), Burke offers another account describing how the various subsystems of peopling processes mediate between "nonsymbolic motion and symbolic action." As he writes in further detail:

> But, whereas the quo modo of the medieval formula was originally treated as but a figurative variation on the theme of "agency" ("He did the job with a hammer and saw, with alacrity"), in time the strategic role of the term began to become apparently. For it designates the point of personal mediation between the reasons of nonsymbolic motion and symbolic action. Its "how" refers to the role of the human individual as a physiological organism, with a corresponding centrality of the nervous system, ATTITUDINIZING in the light of experience as marked by the powers of symbolisticity (Both in themselves and in the realm of the Counter-Nature that has developed as the results, intended and unintended of those powers). Hence our notions of "reality" amount to a tendentious though unstable complex of "personal equations" that are implicit in such simultaneously unique and socially infused "orientation." (Burke, 1937/1984, p. 394)

Ultimately, Burke's metabiology and notion of attitudinizing are remarkably consonant with Bergson's thoughts on agency and innovation. Specifically, they begin with a de-atomized human who travels through successive situations, bringing insights gleaned in the former to bear on the latter. What's noteworthy about these de-atomized models is that they all make space for conditioning and for choice. Atomic humans are neither the passive recipients of environmental conditioning nor the masters of their own destiny. Rather, human entanglement in the world is the result of a complex interplay between conditioned and agentive subsystems.

Memory, De-Atomization, and the Cut Direct

When it comes to better understanding how memory works in the context of the de-atomized rhetor, Bergson will turn out to be a better guide than Burke. This is for the simple reason that we have far more to work with in the former's oeuvre than in the latter's. The relationship between memory and action was a substantive line of inquiry for Bergson for many years. The issue centrally occupies *Time and Free Will* as well as *Matter and Memory*, and, to a certain extent, even continues through *Creative Evolution*. The challenge here is that while Bergson is nowhere near as difficult to parse as Whitehead, his writing is replete with neologisms. Whitehead, at least, had the decency to invent his own terms (e.g., *concrescence*). Bergson, on the other hand, wantonly redefines perception, sensation, and memory, developing his own complex taxonomy of both "pure" variants of each as well as miscellaneous admixtures. Fortunately, a complete understanding of Bergson's taxonomy is not necessary for our inquiry into GAP. At this point, we primarily need the broad brushstrokes. In so doing, I will read Bergson's ideas through an exercise in personal pettiness, one I think we can all appreciate (in spite of its pettiness, or perhaps even because of it).

Several years ago (while employed at a prior institution), I worked as part of a long-term initiative to advance some curricular revisions through the academic governance process. At a departmental meeting, where we had foolishly imagined the revisions would be approved following minimal discussion, one of our own team members sank the proposal. The details are immaterial to the discussion here. Suffice it to say that his remarks were utterly duplicitous and profoundly uncollegial. I don't much imagine there are many among my readers who haven't had a similar experience with academic bad behavior at a department meeting. For the purposes of this thought exercise, you should feel free to mentally substitute the particulars of my experience with your own.

About a week later, I ran into this nefarious individual in the departmental mailroom. He had the audacity to smile at me in greeting. Much to my utter fucking dismay, I smiled back. We've all been here. Someone has done you wrong, is oblivious to that wrong (or worse flaunts that wrong), and you find yourself smiling back against your will. At first, this moment will feel remarkably like the narrative of the iPad baby. It seems to profoundly undercut the broader argument of this chapter. Please bear with me.

From the perspective of a properly de-atomized human/rhetor, there are a number of ways we can account for the unwillingly returned smile. There are, of course, good old-fashioned social niceties. I was raised in the Midwest and have thus been inculcated and indoctrinated into the traditions of midwestern niceness from an early age. I have been interpellated by certain cultural forces that demand that I go along to get along, that I smile. (Of course, the degree of my interpellation pales in comparison to the ways women and people of color are interpellated into regimes of fatuous deference.) But cultural programming is not the only account of the smile-back phenomenon. A more popular (and recent) account involves so-called mirror neurons. Our brains are quite literally hardwired to mirror what is before us. Doing so both foments social cohesion and serves as a defense mechanism. So, in sum, we have two mutually reinforcing systemic mechanisms (the culture of midwestern politeness and mirror neurons) that predispose me to return a smile (even from someone who has recently done me wrong).

Bergson's account of the de-atomized human/rhetor is, quite obviously, not operationalized by either Althusser's theory of interpellation or contemporary neurophysiology. Nevertheless, his account bears a striking resemblance to each of these theories. Waxing poetical, Bergson describes the source of habitual responses as externally received and ill-considered (underconsidered) ideas that float on the surface of our minds like dead leaves in a pond. As he writes in *Time and Free Will* (1910/196),

> But while the cell occupies a definite point in the organism, an idea which is truly ours fills the whole of our self. Not all our ideas, however, are thus incorporated in the fluid mass of our conscious states. Many float on the surface, like dead leaves on the water of a pond: the mind, when it thinks them over and over again, finds them ever the same, as if they were external to it. Among these are the ideas which we receive ready made, and which remain in us without ever being properly assimilated. (pp. 135–136)

As you will recall from chapter 2, Bergson (1896/1911) understands the body to be "a centre of action" (p. 5). It is a conglomerate of subsystems, each engaging in its own ways and times with the subsystems that compose the external environment. As he further elaborates:

> Now we have considered the living body as a kind of centre whence is reflected on the surrounding objects the action which these objects exercise upon it: in that reflection external perception consists. But this centre is not a mathematical point; it is a body, exposed, like all natural bodies, to the action of external causes which threaten to disintegrate it. We have just seen that it resists the influence of these causes. It does not merely reflect action received from without; it struggles, and thus absorbs some part of this action. (p. 57)

The dialectic of reflection and struggle is the key to understanding Bergson's account of the possibility of agency. When our actions reflect off the dead leaves on the surface of our mental pond, we are the "conditioned ones," as Rickert (2013) puts it. But when we struggle against that conditioning, we are sometimes able to bring subsurface subsystems to bear that overcome the surface-level responses.

Returning to my mailroom smile-back encounter, I walked away from that moment positively fuming; I was unwilling to let it go. This scoundrel had slighted me, and I'd be damned if I would not return his pettiness in kind. And so, I committed myself to the cut direct. As most of my readers are probably aware, "the cut direct" was the nadir of Victorian social decorum. To properly execute a cut direct, one must first encounter someone in public view and make clear and obvious eye contact such that it is noticeable to all nearby that that someone had been seen. Then one must cut directly (hence the term) away, declining any social interchange whatsoever. Perhaps the ultimate slight in Victorian England, the cut direct would suffice as a small petty revenge for me in contemporary American academia.

This raises the question, however, of how the cut direct is even feasible. The cultural traditions of midwestern politeness and mirror neurons are two powerful subsystems that coincide specifically to obviate the possibility of the cut direct. If any of my readers have successfully executed the cut direct, you know that it takes a considerable act of will. For Bergson, the wellspring of this (or any agentive act) is memory. The de-atomized body is a center of action, but that action is made possible by utilitarian subsystems that make action possible. The memory subsystems are key here. As Bergson (1896/1911) describes it:

> We assert, out the outset, that if there be memory, that is, the survival of past images, these images must constantly mingle with our perception of the present and may even take its place. For if they have survived, it is

with a view to utility; at every moment they complete our present experience, enriching it with experience already acquired, and, as the latter is ever increasing, it must end by covering up and submerging the former. (p. 70)

In keeping with this account, to execute a cut direct in defiance of cultural programming and mirror neurons, one must keep present in the mind the memory of the original offense. Personally, I find it helps to also keep present in mind the memory of your former failings in delivering the cut direct. Mentally marinating in the memory of your maltreatment (*attitudinizing*, in Burke's parlance) can allow one to short circuit both social niceties and the effects of mirror neurons. The memory subsumes the present experience of the compelling/offending smile reflecting off the dead leaves of your conditioning and allows for new possibilities of action.

Conclusion

So, obviously, this exercise in departmental bickering is not the most important application of Bergson's ideas or the GAP framework more broadly. Nevertheless, it serves as a convenient and accessible thought experiment to counteract the dominance of the iPad baby narrative. Traditional and new materialist accounts of rhetorical agency tend to oscillate back and forth between agent and scenic overdeterminism. As I have argued here, I think this is primarily due to the continued insistence on treating the situation as a momentary dyadic encounter between an atomic agent and a defined scene. Bergson's de-atomized human provides rhetorical theory an analytic framework that allows us to account for both agency and conditioning in our understanding of (rhetorical) action. Despite its petty silliness, the rumination on the cut direct allows us to see both my initial mailroom failure and my subsequent success under the same explanatory heuristic. What's more, it draws our attention to the processual elements of rhetoric in action. In short, the primary insight of this chapter might best be described as follows: just as genres are processes, people are processes too.

One final note on this analysis—one primary goal of this chapter has been to bring a sense of zoom-in de-atomization to rhetorical inquiry. In so doing, I have critiqued Rickert, Cooper, and Boyle for invoking the zoom-in, only to zoom out. Lest I be misread, let me reiterate that the zoom-out approach is a critically important part of de-atomization in RNM. We cannot do this project without zooming out. Indeed, in chapters 5 and 7 of this book, I zoom out as well, with analyses of digital media design and electioneering discourse. The primary intervention of this chapter is to add zooming-in to our repertoire of theoretical and methodological moves. The idea behind it is already present in RNM. My concern is that even though rhetoricians invoke the concept theoretically, the case studies selected all zoom out, thus not fully taking advantage of zoom-in theory. My analysis of the cut direct is meant to provide a model for how a zoom-in perspective can enhance rhetorical inquiry. But it is certainly not intended to be the only model for RNM.

All of which brings us to the larger aims of this book. In some respects, this account of rhetoric in action parallels precisely the overall aim of *Where's the Rhetoric?* To invoke Jensen's historiographic methodologies again, we might describe percolation as a sort of disciplinary attitudinizing. In activating and forcing our attention upon the forgotten memory of Bergson's left-branch legacy, I hope we can better look beyond the dead leaves of our received reading of that legacy. Our efforts to forge a better RNM and a better RGS are sometimes stymied by our presumptions about rhetoric, people, and the world. In much the same way that our developing theory of GAP was stymied by the atomic agent, it has also been inhibited by a limited understanding of *the* situation. That *the* there is the problem. Situations are never isolated events, and agential cuts that treat them as such hinder our understanding of the (rhetorical) possibilities therein contained. Bergson's focus on memory as the wellspring of agency forces us to more substantively address the idea that situations always exist within successions of situations. Indeed, this has always been the key insight of RGS. It is the succession of similar situations that provides a rubric for action—but also the possibility of novelty. Building on the insights provided by our rumination on the de-atomized rhetor and the cut direct, chapter 5 focuses more directly on the processual nature of situations as artificially delimited temporalities within broader temporal successions. In so doing, it blends the insights from chapters 3 and 4 to develop a more complete account of GAP and what it has to offer RGS, RNM, and rhetoric broadly. I also move beyond the more trivial cases of the iPad baby and the cut direct to a careful analysis of new-media design in action. This final distillation of GAP provides the theoretical framework necessary to move into the second part of *Where's the Rhetoric?* and the focus on CR.

CHAPTER 5

FIT FORGING

GENRES GENRE. This is the fundamental precept of GAP. Genres are not textual entities but rather processual structuring templates that persist in the hierarchical assemblages of recurrent situations. In so doing, they provide a framework for situated action. Of course, if genre processes "persist" and if they "provide frameworks," they must constitute powerful structuring structures. For, as you will recall, a Bergsonian relational metaphysics is built on a fundamental presupposition of decay and change. Only the most powerful hierarchies are capable of supporting the kinds of structuring structures that persist and guide action. And yet, we know that creativity and innovation are possible through the agency of memory. New genres emerge and eventually begin genre-ing themselves. Blogs and the tweetorial are two such examples, discussed in chapter 3. And here we have a conflict. In her vision for the next thirty years of GASA, Miller describes this conflict as "the tension between stability and innovation" (Dryer, 2015). As she goes on to ask, "Genres [are] fundamentally stabilized at least to some extent, but at the same time [allow] for change. How does this happen?"

At first blush, this may sound like the same agency question addressed in the previous chapter. It is not. Chapter 4 was primarily concerned with the very possibility that rhetors could defy their conditioning and attempt something new. With the possibility of the attempt—via the agency of memory subsystems—now established, the question remains as to what might allow these innovative attempts to be successful. Just because I was able to execute the cut direct does not mean that I accomplished my goal. Hell, I'm not even sure that my attempted public pettiness was noticed at all. Yet, conventions are sometimes successfully defied, genres do evolve, and occasionally entirely new genres emerge. So, we know that genre innovation is possible. We do not yet have a complete account as to how. This is the primary issue that this chapter works to answer, albeit in a GAP (as opposed to GASA) idiom. In so doing, I argue that when RGS more fully embraces its left-branch Bergsonian heritage, it can better explain how novel genres emerge. Specifically, I argue that moving to a focus on situations and successive processes will give us a great deal more purchase on genre innovation. In making these arguments, I revisit a prior study (Graham & Whalen, 2008) of a multimedia designer working for a marketing and communications firm in the US Midwest. I return to this case study because, on reflection, I too found myself thinking in a Bergsonian direction without even realizing it. In the original article, I suggest that the analysis shows a heretofore (thentofore?) unrecognized form of genre hybridity—gestalt shift genres. Gestalt shift genres are rhetorical responses that begin in the situation of one set of conventions but snap into another set in the midst of delivery. In this case, a single artifact was transmitted as a holiday e-card but became a video game when opened. Through exploring the creativity of the inventional processes that led to the creation of this artifact, we can gain significant insights into the ways that genre-ing processes and media affordances combine in situations to create both constraint and innovative possibility. Specifically, I will show how genre innovation is less a *response* to a pre-existing situation and more a function of forging a fit within an ongoing, unfolding continuity of situations.

Permanence and Change

Dialectics of permanence and change (even beyond *Permanence and Change*) have animated much of contemporary rhetorical theory. Indeed, the tensions provoked by this dialectic have underwritten significant bodies of scholarship in two prominent areas of the discipline: genre and agency. Each of these areas is substantively animated by perceived conflicts between structure and action. This is yet another example of binary metaphysics grafted onto an undifferentiated reality. Much like the case with medium and genre, rhetoricians set up for themselves an insolvable problem by (1) declaring that two sectors of reality are ontologically distinct, and then (2) pitting them against one another. With respect to genre and agency, however, it is quite fascinating to note how similarly the permanence/change dialectic is implemented in each area. In genre theory, rhetors are predisposed toward innovation, but the desire to innovate is willfully curtailed through an act of piety to convention. Likewise, recent debates about agency conceive of rhetor-agents straining at the limits of material-economic structures that prevent them from catalyzing change in the world. As I hope to show below, the largely unrecognized assonance between these two theoretical areas will prove fertile ground for my developing theories of genre, materiality, and rhetorical action. Once again, we will find that Carolyn Miller has been at the forefront of both of these conversations, and that her work channels Bergson's left branch in multiple yet unexpected ways.

Ultimately, the "problem" of agency arises from essentially the same theoretical moves that create the "problems" of genre + medium or constraint versus innovation. The modern Constitution establishes the binary metaphysics that provides the foundation for inquiry, and progress is stymied as we attempt to "solve" the problem we have created. Within agency theory the binary problematic is construed as a result of the collision between critical/cultural theory and classical rhetoric. Specifically, critical/cultural theory comes with readymade models of hegemony and ideological interpellation—structuring structures that are understood to prevent agentive action. This is seen as a significant challenge for traditional rhetorical theory, which is predicated on a model of citizen-orators intervening productively in democratic processes by dint of their rhetorical acumen. Miller's rumination on the agency problematic (and ultimately rejection of its founding theoretical moves) is, indeed, one of the key sources I rely on in making this argument. As she indicates in "Agency and Automation," the agency problematic

> arise[s] from the conflict between realities of political and economic power and ideals of civic participation and social justice. . . . Rhetorical agency is important because it would give voice to the voiceless, empowering subaltern groups, and thus, presumably, weakening structures of institutional, corporate, and ideological domination. (Miller, 2007, pp. 143–144)

Once again, the "dialectical suspension"—to use Ronald Greene's (2004) term—between permanence and change animates significant theoretical activity.

At this point, it is worth noting that I am not the first to suggest that there may be significant value in reading agency and genre against one other. Indeed, reflecting on the agency–genre nexus leads Miller and Shepherd (2009) to attune themselves to dynamism, flexibility, change and flux. As they write:

> More recently, Dorothy Winsor expressed concern that genre theory "underplays the role of agency and change" (1999: 201), and Judy Segal found "an excess of enthusiasm for the generalizing move" at the expense of attention to the local and the particular (2002: 172). In response to these concerns, genre critics and theorists began emphasizing the dynamism, flexibility, and change inherent to genres. Drawing in part on Bakhtin's insights into discourse as a field of both centrifugal and centripetal forces, in part on social theory that explores the relationship between agency and structure, and in part on linguistic studies of variation, this body of work reminds us that genres are continually in flux. (p. 264)

Here again, we see that the most pressing problems of rhetorical theory live in the dialectical suspension between agency and structure. This is a problematic that agency theory may have done a better job, at least so far, of addressing.

Certainly, much of recent agency theory suggests that we need to resolve these tensions through reinterpreting the perceived confrontation between permanence and change. In so doing, this body of work runs in parallel to many arguments from the last chapter regarding genre and medium. For agency, it's not

structure (over here)

and change (way over here),

but rather, as Winsor (2006) puts it, "structure [is] not a bar to agency, but a prerequisite of it" (p. 428). Likewise, Herndl and Licona (2007) read agency authority against one another and ultimately suggest that each is the wellspring of the other. As they write:

> Like agency, authority is a social location, (re)produced by a set of relational practices. The authority to speak—a speaker's authority in discourses and debates—is a social identity that is occupied by a concrete individual but emerges from a set of social practices. In this sense, authority is tied to classi-

cal notions of ethos. Authority is (re)produced by the authority function, and it legitimizes a subject to speak out and act for or against change. (p. 142)

Although the specifics of the relationships are beyond the scope of this book, it's worth nothing that Herndl and Licona's argument participates in another (third-branch) Bergsonian legacy. Ultimately, their approach rejects the vocally anti-Bergsonian Althusser in favor of a Foucauldian theory partially indebted to Bergsonian ideas. Certainly, the resonances between Herndl and Licona's model of agency and the structuring processes of GAP should be evident.

However, it is actually Miller who offers us the most Bergsonian theory of agency. Following her rumination of the limitations of the dialectal suspension, Miller (2007) argues for (1) the relocation of agency in the event (as opposed to the rhetor), and (2) a focus on the "kinetic energy of rhetorical performance." Specifically, Miller challenges rhetoricians to let go of the very idea of agency as a position, to reject the notion that there are entities (rhetors) who have agency and others who do not. Rather, she argues that "we think of agency as the kinetic energy of rhetorical performance" (Miller, 2007, p. 147). In making this move, she reconnects agency theory with the classical Greek notion of *energeia* so as to highlight the active engagement of rhetors in *kairoi*. As she further argues:

> If agency is a kinetic energy, it must be a property of the rhetorical event or performance itself. *Agency thus could not exist prior to or as a result of the evanescent act.* Our talk about agency has tended to essentialize the temporal, condensing into a property or possession of the hypostatized agent what more productively should remain temporalized in the act or performance. (Miller, 2007, p. 147; emphasis added)

For Miller, agency is an emergent property of unfolding situations. The duration of the event itself is the locus of an agency that neither pre-exists nor endures beyond the event. Miller's agency is essentially Bergsonian in its anti-essentialism and focus on the duration of the event. As she goes on to write:

> Interaction is necessary for agency because it is what creates the kinetic energy of performance and puts it to rhetorical use. Agency, then, is not only the property of an event, it is the property of a relationship between rhetor and audience. There are at least two subjects within a rhetorical situation, and it is their interaction, through attributions they make about

each other and understand each other to be making, that we constitute as agency. (Miller, 2007, p. 147)

So, agency is *in* the event, but not fully *of* the event. Again, I'll suggest that this is just like Bergson's notion of duration and OBB's sociomaterial situation. The event is the locus of coming-together-ness, but the phenomena that populate the event are emergent from the interrelationships among nested hierarchies of genre-ing, peopling, and situating processes.

Situated Agency/Invention

As it turns out, the focus on the local site of action with respect to the constraint/innovation dialectic has a longer history in Bergson's thought. Here again, we find that a stronger appreciation of this theoretical legacy can help us avoid the effort required to invent new theories of genre or to import supplementary approaches. Furthermore, when we focus on the loci of situated action, this is where we find the strongest parallels between Bergson's ideas and GASA. In fact, Bergson's theory of intuition bears a remarkable similarity to GASA, especially with the focus on the specific situation and the dialectic between genre-ing processes and embodied action.

Some of the strongest parallels come from Bergson's account of intuition in *Matter and Memory*. As mentioned in the previous chapter, for Bergson memory is the wellspring of agency. And this insight connects very directly to RGS. Memory, in the de-atomized rhetor, is a function of the intuitive recognition of recurrence, but with an eye toward action and response. Just as Miller's theory of genre posits, it is the recollection of recurrence as applied to the current situation that becomes the foundation for effective action. The rhetor recognizes the similarities by calling up images of prior situations and thus extrapolates the best course of action. As Bergson (1896/1911) further describes it, "The recollection of earlier analogous intuitions is more useful than the intuition itself, being bound up in memory with the whole series of subsequent events and capable thereby of throwing a better light on our decision" (pp. 70–71).

To be sure, this model of genre-ing processes is constraining, but it is also generative. As genres genre, they do not only constrain action; they also establish the very preconditions that make action possible at all. The moment of invention involves comparative extrapolation and a response that attempts to satisfy (to return to Whitehead's term) the competing genre-ing, peopling, and situating processes. As Bergson would later describe it in

"The Possible and the Real," creative processes are fundamentally grounded in and a result of recurrent structuring structures. As he writes:

> Artisans of our life, even artists when we so desire, we work continually, with the material furnished us by the past and present, by heredity and opportunity, to mould a figure unique, new, original, as unforeseeable, as the form given the sculptor to the clay. (Bergson, 1911/1946c, p. 110)

As Bergson goes on to argue, it is the very structures that enable the creative mind to appreciate recurrence that make innovation possible. Without recurrence, one would not know that responses were innovative:

> On the contrary we have a surprise interest in familiarizing ourselves with the technique of our action, that is to say in extracting from the conditions in which it is exercised, all that we can furnish us with recipes and general rules upon which to base our conduct. There will be novelty in our acts thanks only to the repetition we have found in things. Our normal faculty of knowing is then essentially a power of extracting what stability and regularity there is in the flow of reality. (Bergson, 1911/1946c, p. 111)

For Bergson, it is this appreciation and intuition with respect to the recurrent that is the fundamental mode of human being in the world.

Miller's original formulation of GASA may, in fact, be at its most Bergsonian when it channels Schütz. While Schütz was not wholly committed to Bergson's ideas, he was most taken with the way that intuition and recurrence play out in social spheres. One of Schütz's principal innovations was to recast memory-images under the rubric of "knowledge stocks." The parallels between him and Bergson are readily apparent when we read his account of how stock knowledge is constituted through recurrent situated action. As he writes in *The Structures of the Life-World*, "Every time in the lifeworldly stock of knowledge is a meaning-context "established" in lifeworldly experiences. Otherwise expressed, the type is a uniform relation of determination sedimented in prior experiences" (Schütz & Luckmann, 1973, p. 230). With Bergsonian memory-images reread as stock knowledge, genre innovation suddenly becomes remarkably easy.

The following passages come from Miller's 1984 article. It's the one place where Schütz survived the peer-review process and continues to make an impact on Miller's more known variants of GASA. As can be seen, the focus on situated action (over discourse systems) is central, and thus the possibility of innovation emerges as a natural condition of the situations:

Alfred Schutz has argued, our "stock of knowledge" is based upon types: "We can . . . imagine a type to be like a line of demarcation which runs between the determinations explicated on the basis of the "hitherto existing" relevance structures . . . and the . . . unlimited possibilities for the determination of experience." In other words, our stock of knowledge is useful only insofar as it can be brought to bear upon new experience: the new is made familiar through the recognition of relevant similarities; those similarities become constituted as a type. *A new type is formed from typifications already on hand when they are not adequate to determine a new situation.* If a new typification proves continually useful for mastering states of affairs, it enters the stock of knowledge and its application becomes routine. (Miller, 1984, pp. 156–157; emphasis added)

Here innovation is a simple act, one born of the situated experiences at play in a succession of situations understood to be genred. Genres continue to genre, of course, but the rhetor with effective action-oriented memory subsystems recognizes that the current genre-ing processes are insufficient to the task at hand, and so s/he simply invents a new type.

Ethnography of Innovation

Ultimately, in reading agency and genre against one another, we can see how central situated action must become to the question of permanence and change. The Bergsonian lineage and the GAP framework suggest that if we are to understand genre change, we must stop looking at genres that *have* changed and begin looking to sites where genres *are* changed. Recentering the focus on the recurring experiences of practicing rhetors will allow us to see how innovation can be understood as an ever-viable response. We can further appreciate how, as structure is a prerequisite to agency, so too is convention a prerequisite for innovation. What follows builds on this line of inquiry by revisiting my earlier ethnographic account of a multimedia designer. In so doing, we can more fully appreciate how the recurrence of structuring structures creates the very possibility of innovative invention, and thus we can further appreciate the return to GAP from GASA.

My original approach to exploring multimedia innovation in action began with many questions about the role of genre in what we were then calling *new media*; I initiated this study by asking to observe Brandon (second author on the original article) during his work for what we pseudonymously dubbed Middle States Graphic Design Services (MSGDS), an advertising, print, and web design firm in the Midwest. At the time of the study, Brandon had been a full-time professional graphic and web designer since receiving his BFA in graphic design four years earlier. Despite his short time with MSGDS, Brandon often served as a project director, working with clients to negotiate a shared vision and to produce an agreed-upon product. In 2005 Brandon earned a prestigious graphic design award in the multimedia category for his work on an electronic greeting-card game like the one I discuss in this chapter.

My approach to developing a more nuanced understanding of Brandon's inventional practices included field observations, interview-discussions, and artifact collection. (We received human-subjects research approval for this project.) The field observations consisted of four visits to MSGDS for six to eight hours at a time, during which I observed Brandon's work on five distinct multimedia projects. These field observations constituted the primary locus of the etic data. In addition to the field observations, I periodically invited Brandon to engage in short read-aloud protocols, narrating what he was doing and why. During this observational period, I also collected various design-process artifacts, including drafts, concept notes, and client and colleague communication transcripts. Also, during this period, we met for seven midday and end-of-day interview-discussions designed to elicit the emic perspective. Each of these interview-discussion periods lasted forty to sixty minutes, except for the observational period follow-up discussion, which lasted approximately ninety minutes. These interview-discussions, which began with a series of open-ended questions that I prepared, helped clarify Brandon's design decisions and underlying rationale.

Our original analysis of these data offered the following conclusions:

1. The impacts of dynamic rhetorical situations and multimodal-multimedia hybridity on communication genres are central considerations during the new-media design process.
2. Current genre and new-media thery underestimates the complexity of the dynamic and nuanced articulations between mode, medium, genre, and rhetorical exigencies.
3. A heretofore underdiscussed type of hybridity is made more prevalent by the affordances of new media.

While we found these contributions useful, with the advent of RNM and GAP, I am now in a position to take these insights further and to do better work for rhetorical theory. In what follows I do precisely this through revisiting the material on one of the e-cards designed by Brandon.

CHAPTER 5

Creativity, Agency, Genre

A thorough analysis of Brandon's situated inventional processes offers an ideal opportunity to explore rhetorical creativity within a GAP idiom. And so I begin with his own account of the most creative part of the design process: the concepting stage. The following vignette is both recollective and representative. It is not entirely true, but it is true to form. It is Brandon's illustrative description of how he began to develop a holiday e-card for the Ryzex Corporation.

> Ryzex [a UPC scanner manufacturer] is one of the few clients I have that gives me almost total creative freedom. Like any artist, I feel that these conditions allow me to produce my best work. When Ryzex said, "We want a game we can send out to our clients and employees," I said, "Okay." It's my job, after all. Working with the copywriter who flourishes most under a similar lack of constraint, we went to work. We came up with some very odd box-and-scanner-themed game concepts: a cowboy riding a box like a bronco, a man riding a box like a spaceship shooting down UPC symbols, a game called *Dance Dance Ryzex*—based on *Dance Dance Revolution* (my personal favorite concept)—and so on, so forth. The concepting stage works a lot like making plans on a Friday night:
>
> DESIGNER: What should we do?
> COPYWRITER: I don't know.
> DESIGNER: Me either.
> COPYWRITER: We could make a *Pac Man* game.
> DESIGNER: That's the dumbest idea ever.
> COPYWRITER: You're the dumbest idea ever.
> DESIGNER: That doesn't even make sense.
> COPYWRITER: You don't even make sense. What if we made a game where you are stuck in a box on its way to China, and you have 2 minutes to escape?
> DESIGNER: That could be cool. What would the graphics be?
> COPYWRITER: Total darkness.
> DESIGNER: I like your concept, but I think it would be cooler if it was something different altogether.
> And so on.
>
> Eventually, we land on a couple of sound concepts, at which point we send them to a copywriter to translate them into good English. A concept is born!

Now it's up to the client to pick one. If the client likes one, perfect. Usually there are tweaks. Sometimes the client wants to merge two ideas, which makes the game strange. "We like concept A, The Beauty Parlor, but can we add these aliens from concept C, Destroy Earth?" Since they are the client, the answer is almost always a resounding "Yes!" After all, creativity is our job.

The processes described shows little resemblance to inventional practices so frequently detailed in RGS. The narrative is not one of working under debilitating constraints; rather, it is a portrait of creative efforts to navigate and innovate within a complex genre-ing and situating processes.

As the vignette suggests, the larger story of this hybrid e-card begins when the Ryzex Corporation, a manufacture of UPC scanners, contracted MSGDS to create a holiday e-card for distribution to employees and clients. In 2008 e-cards were still quite popular, and having a custom-branded e-card created by a professional multimedia design team was a reasonable thing for a company to do. At the time, Brandon's design team was just beginning to explore using Flash to create hybrid e-card games for their clients. Herein we begin to see the complex suite of processes coming into nexus that provided the conditions for Brandon's rhetorical creativity. Brandon was required to meet multiple exigencies: those of the chosen game genre and the concretizing holiday e-card genre. Additionally, the maieutic function (to use Miller and Shepherd's term) of Flash and its dynamic affordances also had considerable bearing on his inventional practices.

Shooting-Gallery Genre-ing

Shooting galleries have a long pedigree in video gaming and beyond. Indeed, their generic history harks back to actual target-shooting activities (cans on a fence or skeets, for example) and has been subsequently remediated through carnival games, video arcades, console games, desktop computers, and mobile devices. In their earliest instantiations at carnivals and amusement parks, simple mechanical mechanisms augmented the traditional cans-on-fence-rail game to provide some level of movement. While physical limitations kept shooting galleries largely the same over much of their life span, the advent of arcade gaming vastly expanded the representational repertoire. No longer limited to pellet and pop guns or mechanical rails and gyros, shooting galleries exploded in their diversity, offering players every available tool from fully automatic machine guns and rocket launchers to sci-fi particle weapons.

While the representational options are now virtually unlimited, the genre of the shooting gallery still typically deploys a few standardized conventions: (1) the player is equipped with a ranged weapon (bow, rifle, space laser), (2) the ranged weapon has built-in limits (range, area of impact, ammunition), (3) there are designated targets (deer, clay pigeons, alien invaders), and (4) there are frequently decoy targets (civilians, hostages, etc). This relatively small number of standardized constraints combined with near-unlimited representational possibilities made the shooting gallery an ideal candidate for an e-card game distributed by a UPC scanner (pricing gun) manufacturer. And this is exactly where Brandon began his design work.

In refashioning these genre conventions for the specific situation, Brandon designed a shooting-gallery Flash game that used Ryzex UPC scanners as ranged weapons and barcode-marked boxes as appropriate targets. Rather than killing wildlife or shooting down clay pigeons, the goal with this game was to scan as many boxes as possible before the gun ran out of charge (weapon limitations). Each "firing" of the UPC gun, rather than epending a bullet, depleted some "charge" from the gun's battery. The game also included a number of decoy targets designed to trick users into scanning the wrong item. In an effort to provoke this confusion, Brandon went with visual similarity and decoy targets including unscannable boxes (no UPC code) as well as other black-and-white-striped items (white tigers, candy canes) that were not UPC codes at all. With these moderate representational changes to the game environment, the game still functioned clearly within the well-established genre conventions of the shooting gallery.

Corporate Holiday E-Card Genre-ing

Like the shooting gallery, the holiday e-card genre has a long pedigree. Combining elements of physical greeting cards and e-mail, the holiday e-card responded to a temporary exigence born from the moment of transition to a more digital communication landscape. As mentioned above, at the time, it was considered acceptable for a company like Ryzex to spend considerable funds in the development of such an e-card. Indeed, the corporate holiday e-card provided Ryzex an important vehicle for responding to multiple simultaneous exigencies: the strong social imperative for extending holiday greetings during the appropriate season, and the cultivation of a certain corporate ethos. There are, of course, two powerful sociological challenges that come with corporate e-cards: (1) not all audiences will share the same communities of faith and correlative holiday seasons, and (2) the tendency of audiences to view all corporate communication in terms of profit motive.

In the first case, simply wishing all Ryzex employees a "Merry Christmas" might respond appropriately to one set of cultural practices but would be inappropriate in a multicultural corporate context. Likewise, a basic e-card might simply be discarded as a ham-fisted sales pitch among client audiences or a poor substitute for holiday bonuses among employee audiences. As it turns out, hybridizing the e-card with the shooting-gallery genre allowed Brandon to more carefully navigate these competing exigencies. That is, making the e-card more game than card allows Ryzex to extend holiday greetings, but in a way that avoids (or downplays) cultural insensitivity and the potential to be read as simply profiteering. A fun game downplays the seriousness of holiday greetings, thus distancing Ryzex from both the cultural and the commercial concerns. Indeed, the first version of the game was entirely free of holiday content. Secularized Christmas elements were only introduced carefully during revision. As Brandon explained during an interview-discussion, "The original game design actually didn't include references to the holidays—they were added later at the request of Ryzex." It was ultimately the decoy targets that carried the bulk of the holiday greetings content—referees wearing Santa hats, convicts holding candy canes, and Siberian tigers sporting reindeer antlers. Representing the holiday content visually—and as a potential target—might have mitigated the appearance of cultural insensitivity, at least among some audiences. Certainly, implementing these design choices seemed safer than adding an explicit greeting such as "Merry Christmas."

Addressing these hybrid, and sometimes conflicting, audiences and contexts in the Ryzex design was further complicated by the multiplicity of purposes for the Ryzex e-card game. The primary, and more obvious, purposes for the game were to express holiday greetings and to entertain Ryzex employees. But on multiple levels, a major purpose in the design was to create and preserve ethos for Ryzex. In many ways this game, which behaves as a holiday card, was the corporation's way of extending empathy and gratitude to its clients or employees. The thought at the time was that this design needed to be implemented in such a way as to exude expense and care (i.e., the trappings of *ethos*) so that the target audiences would perceive the greeting in the spirit in which Ryzex intended it. Consumers today are so inundated with holiday greetings from various firms that they have likely become cynical about the process. The design team and clients alike felt that if this e-card were poorly or ineffectively designed, its recipients might have perceived it solely as a token to increase productivity or sales rather than as a sincere expression of gratitude.

Genre Hybridization

As with any set of design decisions, some were easier than others, and some created path dependencies. The choice to go with a hybrid e-card/game automatically limited the options with respect to a number of media- and technology-related decisions. At the time, Flash was a popular solution for online interactivity, but it was not without its problems. Flash requires appropriate third-party browser plug-ins and a sufficiently robust internet connection to download the interactive content (not so easily guaranteed in 2008). On the surface, these may seem like minor technological issues that hardly warrant consideration here, but the cascading effects of these decisions can—and did—cause significant issues to arise during the course of designing this game. Although Brandon addressed a range of technological issues when he was designing the Ryzex e-card, the issue of file size is a clear example of how technological issues articulate with rhetorical ones. As Brandon noted in follow-up interviews, internet mediation requires constant attention to file size and delivery method. The composition and design of the Ryzex game required Brandon to find a balance between engaging graphical content and the amount of time a user would be willing to wait for a download. The better the graphics, the more intense the interface, the longer it takes for users to access the artifact: something that might cause user attrition. But if the sole focus is on file size and nearly instantaneous delivery, then the final artifact may be insufficient to accomplish its purposes.

Additionally, the deployment of the shooting-gallery genre via desktop computers also required modifications to the genre. The traditional shooting gallery uses an actual firearm or firearm facsimile as interface device. Whether carnival popguns or plastic arcade controls, the gun shape is a key element of the genre. When the game itself is for sale, at sufficient scale, the return on investment can justify the creation of an appropriate gun-shaped interface device, as it did with Nintendo's *Duck Hunt*. But for a holiday e-card/game that was, itself, not sold, there was neither the time nor the resources available to provide every user a controller in the shape of a UPC scanner. Subsequently, Brandon was forced to find ways to represent the scanner within the screen elements of the game, knowing that users would be interacting with a mouse. Brandon decided to rely primarily on the targets of the gun to indicate that the user was operating a pricing gun. That is, since the users were targeting UPC-coded boxes rather than clay pigeons or some other conventional target, their appreciation of the primary game tool should be different. Additionally, the single red line of a UPC scanner was used as cursor, in lieu of the more traditional gun sight.

Fit Forging in Action

The case of the hybrid Ryzex e-card/game provides a useful illustration of the dynamics between constraint and creativity in communication and design. In developing this artifact, Brandon had to confront a vast and disparate array of dynamically interacting genre-ing and situating processes. These include complex audiences (company officers, employees, and clients), purposes (holiday greetings, entertainment, ethos/branding), contexts (American holiday culture, secular corporate culture), conflicting generic conventions (shooting galleries, e-cards), and particular media ecologies (Flash, the internet circa 2008). In our original account of this complex inventional environment, we developed the articulation map shown in Figure 5.1 as a way of conceptualizing the competing exigencies of the design.

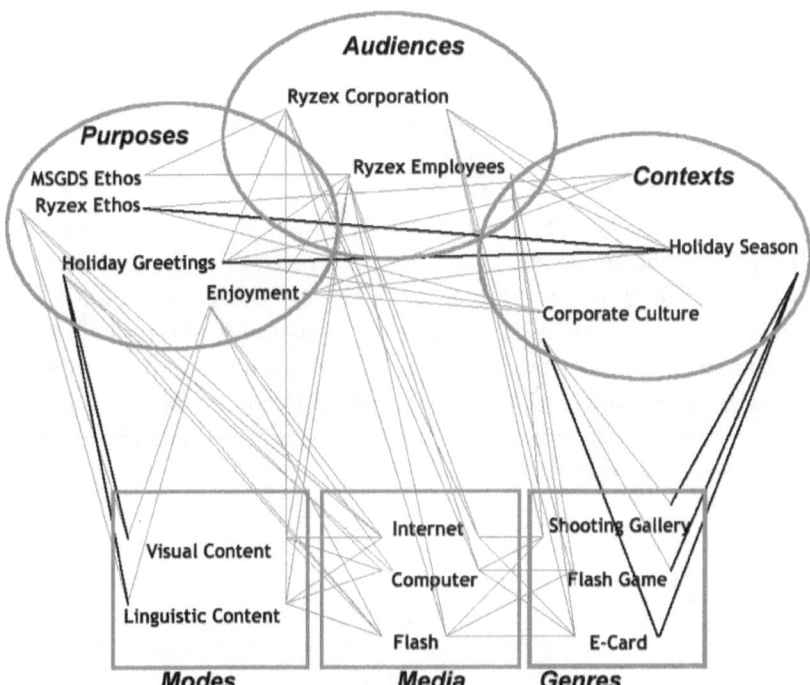

FIGURE 5.1. Graham and Whalen's (2008) schematic of e-card/game mode, medium, and genre interaction

As we described it at the time,

> the connecting lines represent specific articulations between design issues; the darker connecting lines represent the specific articulations in play for one design decision—determining how to encode the holiday content. The diagram illustrates the cascading nature and complexity of new-media design decisions and how particular articulations need to be understood and anticipated in making particular design decisions. Figure 5, despite its dizzying complexity, does not completely represent Brandon's design process in general; it is a representation of one instantiation of his design process. (Graham & Whalen, p. 87)

In the diagram, we can see the force of the modern Constitution playing out in the analysis. I committed precisely the same error that I attribute to the tradition of Burke-Received and its realization in GASA. I grafted a binary metaphysics onto a relational metaphysics, taking a productively integrated sociomaterial situation and dividing up the nodes into pre-identified categories. With the benefit of this new analysis, however, we can reinterpret Figure 5.1 as a complex situation composed of multiple genre-ing processes of becoming. It represents the nexus of genre-ing structures that helped shape Brandon's design process.

As an act of creativity, then we can now understand Brandon's design work as the realization of conjunction out of disjunction. The Ryzex e-card/game provided a mostly coherent unity (a satisfaction) that forged a rhetorical fit out of the competing structuring structures of pre-existing genre-ing and media processes. There was no possible way to simply respond to a pre-existing situation. Rather, the situation itself had to be modified as it unfolded. Thus the apparent shift between the e-card and the game. Brandon forged a new-media apparatus that evoked within its audience a succession of durations appropriate to the unique admixture of genre-ing processes. So harking back to my earlier definition of rhetoric in chapter 3 (the attempt to effect a satisfaction), we now have a new term of art within the GAP framework:

> **Fit Forging:** Action that effectively shifts the dynamics of an unfolding situation to fit the unfolding "response."

This concept and my description of Brandon's work here parallel Burke's discussion of evolutionary change in his rumination on metabiology. As he writes, "Let a certain new kind of grasshopper come into being, for instance, and you have a new set of 'principles' which move certain bits of the universe about in certain ways" (Burke, 1935, p. 297). The emergence of novelty, itself, can catalyze changes in the structuring structures of the universe. A new species' evolutionary niche does not always predate the emergence of that species. Fittingness can be forged.

As it turns out, the account here is also remarkably consonant with other rhetorical studies of inventional practice, even those that do not use a Bergsonian perspective. For example, Brian McNely, Paul Gestwicki, and Ann Burke (2013) draw on visual ethnography and writing, activity, and genre (WAGR) frameworks to describe the creative inventional practices of educational game designers. As they write:

> Artifacts, tools, symbol systems, historical contexts, cultures, and discursive norms combine to shape what it means to do the everyday work of game development. Spinuzzi ("Compound Mediation") uses the term compound mediation to "refer to the ways that people habitually coordinate sets of artifacts to mediate or carry out their activities" through an ecology of genres (98). Stated another way, an individual's genre ecology itself mediates activity in a given work or learning scenario rather than individual tools (100). . . . Genres, genre practices, and genre knowledge thus interact, overlap, and may even contradict one another or form new, hybrid assemblages.

Compound mediation and the creation of hybrid assemblages that resolve (or minimize) contradiction are key elements in the analysis here. As such, the transformation from disjunction to conjunction is powerfully evident as a novel fit is forged from competing exigencies.

Likewise, Stacy Pigg's (2014) ethnography of a "dad blogger" provides an account of creativity and rhetorical invention that exceeds the limits of a norms/conventional framework. Pigg argues persuasively that effective symbolic-analytic practices move "beyond understanding social norms and maintaining a presence in relationship to them; they must leverage them toward future action" (p. 81). Indeed, her account of the relational networks entered into by her primary subject (Dave) is remarkably Bergsonian in its orientation. As she describes it:

> What resulted between Dave and other dad bloggers was a reciprocal exchange of readership and knowledge that could be understood as a temporary alliance maintained through shared attention and practices. However, maintaining a presence or becoming part of a community was not the

> end goal for Dave's work; he learned and practiced participatory norms to use them to launch his writing.... Once writing was completed, for example, Dave leveraged social norms to garner notice from other dad bloggers. First, he posted kairotically (see Sheridan, Ridolfo, & Michel, 2012), timing his contribution to coincide with times of high readership. "Fatherhood Fridays," which drew on Twitter's tradition of using Fridays to share recommendations for new followers, were high on his list: "I've had 120 hits on Fridays. I have huge days on Fridays." This sense of timing motivated choices about what work to complete when: He posted in times of high potential activity to garner individual attention from the network. During his observation, for instance, Dave was motivated to finish his blog posting early during the day on Friday to have a new post online during Fatherhood Friday. (p. 81)

Like OBB's situation, Pigg's account of social media networks is one of "temporary alliances" that tend toward entropy. Dave's creative activity is future-oriented. It is centered around forging a new fit that resists the entropic forces of social media networks and entrepreneurial writing. Pigg's account details a complex interactional space where Dave must work to transform the disjunction of community norms, writing conventions, and media affordances into the type of conjunction that leads to ensuring success (stabilized community membership and correlatively high readership rates).

What's more, inventional spaces are not the only loci where this Bergsonian approach to genre proves productive. New scholarship in what is becoming known as "circulation studies" demonstrates remarkable parallels with my account of Brandon's inventional activities. For example, Jenny Edbauer Rice's (2005) canonical exploration of the rhetorical ecologies of "keep Austin weird" evinces a similar focus on creativity located in intra-active event-spaces. As she writes:

> Rhetorical ecologies are co-ordinating processes, moving across the same social field and within shared structures of feeling. The original call of Austin's "weird" rhetoric, for example, has been affected by the actions, events, and encounters that form "small events loosely joined" as a kind of rhetorical-event neighborhood. Even when a multi-national corporation like Cingular coopts the phrase, placing it within a completely antithetical context from its origin, we find that Cingular's rhetoric adds to the (original) rhetoric of "weirdness" in Austin. They mark two different situations, of course—complete with different exigence, audience, rhetors, and constraints. But Cingular's rhetoric co-ordinates within the same neighbor-

hood as the anti-corporate rhetoric. Thus, in the course of this evolution, the "weird rhetoric" receives what we might call an extended half-life in its range of circulation and visibility, as well as a changed shape, force, and intensity. Like a neighborhood, the amalgamation of events can both extend the street's visibility (or impact) and its very contours. (p. 20)

The link to Bergson's right branch is evident here. Edbauer Rice's rhetorical ecologies are built on a Deleuzian framework, and thus there is a clear intellectual trajectory between Bergson and Edbauer Rice. Subsequently, her ecological framework is attuned to the entropic forces surrounding public rhetorics and thus also locates creative power in the invention of rhetorical artifacts with staying power, as it were. The disjunctive experiences of migration, gentrification, Austin community movements, and corporate branding are forged into a conjunction located in a rhetorical-event neighborhood.

Likewise, Laurie Gries's *Still Life with Rhetoric* integrates Edbauer Rice's rhetorical ecologies with process-philosophy-inspired new materialisms to create yet another parallel account of rhetorical creativity. In so doing, she describes rhetoric as "an emergent process distributed across a complex web of physical, social, psychological, spatial and temporal dimensions (Edbauer Rice 2005, 12–13; Syverson 1999, 23)" (Gries, 2015, p. 15). This approach to rhetorical activity attunes Gries to rhetorics of circulation, and here the Bergsonian overtones of her scholarship become most evident. For Gries, circulation

> refers to spatiotemporal flows, which unfold and fluctuate as things enter into diverse associations and materialize in abstract and concrete forms. From a new materialist perspective operating in conjunction with a rhetorical ecology model, things must be studied as divergent, unfolding becomings in order to account for their unique, distributed rhetorical ontology. (p. 19)

The account here, thus, coordinates quite effectively with Miller and Shepherd's (2009) analysis of the emergence of the genre of the public affairs blog. They too offer a description of creativity and novelty born of the attempt to unify competing technological, cultural, and rhetorical strands. As they clarify:

> New technological capabilities, or affordances, helped make blogging a fitting rhetorical response to the recurrent exigence we have identified. For

an exigence characterized by the corporate commodification of news, perceived loss of authentic public engagement, and a shared sense of political impotence, blogs provided ways to engage issues, to participate in discussion, to undercut corporate media homogeneity, and to turn audiences into participatory communities. These effects addressed directly the growing unease with public discourse. The interactive capabilities, the immediacy of response, and the ease of access all contributed to the hope that blogging could support what Benjamin Barber has called "strong democracy," which he characterizes in rhetorical terms as "a democracy that reflects the careful and prudent judgment of citizens who participate in deliberative, self-governing communities (1999: 585)." (pp. 278–279)

Creativity is the required response to the entropic forces that arise from social, cultural, or technological perturbations. The post-9/11 media landscape dominated by fractured trust and an erosion of democratic norms provided the necessary preconditions for generic innovation. The public affairs blog forged for itself a new fit and stabilized within this novel admixture.

Coda

Finally, let me close this chapter by returning briefly to agency. Above, I have argued that reading agency through genre and genre through agency provides better purchase on enduring rhetorical debates over the conflict between change and stabilization. A rhetorical approach embedded in process philosophy allows for a better and more productive way of addressing this supposed conflict. As I have argued elsewhere (Graham, 2016), one of the fundamental issues with respect to the agency problem for rhetorical theory is that fact that it is typically presented in a synchronic framework. Synchronic structuralist theories of identity and subjectivity entirely disrupt the notion of rhetorical agency. Such theories of ideological interpellation or hegemony are meant to explain why agency has not occurred. As such, they lock analysts' attunements to the stabilizing forces that prevent change. Interestingly, many accounts of agency are also essentially synchronic. Many treatments of agentive acts focus on kairotic moments. These are singular events, isolated in time, where a prepared rhetor responds. But agency is fundamentally about change. As such, it is essentially diachronic. Agency is about differences during and between successive events. It is about the destabilization of stabilizing forces. Yet it is also about re-stabilization. If change is to be change, it must endure. To understand agency and innovation, one must appreciate how invention plays out across successive durations, to use Bergson's term of art.

In my previous writing on agency, I have argued that a review of the literature on agency will show that rhetoricians who purport to address the one thing that is "agency" are actually exploring multiple interrelated and successive phenomena. In making this claim, I outlined four agency maxims that can be distilled from the literature: "1) Agency is the process of instantiating change in the status quo. 2) Change arises from series of rhetorical events over time. 3) Although the overall agentive program resists authoritative forces, the constitutive rhetorical events frequently rely on those same authoritative forces. 4) A change becomes the status quo when the (new) authoritative structures operate to maintain the change" (Graham, 2009, pp. 379–380). This analysis here suggests that these maxims might be rewritten to apply equally to **genre change:**

1. Genre innovation is the process of instantiating change in the structuring templates of recurrent situations.
2. Genre innovation arises from perturbations in series of events over time.
3. The new structuring templates of emerging genres arise from transforming disjunctive pre-existing structuring templates into novel conjunctive structuring templates.
4. New genres become stabilized when they themselves begin to genre.

As I close this chapter, I want to draw the reader's attention to one significant ramification of GAP and its theory of genre change: the critical importance of diachronic analyses. Rhetorical inquiry's traditional focus on "the" situation often results in fairly synchronic analyses of moments of rhetorical activity. Indeed, much in the way of neoclassical analytic terms attune critics to relatively isolated moments. The original Aristotelian ethos is invoked in the moment of oratory, rather than a function of the author's actual character over time. Kairos, and the analytic criterion of "fittingness," is often expressed in momentary metaphors—the instant the warp and woof make threading the needle possible; the moment where an arrow can penetrate a shield wall. As the ethnography of innovation, above, describes, genre change is a process within processes. Brandon relies on memory and creativity to forge a new fit in an actively unfolding situation. Midair refueling might be a better metaphor than weaving or combat archery. What's more, there is a second dimension of diachrony in my final account of genre change. There are the unfolding processes of memory and creativity where rhetors attempt to forge new fits. There are also the larger unfolding processes of sociomaterial structures whereby innovative responses begin to exercise their own maieutic effect on subsequent genred activity. Here we come closest to the original linguistic sense of diachronic.

In the next two chapters, I argue that new methods of inquiry are necessary for rhetoricians to effectively attend to this dimension of diachrony. Just as field methods like ethnography make it easier for us to attune ourselves to the unfolding processes of invention, methods that can evaluate scope, scale, and change are required for us to properly appreciate longitudinal change in certain structures. And, so finally, we return to the problem of CR invoked in the introduction. Computational methods are not the only methods available for tackling structural change, but they do offer some powerful affordances toward that end. Thus, in chapter 6 I address the epistemic challenges of CR for rhetorical inquiry, and in chapter 7 I demonstrate how CR and traditional rhetorical criticism can work hand-in-glove to explore genres and genre change in a GAP idiom.

CHAPTER 6

THE SCIENCE OF INTUITION

> Formalized procedures and language, including quantification, overcome physical and temporal distance, disparities of experience and background, and absence of a shared natural language. To increase the scope of their communication, professionals reduce their reliance on the sort of intimate, personal knowledge and judgment that can only build up over time in small, tight-knit, and highly interactive groups.
> —CHARNEY, 1996, P. 577

> The positivistic overreaction argues that scale (Smith 2012) is computation's main bounty—all of Faulkner in a nanosecond. . . . Assumptions like these, says Susan Witting (1997), turn words into numbers efficiently, but too often forsake the text itself.
> —HART, 2015, P. 154

ONE DAY—longer ago than I'd care to admit—in my high school chemistry class, the teacher offered a brief lecture on "The Hierarchy of the Sciences." He explained how we should understand that there is a steady progression of increasing accuracy up a pyramid of scientific inquiry, and that furthermore each step up the pyramid is a truer expression of the science below. Specifically, we were told that biology is really chemistry; chemistry is really physics; and physics is really math. Nearly a decade later, in another classroom—this time a graduate seminar in the history of science—my professor (who really should have known better) presented the exact same hierarchy as a true account of the world. Around the same time, while attending an interdisciplinary graduate student conference, I saw a biologist and a physicist nearly come to blows in a bar over the relative size of the error bars[1] in their respective disciplines and what that might mean for whose field was better. In the intervening years, I took classes with a philosophy professor who also taught the hierarchy of the sciences but ended the hierarchy one step further with the assertion that math is really philosophy. I kind of liked this version, of course, and I think Bergson would have as well.

Nineteenth-century philosopher and sociologist August Comte is largely credited as the originator of this kind of hierarchy of the sciences, and his devotion to positivism is evident in its construction. Comte argued that each science progressed through a series of evolutionary phases toward increasing positivity or exactness. That is, as a science matured, it would be able to make more accurate and objective claims about the world. However, it's worth noting that the contemporary mythological hierarchy of scientists and science teachers inverts Comte's hierarchy where physics and mathematics were foundational, albeit more positivist. Regardless of the structure of the moment, Comte's hierarchy (or something quite like it) has been used to authorize boundary work (see chapter 1) in academia for some time.

Within rhetoric, disciplinary hierarchies are (at least, ostensibly) out of vogue, but questions about epistemic authority still persist, and often function as an inevitable part of boundary work. Indeed, the opening epigraphs to this chapter showcase enduring epistemological debates in the discipline. In the first passage, Davida Charney calls on rhetoricians and technical communicators to accept that "empiricism is not a four-letter word." She reminds us of the ways that quantification and rigor can improve both inquiry and dissemination. More recently, Roderick Hart cautions rhetorical DHers against the dangers of overly positivist approaches to text analytics. Each scholar advocates the use of rigorous methodologies and is more than willing to deploy quantification in their inquiry. Yet, at the same time, long-standing disciplinary concerns about quantification and positivism force careful hedging even in the midst of quantitative advocacy. Now certainly, there is good reason for concern. The issue of the truthiness and its relationship to power in and beyond the sciences is no small matter. Epistemic authority, generally warranted through appeals to positivity and/or exactness, has absolutely been used in a wide variety of unethical pursuits, from eugenics to predatory pharmaceuticals marketing. The Strong Programme of social construction and the corresponding rhetorical turn were important

---

1. Error bars are lines drawn across individual points on a scatter plot. They indicate how uncertain any given measurement is, and as such they serve as a synecdoche for "exactness."

both for disrupting these power dynamics and for offering rhetoric its own, albeit localized, epistemic authority.

Nevertheless, the move toward CR and the emerging focus on quantification suggest that these epistemic issues need to be revisited in rhetorical studies. Ultimately, the role of CR in rhetoric will always be suspect as long as the epistemic authority of rhetorical inquiry is built primarily on the construal of quantification as an unethical power grab. Rhetors deploying this kind of boundary work in our discipline are enacting something like a reversal of Comte's hierarchy, where increasing positivity is rendered as increasing self-delusion (at best) or increasing dishonesty (at worst). Nevertheless, there is good reason to embrace the idea that CR methods may provide useful insights for rhetoric. However, if they are to do so successfully, CR must be built on an epistemic foundation that avoids the positivist overreaction, on a foundation that does not merely constitute backsliding into some sort of misguided/inverted hierarchization effort.

Once again, in suggesting one possible pathway toward greater disciplinary cohesion, I argue that we can take inspiration from Bergson, in this case from his notion of intuition.

> **Intuition:** An experiential approach to metaphysical inquiry characterized by a general aim of identifying how abstract representations of reality distort our understanding of reality.

Much of this book has been about Bergson's intuition. Indeed, chapters 3, 4, and 5 are, in many ways, exercises in Bergsonian method as applied to RNM and RGS. Essentially the aim has been to explore rhetor and audience experiences of genre so as to clarify where common metaphysical representations (e.g., binary metaphysics) have led us astray.

In this light, and given that intuition is Bergson's preferred method of inquiry, the move toward quantitative approaches might seem odd. However, as Deleuze was quick to remind us, Bergson was actually far more committed to scientific inquiry than one might generally suspect. In an effort to correct the gut reaction that Bergson might be antiscience, Deleuze (1991) has this to offer:

> Rather, [Bergson] thought that the Absolute has two "halves," to which science and metaphysics correspond. Thought divides into two paths in a single impetus, one toward matter, its bodies and movements, and the other toward sprit, its qualities and changes. (p. 116)

Interestingly, we find a similar corrective (vis-à-vis Burke) in Duncan's (1965/1984) introduction to the third edition of *Permanence and Change*. Debra Hawhee's corrective account of Burke's investments in epidemiology and metabiology notwithstanding, many in rhetoric tacitly assume that Burke was antiscience. However, Duncan argues that Burke was "not against science, even science that tells us the world must be regarded as a great machine" (p. 2). Instead, Burke (or at least OBB) was more concerned with overly narrow positivist notions of science and hoped to help scientists think through the myriad ways their inquiries fit into larger systems.

In what follows, my aim is to demonstrate the Bergsonian tradition's significant affinity for scientific inquiry. From this line of thought, I will further show how foundational contemporary rhetorical theory and related science studies neglect this tradition by reading all science as a positivist caricature. To disrupt these problematic presuppositions, I offer an autoethnographic account of one methodological area where rhetoricians are already somewhat more willing to go quantitative—content analysis and interrater reliability. In so doing, I argue that (1) rhetoric's history with content analysis provides a model for how rhetoric can productively combine its intuitive arts with a more scientific project; and (2) more recent science studies' insights about the nature of scientific inquiry can provide an appropriate alternative epistemic framework for CR, one that can allow for normative judgments about truthiness without replicating antiquated positivist hierarchies and ideologies.

Dropping Science

The Beastie Boys' (1989) song "Sounds of Science" refers to dropping science in the sense of dropping the bass or the beat. That is, science is dropped *into* the situation or duration. This is the sense of dropping science that I intend in the chapter as a whole. But, oddly, *dropping* can be its own antonym, and for the next few paragraphs I need to discuss that other form of *dropping*. Here I refer to when science got dropped (or maybe drop-kicked) by rhetoric. In many respects the modern era of rhetorical inquiry has been authorized by the dropping of science. The rhetorical turn which I discussed in chapter 2 results in far more than reinscribing the metaphysical binaries of the modern Constitution. The rhetorical turn was not simply derivative. Its innovation was to leverage the modern Constitution to drop science down in disciplinary hierarchies, to replace exactness with other measures of epistemic prestige and authority.

Two foundational texts in the contemporary rhetorical tradition are largely credited with dropping science. Robert Scott's (1967) "On Viewing Rhetoric as Epistemic" and Carolyn Miller's (1979) "A Humanistic Rationale for Technical Writing" serve both as touchstones in our disciplinary histories and primary loci of hierarchal realignment. Indeed, both Scott and Miller partially ground their arguments against (positivist) science in a concern over what scientific epistemologies mean for rhetoric. For example, Scott laments that

> the art of persuasion is granted sufferance only on the grounds that men are not as they ought to be. Were all men able as some men are to reason soundly from true premises, then rhetoric would be superfluous. (pp. 9–10)

Similarly, Miller (1979) is concerned that positivist epistemology construes language as grounded in "personal psychology" and thus "is largely a distraction for science" (pp. 612–613).

Ultimately, Miller is even more direct than Scott with her frustrations about where positivist epistemologies place rhetoric in the hierarchies of academia. In so doing, she further argues that the technical communication wing of the discipline runs the risk of internalizing its own marginalization when it accepts disciplinary hierarchies based on exactness. As she writes:

> The most uncomfortable aspect of this non-rhetorical view of science is that it is a form of intellectual coercion: it invites us to prostrate ourselves at the windowpane of language and accept what Science has demonstrated. After all, if we do not see the self-evident, there must be something very wrong with us. I believe that this mystique of absolute scientific truth is as much responsible as our technical achievements for the power of science and technology in our culture today. If rhetoric is irrelevant to science, technical and scientific writing become just a series of maneuvers for staying out of the way. A rhetorical discipline built on positivist theory must founder on this self-deprecation at its center. But because there has been no alternative basis for the discipline, technical writing as it is commonly taught is shot through with positivist assumptions, which destroy its aspirations toward disciplinary respectability and relegate it to its status as a skills course. (Miller, 1979, p. 613)

This is certainly no way to run a discipline, and furthermore, it creates a deeply problematic pedagogical foundation. And so, as a boundary-enforcing corrective, Miller (like Scott) drops science down a peg.

Essentially, both Scott and Miller make the same theoretical move. They recenter epistemology not in exactness or positivity but rather in rhetoric and consensus. Scott (1967) overtly rejects the notion that one "must consider truth not as something fixed and final," arguing instead that it is "created moment by moment in the circumstances in which he finds himself and with which he must cope" (p. 17). This position leads ultimately to his argument that "in human affairs, then, rhetoric, perceived in the frame herein discussed, is a way of knowing; it is epistemic" (p. 17). Likewise, Miller (1979) suggests that science, itself, is a fundamentally rhetorical enterprise: "Science, then, is not concerned directly with material things, but with these human constructions, with symbols and arguments" (p. 616). As a result, "Scientific verification requires the persuasion of an audience that what has been 'observed' is replicable and relevant" (p. 616).

Without a doubt, dropping science through arguments about the problems of positivism and the inherent rhetoricity of knowledge production have been instrumental in authorizing large swaths of inquiry. As a result, the theoretical positions that underlie these articles have established, in our disciplinary zeitgeist, a profound distrust of positive knowledge claims and quantitative argumentation. The essential presumption of our discipline is that most knowledge claims are inherently facile and based on laughably ignorant epistemological foundations. As mentioned above, the Bergsonian tradition is not nearly so committed to this portrayal of inquiry as an adversarial hierarchy. Rather, different disciplinary methods and projects must advance in concert so as to be mutually informative.

Abstraction and Intuition

Although I will eventually reject Scott and Miller's rejection of science, there is much to admire in their arguments. Certainly science, when viewed through a positivist lens, necessarily construes rhetoric as largely irrelevant window-dressing. And Miller is quite right that this attitude has significant deleterious effects for the study of rhetoric as well as rhetorical pedagogy. Ultimately, my rejection of their rejection is not a rejection of these concerns. Rather, it is an objection to what has become a totalizing view of all science as positivistic. An unfortunate side effect of the popularization of science through positivist frameworks has been that the popular rhetorics about science (e.g., Comte's hierarchy) are quite a bit more positivistic than the everyday practice of science.

While the actual language of Miller's (1979) article demonstrates her sensitivity to this issue, much of the nuance has been lost in how her article has been received by the discipline. Indeed, rhetoric largely followed the same path as history and sociology of science in its willingness to read the rhetorical/linguistic/cultural turn as a rejection of science *in toto*. Our received reading of Miller looks very much like the received reading of Kuhn in cognate disciplines and is likely one Miller herself would reject. With the benefit of an additional thirty years of inquiry in rhetoric of science and science studies, it's even easier to see the limitations of our old narratives. In many ways, science isn't science anymore. That is, the caricatures of science used in rhetoric of science (which are based on nineteenth-century scientism) are not particularly representative of contemporary scientific practices or ideologies.

I was recently asked to write an essay for *Theory and Event*, exploring the resonances between my own work and Samantha Frost's new book, *Biocultural Creatures*. The exercise provided me a valuable opportunity to really explore how far science has come since it was the science so often caricatured and pilloried by rhetoric. Indeed, one thing that stood out was how very much the latest sciences have started to look a lot like new materialisms. As I write in the essay:

> These latest insights of biology and biochemistry resonate productively with new materialists' conceptions of the human because, as Frost points out, both initiatives understand the human as "a creature embedded in and composed by the social and material contexts of its existence, an agent whose actions are dependent on and conditioned by manifold networks of ecological, institutional, social, and symbolic relations." . . . The new biochemistry of epigenetics and the biopsychosocial model of pain medicine are fundamentally nonmodern. At a profound level, they reject the binaries and reductionism of the modernist project and so have the potential to transcend the ideologies of scientism without rejecting science, whole cloth. (Graham, 2017, p. 534)

What I didn't know when I wrote this was that in arguing that contemporary accounts of scientific practice look like new materialisms, I was inadvertently arguing that contemporary accounts of scientific practice look like the kinds of science Bergson found most appealing.

Here it must be noted that at the time Bergson was writing, positivism was new. It was a proposal for how to do science, and not yet one that had been broadly accepted. As a result, his view of science wasn't so powerfully informed by our contemporary popular rhetorics of science and so he was comfortable noting that "modern science is neither one nor simple" (Bergson, 1903/1946, p. 233). With his sense of the differences between scientific practices animating his ideas, Bergson was open to a version of inquiry that hybridized metaphysical and scientific inquiry. As Deleuze (1991) describes it, "Scientific hypothesis and metaphysical thesis are constantly combined in Bergson in the reconstitution of complete experiences" (p. 118). While Bergson's preferred sciences tended to be theoretical, he also made room for the utility of quantitative inquiry.

Utility is the key word in the last sentence. Bergson (1903/1946) focuses on intuition as the principle method of metaphysics precisely because metaphysics "does not aim at any application, can and [so] for the most part ought to abstain from converting intuition into symbol" (p. 225). However, when the aim is action, quantitative inquiry is a critically useful tool for tracing the processes of becoming. As Bergson writes:

> Modern mathematics is precisely an effort to substitute for the ready-made what is in process of becoming, to follow the growth of magnitudes, to seize movement no longer from outside and in its manifest result, but from within and in its tendency towards change, in short, to adopt the mobile continuity of the pattern of things. (Bergson, 1903/1946, p. 225)

For Bergson, quantitative approaches offer a way to chart the kinds of diachronic processes alluded to at the end of the last chapter. Quantification can help identify the emergence of patterns in the processes of becoming. Here Bergson describes the epistemic act of abstraction, which he construes as the primary useful mode of scientific and mathematical inquiry.

> **Abstraction:** The process of distilling intuitive insights into formalized representations so as to better support future situated action.

Something remarkably like Bergson's embrace of then modern mathematics occurs in Miller's (2016) "Genre Innovation: Evolution, Emergence, or Something Else?" In the article, Miller argues for an approach to genre innovation grounded in another diachronically focused mode of inquiry, in this case biological evolution. Importantly, however, her invocation of evolutionary thought is not grounded in popular or tacit understandings of what evolution is or means. Instead, she is careful to point us toward contemporary philosophies and epistemologies of evolution grounded in population thinking. As she describes it:

> Evolution, in contrast, gives us a population-based model of genre, focusing our attention on diachronic change and relatedness, as well as on the variation among instances, giving us incremental processes and empirically fuzzy boundaries between apparent genres. Evolution invites us to look for mechanisms that enable or promote change, as Fowler suggests with his list of the processes by which literary genres are transformed. (Miller, 2016, p. 15)

Although the article does not go so far as to argue for a mathematical approach to genre, it is striking that Miller's evolutionary genre theory is population-based as opposed to Lamarckian. In Lamarck's theory of evolution, it is the individual that drives change. Giraffes have such long necks because they spend their entire lives stretching to reach the highest branches. This effort is passed down, somehow, and the children of the stretchiest giraffes start off a bit taller. In contrast, a population-based approach to evolution situates adaptation and speciation as the result of a complex, dynamic web of environmental pressures. Likewise, for Miller, it is not solely the drive of individual rhetors seeking to reach new heights that causes genre innovation but rather a constellation of forces on a variable population.

Ultimately, this provides a powerful entrée for CR in that CR affords us the technologies necessary to track population variances in situated responses. The population approach underscores Bergson's suggestion that intuition and abstraction must work hand-in-glove when the aim is situated action. The insights of our rhetorical intuitions must combine with representative abstractions of population variants to provide an effective foundation for response. What's more, Miller's suggested population approach fits perfectly within the GAP theoretical framework I have been developing. Both the de-atomized rhetor and the possibility of fit forging are derived from Bergson and Burke's interest in emerging evolutionary theory as applied to human action. Thus, in what follows, I reflect on some of my own work in content analysis and interrater reliability to demonstrate how rhetorical intuition and abstraction might effectively coordinate in an extended Bergsonian tradition.

The Science of Intuition

Since 2011 I have been working as part of several teams to better understand the patterns of discourse at US Food and Drug Administration (FDA) drug advisory committee meetings. Drug advisory committees are independent bodies of biomedical experts and patient and consumer representatives who evaluate questions of regulatory policy for the FDA. Advisory committee meetings are structured like a legal proceeding, where a series of pro, con, and supporting presentations are offered to the advisory board, followed by intermittent periods of cross-examination. The most common form of advisory committee meeting evaluates whether a new drug should be approved for the market. In these cases, the drug manufacturer offers an affirmative presentation laying out evidence for the drug's safety and efficacy. A group of FDA scientists provide a counter presentation highlighting any concerns about the suitability of the drug for market. The advisory committee questions both groups of presenters, and there is generally a public comment period where patients, practitioners, and advocacy organization representatives offer additional perspectives on the drug's safety and efficacy.

Pursuing these questions has always been a collaborative endeavor, and I have worked with research teams at my then home institutions (the University of British Columbia and the University of Wisconsin-Milwaukee) as well as with a remote collaborator from The Ohio State University. Regardless of the driving research question at any given phase of the project, the driving goal has been to understand patterns of discourse across increasingly large samples of advisory committee meetings. This necessarily led to various content-analysis coding schemata. My work on drug advisory committees has had two primary motivating questions, the first having to do with patient voice and the second addressing financial conflicts of interest. Regarding the first aim, my collaborator described the intent of the project thusly: "Our goal is to analyze how the FDA's deliberative procedures afforded the capture of key stakeholder discourse and whether that discourse is meaningfully incorporated into final policy decisions" (Teston & Graham, 2012, p. 2). Over the lifecycle of the project, my interests expanded to include more complex questions regarding the influence of different stakeholder makeups on advisory committee deliberation and decision-making. As a later article put it:

> Specific research questions include (a) Does the presence of (more) patient representatives change the nature of the debate? (b) Does an increase in the number of financial conflicts of interest among adjudicators change the outcome of committee meetings? (c) Do drug manufacturers adapt their presentations to the types of questions under consideration or the demographics of the adjudicators? (Graham et al., 2015, p. 71).

A still later iteration of the project turned our analysis back on the predictive theses of rhetorical theory to evaluate

TABLE 6.1. Coding Domains and Representative Content Codes

CODING DOMAIN	REPRESENTATIVE CONTENT CODES
Official FDA position	Advisory committee member, drug sponsor, FDA employee, patient representative, non-party presenter
Stakeholder status	Biomedical expert, patient, FDA administrator, patient ally, patient advocacy organization representative
Forms of evidence	Safety data, efficacy data, preclinical data, pathological data, patient testimony, provider experience
Modes of reasoning	Probabilistic, experiential, economic
Site of practice	Clinical laboratory, patient–provider encounter, pharmacy, medicine cabinet
Conflict status	Financial relationship with drug sponsor, financial relationship with competitor, conflict intensity (±$50,000), conflict type (personal or imputed)
Rhetorical constructs	Stasis questions (fact, value, jurisdiction); Toulmin model (claim, evidence, warrant)

a central assumption of [Rhetoric of Health and Medicine] that the inclusion of patients in clinical and health policy decision-making will invariably catalyze an increase in the amount of time spent discussing those unique domains to which patients have access and doctors do not. (Graham et al., 2018, p. 64)

Addressing these shifting research questions required visiting and revisiting the artifacts of analysis. Likewise, along the way my collaborators and I were required to imagine and reimagine new ways of accounting for and representing the complex texts we sought to understand.

Ultimately, over the life of the project, we have used a variety of traditional, directed, and summative content-analytic approaches to understand the nature of deliberation at drug advisory committee meetings. We coded transcripts for who was speaking, what their stakeholder status was, forms of evidence offered, evidentiary logics deployed, rhetorical stases, Toulminian warrants, and so forth. A full accounting of each coding schema used would require about twenty pages, so I've provided a list of representative coding domains in Table 6.1.

The various coding schemata were applied to approximately a dozen different samples of advisory committee meeting content. Many samples were coded once in the pursuit of answering a single research question. Other samples were coded repeatedly according to multiple different schemata as part of different phases of the project. At present, I'd estimate that my collaboratories and I have coded about twenty million words of advisory committee discourse over the life of this project.

Ultimately, our efforts to make sense of FDA discourse began—as many similar projects do—in a very inductive register. The initial publication of coding activities was essentially an exercise in traditional qualitative content analysis and grounded theory. This is something we worked to surface in the methodological discussion. As we described it:

> We chose to deploy a hybrid methodology combining grounded theory with rhetorical stasis analysis. Miles and Huberman (1994) outline a set of analytic moves characteristic of qualitative data analysis. These include the "affixing" of codes to field notes from observations or interviews, "noting reflections," identifying "similar phrases, relationships," and "patterns, themes, distinct differences between subgroups, and common sequences," then confronting "those generalizations with a formalized body of knowledge in the form of constructs or theories" (9). (Teston et al., 2014, p. 153)

What I wish to suggest here is that the inductive approaches to qualitative content analysis are essentially intuitive. Like Bergson, I reject the idea that intuitive means instinctual or noncognitive. Rather, rhetorical training provided the coding team a suite of intuitive methodologies that we were able to deploy so as to abstract patterns from our engagement with the series of recurrent rhetorical situations that make up drug advisory committee meetings.

However, as the research questions shifted from exploratory to evaluative, the needs of the project changed, and subsequently the methods deployed took on a more quantitative character. The 2015 *TCQ* article presents the results of an entirely new coding exercise deployed on a much larger sample of drug advisory committee meetings. The increase in scale required an increase in quantification to make sense of the data. As a result, the methodological emphasis on the intuitive part of the exercise is somewhat diminished in the final write-up. Nevertheless, we felt it was critically important to link our quantitative results to a strong foundation in rhetorical intuition. Thus, the aim was "to offer encompassing conclusions about larger data sets without losing the craft character of rhetorical inquiry" (Graham et al., 2015, p. 72). The most recent contribution to the project underscores our efforts to manage the dialectic between intuition and quantification. As we wrote:

> In working to meet this difficult balance, our approach here began with lengthy traditional rhetorical analyses of discourse wherein the develop-

ment of coding categories and the subsequent quantification was resisted as long as possible. However, in keeping with the postcritical tradition, the ultimate quantification of the data is a critical part of our goal to offer findings in ways that the medical community may find more inherently persuasive. (Graham et al., 2018, p. 67)

Here we describe the third and most extensive recoding activity. The methods discussed here were applied to the largest yet section of FDA discourse and probably represent the upper limit of what's possible without scientist levels of grant funding or automated computational assistance.

In content analysis, intuition is represented quantitatively in two different modes. The first mode I discuss below, interrater reliability, offers a quantification of intuition itself and provides a metric that aims to account for the many perturbations that may occur when different rhetorical-analytic subsystems (raters) enter the research situation. The second mode includes representation of the data themselves. Accounts of content frequency by code are essentially aggregations of intuitions rendered symbolically so that the patterns, abstracted for the local sites of situated action, become more clearly visible.

Quantifying Intuition Itself

Interrater reliability (sometimes called *intercoder reliability* or *interrater agreement*) refers to a suite of methodological practices designed to underwrite the quality of heuristics that support human judgment in a variety of domains. As content-analysis pioneer Klaus Krippendorff (1980) describes it:

> The ultimate aim of testing reliability is to establish whether data obtained in the course of research can provide a trustworthy basis for drawing inferences, making recommendations, supporting decisions, or accepting something as fact. (p. 146)

That is, interrater reliability is construed as one warrant for epistemic authority and trust. Originally developed for psychological research and clinical practice, interrater reliability is designed to lend trustworthiness to scales and inventories that support situated action (diagnosis in clinical psychology). That is, the goal is to ensure that different psychologists working with different patients in different contexts will arrive at the same diagnosis using the same diagnostic instrument.

In psychology most (if not all) approaches to interrater reliability are statistical. Interrater-reliability metrics (often κ-statistics) provide a measure of consensus that corrects for chance. Correcting for chance is an essential improvement over other measures of consensus. For example, with percent agreement, the proverbial (and much maligned) team of monkey coders would achieve 50 percent agreement.[2] Different interrater-reliability metrics are available for a wide range of methodological designs. The number of raters, the presence or absence of missing data, the use of binary (yes or no) or continuous (a numerical scale) rating designs, and other similar design decisions all contribute to decisions about which interrater-reliability metric is most appropriate. Those interested in assessing interrater reliability can choose from among a wide range of κ-statistics, α-statistics, and correlation coefficients depending on study design.

Although reliability is often discussed in terms of the statistics that measure it, the phenomenon evaluated is far more complex. As Holsti (1969) describes it:

> Reliability is a function of coders' skill, insight, and experience, clarity of categories and coding rules which guide their use; and the degree of ambiguity in the data. Because the nature of the data is usually beyond the investigator's control, opportunities for enhancing reliability are generally limited to improving coders, categories, or both. (p. 135)

This conception of interrater reliability centers itself firmly within the realm of content-analytic methodologies more familiar to rhetoricians. While there are a wide variety of different approaches to content analysis, at their core they are quite similar and involve the development of a schema of codes for identifying patterns in discourse. Traditional qualitative content analysis and grounded theory are among the most common forms of content analysis. These methods use collected textual artifacts from communities or domains of interest to inductively identify common themes across an artifact population. The practice of content analysis primarily involves assigning codes to sections of discourse in the artifact population. Historically, this was often accomplished by use of color-coded highlighting or through literally cutting up artifacts into units of analysis (sentences, paragraphs,

---

2. Although it is considered problematic to report percent agreement alone, the value is often reported alongside interrater reliability metrics that correct for chance. Agreement values may be artificially suppressed when agreement is high within a relatively small sample or in cases of cell asymmetries.

t-units[3]) and placing the text fragments in piles corresponding to thematic codes. More contemporary content analysts use one of many available qualitative analysis software programs that allow codes to be attached to units of interest as metadata.

Regardless of the physical practice, content analysis is much like psychological diagnosis, as the aim is to create a heuristic (coding schema) that supports consistent intuitive judgments (theme or feature identification) across a variable population of artifacts divided into units of analysis. However, unlike in psychology, agreement statistics are not the only methodological approach used in content analysis. Some content analysts use one of several methodological designs that engineer 100 percent agreement. Two common approaches are (1) consensus-based coding, where analysts discuss each code and the assignment of each code to each unit and only assign that code in cases of agreement; and (2) coder dropping, a practice where more analysts are used than needed, and those that disagree are removed from the final report.

In rhetoric, it's also not uncommon to use a single-rater design, which would, of course, result in either perfect agreement or no agreement—depending on your perspective. Certainly, one reason this is the case comes from the traditional solo-practitioner humanistic orientation of rhetorical theory. However, I suspect that deeply ingrained rhetorical skepticism about quantification may also explain why many in rhetorical studies eschew interrater-reliability metrics.

While consensus-based coding methods are an effective way to ensure high degrees of interrater reliability, some worry that the practice compromises the integrity of the study. If agreement is uniformly high, it may indicate that no meaningful judgments are being made. That is, why should we go to the effort of creating a schema, training raters, and assessing reliability if themes are easily identified? Additionally, focusing only on using reliability metrics to underwrite completed research neglects the powerful utility of interrater reliability during schema development and refinement. Interrater-reliability assessments, deployed early in a project, help analysts calibrate intuitive judgments. That is, they can help determine when raters need additional training and/or when coding categories need to be refined, subdivided, or otherwise changed before the study is complete.

Over the course of my research on FDA drug advisory committees, I have profoundly changed my relationship to and my understanding of interra-

---

3. A *t-unit* or *utterance* is a variable length of text defined by a change in speaking subjects. That is, a t-unit is all the things one person says until s/he stops to listen to another speaker.

ter reliability. Different phases of this project and different coding schemata required fundamentally different approaches to guaranteeing the reliability of the research practices deployed. In part, this was a function of audience. Certainly, journals in health communication and medical sciences required a rather more particular approach to interrater reliability than did journals in rhetorical studies or medical humanities. But I can no longer see the different approaches to interrater reliability as a function of different disciplinary audiences. Through engaging with these different disciplinary practices and collaborators from health communication, specifically the quantitative side of health communication, I've developed a rather different understanding of the function of interrater reliability in rhetorical research. Initially, I understood interrater reliability to be a necessary fiction. As a devotee of social constructivist theories of epistemology, I understood interrater reliability to be a fictional statistic designed to lend authority to research practices that otherwise wouldn't have them. It seems to be little more than a modernist conceit employed uncomfortably as part of a postmodern research practice. I now have a much more robust appreciation for the humble kappa statistic.

Content Quantified

Following successful coding exercises, the other quantitative benefit of content analysis is that, in some cases, it can be used to effectively create a representative abstraction. That is, the quantitative representation of content-analytic exercises aggregates intuitions in order to provide a snapshot of the patterns of discourse studied. This idea that the goal of rhetorical inquiry practices is to create a representation of artifacts studied is not a new one. Indeed, how should we understand a close reading if not as a representation of the intuitive experience that follows traditional rhetorical criticism?

This idea is, perhaps, presented most clearly in Carl Herndl's (1991) account of ethnographic practice and its use in rhetorical inquiry. Herndl's goal in his article is quite similar to the goal of this chapter. It serves as a justification for importing what some might consider a social scientific research method (ethnography) into a traditionally humanist space (rhetoric). Ultimately, "Writing Ethnography: Representation, Rhetoric, and Institutional Practices" rejects the idea that ethnographic researchers are positivist or should be understood though that lens. Drawing on insights from postmodern ethnographers in anthropology, Herndl argues that accounts of ethnographic research are predicated on the inscription of field notes. In short, ethnographers create a representation (field notes) of their data (observations) and then draw conclusions from those representations. Content-analysis pioneer Krippendorff (1980) offers a similar account of his research in his textbook, where he argues, "As a research technique, content analysis involves specialized procedures for processing scientific data. Like all research techniques, its purpose is to provide knowledge, new insights, a *representation* of the facts" (p. 22; emphasis added).

Ultimately, my research on the FDA has been about providing quantitative representations of patterns of discourse. Sometimes this is expressed in a specifically genre idiom. Other times it is not. In my 2015 *TCQ* article, the primary representational outcome was what my team and I dubbed a genre *fingerprint*. That is, we distilled the collected intuitions of our coding practices into a single data display. As we described that display:

> Figure [6.1] provides what we believe to be a novel and productive approach to genre analysis in rhetoric and technical communication. Essentially what this figure offers is a visual representation of the assessed genre conventions in sponsor presentations at ODAC meetings. Although traditional, inductive approaches to genre analysis select exemplar artifacts and provide a nuanced discussion of common responses across those exemplar artifacts, Figure [6.1] represents a complete analysis of the responses to the rhetorical situation during a 4-year period. Rather than typical or conventional being identified as a result of rhetorical analysis of prototypes, typical arguments are here identified graphically by describing their typical distribution. This offers great potential for identifying truly typified responses and could be used heuristically in the development of future sponsor presentations (and similar statistical models could be developed other technical communication genres). (Graham et al., 2015, p. 86)

Ultimately, I would describe the genre fingerprint as an abstraction, as a representative aggregation of intuitions. Although the language did not survive through to the final article, that is precisely how my co-authors and I described it during the initial submission of the manuscript. That version of the article included the following description of the relationship between our more scientific approach and the intuitive methods of rhetorical inquiry:

> Thus, the definition of a genre should be said to be representative of the collected responses to a recurrent situation. Subsequently, we would argue that the claim to typification in traditional TC/rhetorical genre analysis is perhaps a bit overstated in that it is grounded in the description of some small number of artifacts that, which are taken inductively to be "represen-

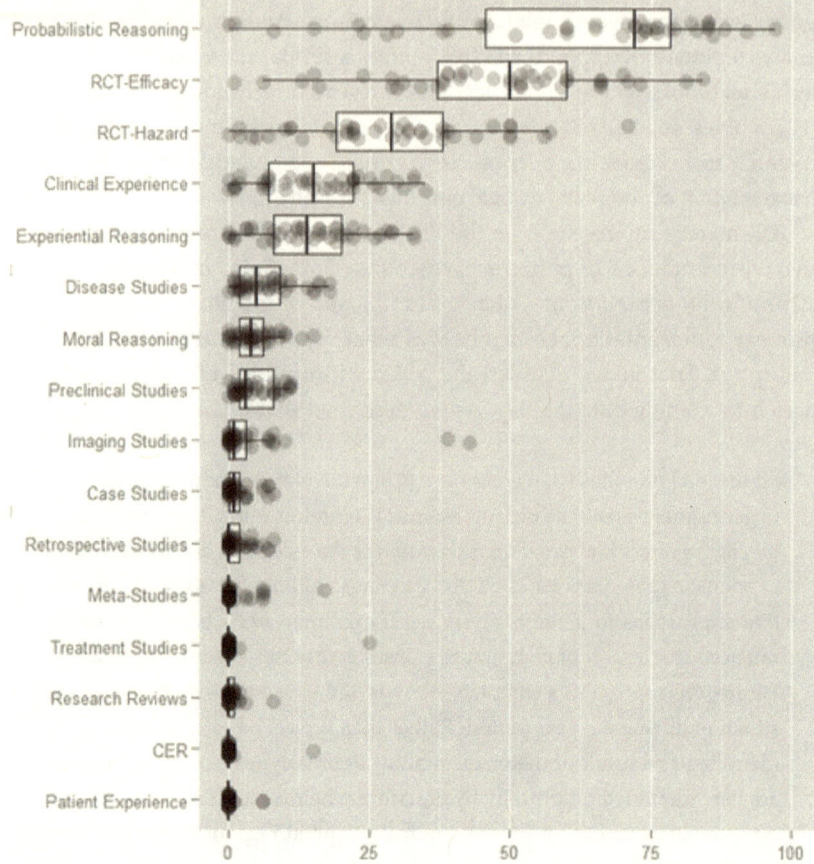

FIGURE 6.1. Graham et al.'s (2015) genre fingerprint. © 2015 Association of Teachers of Technical Writing, https://www.attw.org, reprinted by permission of Informa UK limited, trading group, https://www.tandfonline.com on behalf of Association of Teachers of Technical Writing.

tative" of the broader population of recurrent responses. Due to the smaller number of artifacts, researchers often must rely on *intuition*, challenging the establishment of a critical distance and the ability to move beyond what Bazerman refers to as a "'naturalized' user's view of genres and activity systems to a more carefully researched, observed and analyzed knowledge" ("Speech Acts" 321). (Graham et al. [Draft], 2014, p. 22; emphasis added)

Ultimately, the special issue editors were concerned with what might be implied by the use of the word *intuition*. They offered the same criticism that others had of Bergson's use of the term, reading it as "without inference or the use of reason."

To be completely clear, at the time I was channeling Charles Sanders Peirce's notion of intuition and not Bergson's. While these two senses are not altogether different, my use of the Peircean construct was neither appropriately surfaced in the manuscript nor sufficiently important enough to the claims of the article to keep in the face of the editors' reasonable critiques. However, when I mentally reinfuse the italicized word above with the intuition of the Bergsonian tradition, I find that it is precisely what I mean to say with respect to one part of the relationship between rhetorical intuition and quantitative abstraction.

The representation of aggregate intuitions has the potential to reflect back on the intuitions themselves. This should not be read as some sort of facile falsificationism, but it's not entirely unrelated either. Abstraction and intuition can work together dialectically in rhetorical inquiry. The scientific aggregation of intuitions can augment and improve any generalizations (recommendations for situated action). Without the perspective of aggregation, it is more difficult to know whether intuited conventions are indeed conventions or whether deploying those conventions will lead to success. Indeed, this is one of the primary affordances of integrating intuitive and scientific inquiry. As we argued in the final version of the 2015 article, our approach "to genre analysis offers the potential to identify which features (or perhaps which violations) of conventional responses are mostly likely to result in the designed outcome among the audience" (Graham et al., 2015, p. 91). Quantification allows researchers to track permutations in recurrent situations and, therefore, to assess whether certain changes are more likely to result in different responses to what might otherwise seem to be a stable recurrent situation. In the end, we were able to show that certain less common responses to the recurrent rhetorical situation were statistically associated with a greater likelihood of success (i.e., the FDA voting in favor of the petitioner). And thus, through dropping science into our intuitive inquiry, we have a stronger foundation for recommendations related to future situated action.

A Durable Rhetorical Epistemology

While this action-oriented account effectively meets Bergson's demands for when abstraction and intuition might be used effectively together, it does not yet adequately address the epistemological concerns that began this chapter. Where do quantitative content analysis and interrater reliability fit within a rhetorical epistemology that rejects positive knowledge? Nowhere, of course. However, as suggested by Charney in the opening epigraph, the rejection of positivism does not have to be the rejection of empiricism. Furthermore, as the last thirty years of science studies attests, the rejection of positivism does not have to be the rejection of science either.

After the brief detour through hardline antirealism, science studies became increasingly interested in understanding how epistemic authority is conferred in the sciences. Using a range of complementary theoretical and methodological approaches, scholars like Andrew Pickering and Bruno Latour ended up converging on similarly theories of recalcitrance as the primary driver of epistemic authority. Latour's (1987) *Science in Action* articulates this new epistemology of recalcitrance, perhaps most directly in his attempt to account for the durability of scientific claims. As Latour (1987) writes:

> Laboratories are now powerful enough to define reality. To make sure that our travel through technoscience is not stifled by complicated definitions of reality, we need a small and sturdy one able to withstand the journey: reality as the Latin word *res* indicates, is what *resists*. What does it resist? Trials of strength. If, in a given situation, no dissenter is able to modify the shape of a new object, then that's it, it is reality, at least for as long as the trials of strength are not modified. (p. 93)

According to Latour, reality is real because of its recalcitrance. It is obstinate in the face of new theories and new experimental designs (trials of strength). It takes great effort to reliably and durably articulate a scientific claim to a facet of reality, and it is precisely this difficulty that underwrites scientific authority.

In this epistemology, science studies move past ludic antirealism to a new approach where scientific claims or facts are understood to be made, but not made up. Here Latour famously invokes the assertion that *un fait est fait*. Drawing on the Romantic etymology that provides a common origin point for both *un fait* (a fact) and *fait* (third-person present indicative conjugation of *faire*, to make), Latour reminds us that facts are made, or as he prefers it, facts are fabricated. Where Latour focuses on a metaphor of industrial fabrication, Andrew Pickering (1995) opts for the more colorful notion of *mangling* to account for the practical creation of facts. And these two are certainly not the only STS scholars to invoke this version of pragmatic realism via fabrication. Annemarie Mol's (2002) more contemporary theory of multiple ontologies relies on the same underlying premise that "enacting reality involves manipulations" (p. 89). I will return to the details of the manipulations, fabrications, and trials of strength below, but first it is necessary to address how they function as the guarantor of epistemic authority in scientific discourse.

Here, despite very different cases, methods, and theoretical orientations, Pickering and Latour converge on the same basic construct. For each, the practical manipulations of fact fabrication are translated through progressive orders of discourse as bodies of scientific theory are assembled and established. In the two excerpts below, the powerful similarities between Pickering and Latour's account become evident. As Picking (1995) writes:

> Scientific knowledge—from the realms of high theory to the humble domain of empirical facts—should be understood in terms of representational chains ascending and descending through layers of conceptual multiplicity and terminating in captures and framings of material agency, with the substance and alignment of all the elements in these changes formed in mangling. (p. 101)

Where Pickering focuses on the body of scientific knowledge and Latour on an individual claim, it's clear that both are reciprocally created and imbued with authority through multiple nested layers of material and discursive practices. Latour's (1987) account is as follows:

> What is behind the claims? Texts. And behind the texts? More texts, becoming more and more technical because they bring in more and more papers. Behind these articles? Graphs, inscriptions, labels, tables, maps, arrayed in tiers. Behind these inscriptions? Instruments, whatever their shape, age and cost that end up scribbling, registering and jotting down various traces. Behind the instruments?.... Trials of strength to evaluate the resistance of the ties that link the representatives to what they speak for. (p. 79)

In either case, scientific practices (mangling, trials of strength) are those that extract a recalcitrant reality for use in orders of discourse. Facets of reality or phenomena under study are captured and made visible through the agency of scientific instruments and inscriptive practices, and the authority of the eventual claims made are nested in those investigational practices in the liminal spaces between a recalcitrant reality and a scholarly discourse. As Latour (1999) later describes it, the principal aim of a scientific practice is "to associate elements into a durable whole, and thus to gain existence" (p. 162).

If these trials of strength, mangling practices, or elemental associations are the bedrock of epistemic authority, then it is incumbent on us to understand how they function. While Latour, Pickering, and other science scholars each offer their own notion of and metaphors for the processes of fact fabrication, Pickering's mangle will be most useful for the purposes of this chapter. In *The Mangle of Practice*, Pickering seems to address the aforementioned and long-standing problem of realism in scientific inquiry. In so doing, he focuses on the realest of the real, high-energy physics. The book ultimately traces several important microhistories of fact fabrication including efforts to capture cosmic rays, the search for empirical evidence of quarks, and the construction of quaternions. In each of these cases, Pickering documents how physicists had to go to great lengths to "capture" natural agency. Cosmic rays, quarks, and quaternions are not easy to find. They are too small for the human eye, generally buried in other natural phenomena, and don't always show up when scientists want them to. Pickering's exegesis on the bubble chamber is perhaps most instructive.

Bubble chambers were a popular instrument in high-energy physics in the 1950s and 1960s. Large vessels filled with superheated liquid and attached to a camera, bubble chambers are designed to capture the most elusive of phenomena. When a cosmic ray or high-energy particle passes through a bubble chamber, it makes a visible track through the superheated fluid, and that track can be photographed and used for subsequent scientific scrutiny. While bubble chambers are a useful investigational tool, they are not unproblematic. Cosmic rays and/or high-energy particles of interest are not always present at any given location. Furthermore, bubble chambers require extensive tuning and calibration in order to capture traces of particles of interest. Using bubble chambers to fabricate facts requires longstanding engagement with a recalcitrant reality. As Pickering (1995) puts it, "We should understand the history of the bubble chamber as a more-or-less violent tuning process involving the continual reconfiguration of material setups in the pursuit of an intended capture of material agency" (p. 51). The bubble chamber is set and reset, tuned and retuned until the settings are optimally aligned with the phenomena under study.

Ultimately, it is Pickering's (1995) reflection on the history of bubble chambers that leads to the development of the operant metaphor of the work—the mangle:

> I find "mangle" a convenient and suggestive shorthand for the dialectic, for me, because it conjures up the image of the unpredictable transformations worked upon whatever gets fed into the old-fashioned device of the same name used to squeeze the water out of the washing. It draws attention to the emergently intertwined delineation and reconfiguration of mechanic captures and human intentions, practices, and so on. The word "mangle"

can also be used appropriately in other ways, for instance, as a verb. Thus I say that the contours of material and social agency are mangled in practice, meaning emergently transformed and delineated in a dialectic of resistance and accommodation. (p. 23)

Whether the driving metaphor is the mangle, trials of strength, or the less violent "translation" that Latour would eventually adopt, our theories of fact fabrication are built on this intersection between instrument, investigator, and phenomenon.

Importantly, an epistemology of recalcitrance is not solely a feature of science studies scholarship. Burke, too, identified recalcitrance as central to inquiry and invention. Michelle Gibbons's (2018) "The Recalcitrant Invention of X-ray Images" offers the following account of Burke's theory of recalcitrance from *Permanence and Change*:

Recalcitrance compels revision, inducing adjustments and alterations. In places, Burke uses terms like "shaping" and "reworking" to characterize its effects (p. 258). Burke emphasizes the conservative nature of this transformation, referring to it, in places, as a corrective, and describing it as a force that results in more practical assertions (pp. 255–256). In this way, it acts as a capacious force that shapes our generative extensions in the world in a powerful, but often inscrutable fashion. (p. 4)

The parallels between this and Latour's trials of strength or Pickering's mangle are readily apparent. Indeed, Gibbons notes them herself, especially with respect to the mangle (p. 12, fn 2). Whether working from a science studies or Burkean perspective, the reciprocal agitation between theory and a recalcitrant reality define inquiry and invention as features of engaged practice.

Thus, the new epistemology of recalcitrance is clearly antipositivistic, and yet it still provides a foundation for making claims about the durability and reliability of knowledge. And here is where we can return to content analysis and interrater reliability. Viewed through the lens of science-in-the-making, content analysis is a mangling process. It is a process of fact fabrication built from the intersection between instrument (coding schema), investigator (rhetorical critic), and phenomenon (discourse). Under this model, interrater reliability becomes a trial of strength. It is a guarantor of epistemic authority, not because it is quantitative but because it is recalcitrant. It forces investigators to assess and reassess the fitness of their theories (coding categories) to the resistant reality (discourse) they wish to understand.

Viewed this way, quantitative content analysis and interrater reliability are not pretentions to positivity. They are not fictions of exactitude. Rather, they are about process and practice. They are about underwriting the reliability of an inquiry practice. They are about demonstrating that inquiry practice represents a recalcitrant data set in a durable and useful way. Quantitative content analysis and interrater reliability set up the conditions for inquiry such that the findings bear up under scrutiny, such that they are more likely to survive subsequent trials of strength such as peer review.

Conclusion

Ultimately, an epistemology of durability provides an appropriate and effective foundation for CR. Quantitative content analysis and similar approaches within the broader CR rubric are ultimately about calibrating intuitive and scientific practices against one another. This is an exercise in durability, to be sure, but it is also an exercise in utility. The goal is to develop a durable abstraction of patterns in discourse so as to provide the possibility of effective situated action. Just as interrater reliability can augment and shape intuition in research, the results of quantitative content analysis can augment and shape intuition in situated action. Armed with an aggregate abstraction that represents patterns of discourse and articulates those patterns of discourse to perturbations in common across recurrent situations, a rhetor may be better prepared to select the appropriate response for a particular situation.

Exploring the relationships between intuition, abstraction, and CR is a primary aim of the next chapter. In the chapter, I offer constative analyses of related events in series of recurrent rhetorical situations that make up presidential primary contests. In so doing, I will explore what are largely understood to be extravagant violations of the generic conventions of presidential discourse. I will investigate some of the most off-color moments in the off-color campaign that culminated in the election of Donald Trump to the office of president. Ultimately, my aim is to demonstrate precisely how intuition and abstraction can work in tandem to optimize our understanding of how genres genre in complex discursive landscapes.

CHAPTER 7

CHASING SATISFACTION

> I have to say this, he hit my hands. Nobody has ever hit my hands. I've never heard of this one. Look at those hands. Are they small hands? And he referred to my hands if they're small, something else must be small. I guarantee you there's no problem. I guarantee you.
> —DONALD TRUMP, MARCH 3, 2016[1]

THERE'S A GENERAL SENSE that there was something uniquely horrid about the 2106 American presidential election. No, I'm not talking about the outcome itself, Russian interference, or even the specter of treason. Rather, here I refer to that general sense of revulsion at the tone of our electoral discourse. The opening epigraph to this chapter comes from a nationally televised Republican primary debate. In the above excerpt, Donald Trump assured voters that his penis was sufficiently large for the office of president. Nearly four years and countless other presidential indiscretions later, I am still flummoxed by this event. Making sense of it within the broader American political landscape challenges many, if not all, of my prior assumptions about electioneering, political rhetoric, and genre. Indeed, the conventional discursive registers of academic may well be insufficient to process this information. In truth, the best purchase I can get on my feelings here pretty well amounts to, "I have seen some shit, but...."

Of course, this (or something like it) is the mantra of political junkies throughout the Trump era. Hardly a week of his candidacy or presidency has gone by without us being able to watch Candidate Trump, President-Elect Trump, and finally President Trump use both hands to grab ahold of

---

1. Transcripts of debates used in this chapter were drawn from the UC Santa Barbara American Presidency Project.

what was once presumed to be a third rail of American politics. His Twitter feed is an open sluice gate of racism, misogyny, fat-shaming, invective, inanity, and duplicity. He harassed a Gold Star family. He disparaged a POW. He called for the incarceration of his political opponents. He accused the entire American intelligence establishment of lying about Russiagate. He bragged about committing sexual assault, on film. He told us he has a big dick.

Donald Trump once claimed he could shoot a man in the street on a busy day and not lose voters. Sometimes I fear he's right. In my darker moments, I worry that Trump may prove the truth of one of politics' most revolting adages: the only truly unrecoverable political error is to be "caught in bed with either a dead girl or a live boy."[2] At the time of this writing, Trump's failures to adequately respond to the coronavirus pandemic are only just coming to light. Perhaps they will be significant enough to erode political support. Obviously, the Trump era forces us to confront untold serious issues in contemporary society, the least of which may be challenges to core presuppositions in rhetorical theory. Nevertheless, Trump's rise to power and enduring success offer a powerful challenge to genre as traditionally conceived. Unless we accept that there are only two legitimate third rails of politics (dead girl and live boy), Trump has defied every insight of genre theory. He obliterated every rule, trounced every convention, and in so doing has achieved considerable rhetorical success.

The armchair analysis I offer here has been a central feature of the punditsphere. TV talking heads and op-ed typing fingers regularly remind us that political rhetoric has reached the apotheosis of negativity. However, rhetoricians are more divided on the extent to which the Trump era represents a new low in political discourse. On one end of the spectrum, Joshua Gunn begins his 2018 rumination on perversion in Trump's rhetoric with a very reasonable hedge: "Unquestionably by the time this chapter appears in print, US President Donald J. Trump will have said something more obnoxious than when I originally composed it" (p. 161). For Gunn, not only does the Trump era signify a new era of boundary transgressions, it is an era where the limits of discourse are bound to be broken over and over and over again. In contrast, Jennifer Wingard (2018) argues that

---

2. The origin of this little gem is former Louisiana governor and member of Congress Edwin Edwards. Bragging to reporters on the eve of a 1984 election, Edwards joked, "The only way I can lose this election is if I'm caught in bed with either a dead girl or a live boy."

> Trump's use of exclusionary rhetoric, which echoes decades of Republican messages, helpfully demonstrates something about this supposedly shocking rhetoric. In fact, Trump is not an outlier, but instead is committed to the GOP's rhetoric of exclusion and vilification of specific groups in order to solidify an imaginary US citizenry that is under siege. (p. 46)

Read against each other, there are striking contrasts between these portrayals of contemporary political rhetoric. Trump is revolutionary in his obscenity and derivative at the same time. He is both shockingly new and simply old hat.

To this dyad, let me add one more voice: that of Anna Young (2018). Her essay *Faking the News* opens with a haunting rumination, one that I imagine echoes the feelings of many of my readers. As she writes:

> When I agreed to be on the conference panel that led to this chapter and this book, I thought it would be an opportunity to reflect on what has to be the most turbulent and exhausting political experience of any presidential campaign in my life-time, at least to date. I thought I would be looking back, in other words. Having to reckon with the subject of Donald Trump as president on a minute-by-minute basis across a spectrum of media has been difficult. (p. 21)

I have to assume that there's a "—to say the least!" that got edited out of the end of this passage somewhere along the way. Imagined revisions aside, this passage helps cast in relief an important distinction for this chapter. Regardless of the "true uniqueness" of the 2016 campaign's negativity, there was a perception of newfound uniqueness, and that perception seems to have exerted an effect as part of larger genre-ing processes of the campaign.

This is precisely where intuition and more scientific approaches to genre must work together. A comparative claim like "this campaign was more negative than any previously" will require a quantitative representation of the aggregation of intuitions. Yet, that aggregation may well not show the processual influence of negativity on the campaign. Put another way, the science of genre can help provide insights into the attempted satisfactions of political rhetoric, but only intuitive genre studies can tell us about all the structuring structures that combined in the crucible of the situation. We must bring these two sides of genre together in order to have a satisfying explanation.

From the Science of Intuition to Science and Intuition

The principal goal of the previous chapter was to demonstrate how scientific approaches and intuitive approaches can work hand-in-glove. In so doing, I focused specifically on the particular (and maybe peculiar) example of interrater reliability. This is a useful example of the benefits of comingling scientific and intuitive approaches because of how closely they work together. Interrater reliability does not work without the intuitive judgments for which it seeks to underwrite. The subsequent quantification of the content analysis follows a similar pattern. Intuitive judgments are aggregated and quantified for future use. Now, here I am in great danger of being misunderstood. Many who discuss the qualitative-quantitative "divide" in contemporary research do qualitative research a great disservice by relegating it to the role of hypothesis formation. Of course, once the hypotheses have been established, the real work of quantification can begin. Let me be clear: this is not at all how I aim to construe the relationship between scientific abstraction and intuition in rhetorical studies.

Additionally, the somewhat peculiar example of content analysis and interrater reliability may suggest that I think all rhetoricians should shift to a content-analytic approach. It might be read as suggesting that our intuitions should always be verified in a sequential progression from intuition to abstraction, and that subsequently all rhetoricians must make themselves over as social scientists. To be clear again: this too is not at all what I mean. Rather, I began my inquiry into CR with content-analytic methods because it is where the gap between qualitative and quantitative is smallest. You can read this again as me taking inspiration from Latour's pedocomparator. Where the gap is small, the challenge of bridging the chasm does not seem so large.

Ultimately, however, my argument is that the dialectical relationship between CR and more traditional approaches to inquiry needs to happen at the disciplinary level. Intuitive and computational insights have a lot to offer one another, and yet, one of my greatest worries is that the boundary work discussed in chapter 1 will end up causing a speciation event where CR becomes its own separate discipline, publishing in its own separate journals. Such a move would greatly diminish the productive synergy that can come from keeping CR and more traditional approaches together. While the previous chapter argued that the Bergsonian lineage authorizes keeping CR and traditional rhetorical methods together, this chapter extends that work by demonstrating the utility of doing so. Thus, rather than offer another account of content analysis in action, this chapter seeks to model what two studies (using two completely different methods run in parallel) might say to one other. So here I will conduct a CR analysis of negativity in the 2016 presidential primaries and an intuitive GAP inquiry into perhaps the most negative event of that same campaign season. The goal here will not be to present one approach as better, or more accurate, or more useful, but rather to demonstrate the potential benefits of allowing both lines of inquiry to proceed within the boundaries of contemporary rhetorical studies.

For each of the following studies, the goal is to tackle the question posed in the introduction to this chapter: how should we understand the negativity in the 2016 primary election? The question is phrased vaguely here on purpose. I mean to articulate an area of inquiry and *not* a research question. CR and intuitive GAP do not and cannot answer the same research questions. And this is precisely why they must work together in their inquiry. While each approach can address the same area—broadly conceived—the particularities of the research questions and sites of inquiry must be adapted to the affordances of each method. Subsequently, my CR study will attempt to answer the comparative question in the introduction: was the 2016 presidential primary actually more negative that prior campaign cycles? The affordances of aggregation and quantification embedded in CR will allow us to answer this question in a way that intuitive approaches could not. In contrast, my GAP analysis will zero in on a particular moment largely considered to be the low point of the campaign, the lead-up to Trump's penis retort. The intuitive approach can provide us unparalleled insights into the way structuring structures configure the situated response of a local situation. CR, of course, does not give us much purchase on this question. Finally, this chapter will close with an exploration of what each of these two studies say to one another.

How Low Can We Go?

Is political discourse careening out of control? Was the 2016 primary campaign the nadir of civility and the end of deliberative democracy as we know it, or was it simply more of the same? Was it merely the latest iteration in an enduring deliberative environment that has long been marked by divisiveness, incivility, and ad hominem attacks? CR is, of course, well suited to address this question. It is precisely the kind of narrowly defined, comparative question that computational methodologies are designed to tackle. As mentioned above, we will not learn much about the nuances of any particular rhetorical situation, but we can derive a compelling quantitative assessment of negativity over time.

In so doing, the first task was to identify a longitudinal sample of comparable electioneering discourse. To that end, this analysis focuses on the last seventy-six presidential primary debates. I have chosen presidential primary debates as a way of collecting a deep sample of similar campaign events over a long period. The fragmentary record on stump speeches and campaign advertising would make using either to compose this corpus difficult. Furthermore, the more structured format of debates should provide a check on negativity. Yet—at the same time, we know Trump's argument about penis size was during a primary debate. This suggests that we should be able to find increasing negativity in the data set, if the hypothesis is correct. This sample includes all televised debates for the Republican and Democratic parties in the 2008, 2012, and 2016 electoral cycles. The total time range is an approximately eight-year period from May 2007 to October 2016. I have selected this time frame because given claims about each successive primary season being "worse than ever before," an eight-year progression should be sufficient to observe increasing negativity.

The negativity of each primary debate was evaluated using the RSentiment package (Bose, 2018) in the R development framework. Most sentiment analysis is conducted at the word level. However, word-level sentiment analysis does not effectively capture negation. That is, it doesn't know how to discriminate between "good" and "not good." The sentence-level approach available in the RSentiment package allows the tool to discriminate between positive and negative sentences as opposed to words, and thus it has the ability to identify negation. The RSentiment approach was developed by combining word-level sentiment analysis with Natural Language Processing (NLP) techniques so as to effectively evaluate sentiment at sentence-level granularity (Bose, Saha, Kar, Goswami, Nayak, & Chakrabarti, 2017). RSentiment is an unassisted sentiment-analysis technique that begins by assigning each word in a unit a sentiment score (Positive, Negative, Very Positive, Very Negative, or Neutral). Word-level sentiment analysis in RSentiment is based on the canonical Liu-Hu opinion lexicon (Hu & Liu, 2004; Liu, Hu, & Cheng, 2005).

RSentiment's NLP framework then evaluates each sentence for negation or sarcasm and assigns a numerical score to indicate the unit's overall sentiment. The rating scale is continuous, with positive values indicating positive sentiment and negative values indicating negative sentiment. A score of 0 is neutral. RSentiment also assigns a score of 99 to any text unit that is likely to be "sarcastic." However, my experience is that the tool does not effectively identify sarcasm so much as it identifies sentences that it has difficulty parsing. Thus, all sentences rated 99 were removed from my analyses. Despite this limitation, a comparative assessment of RSentiment's accuracy found that it was more effective than other popular variants of analysis (Bose et al., 2017). An illustrative sample of sentences in the primary debates data set is provided below, each with its assigned sentiment score.

- [Sentiment Score: –8] You know I understand why Donald made the comments he did and I understand why Americans are feeling frustrated and scared and angry when we have a president who refuses to acknowledge the threat we face and even worse, who acts as an apologist for radical Islamic terrorism. Ted Cruz, 1/14/2016
- [Sentiment Score: –7] You know, we have a foreign policy where we blow up bridges overseas; and then we tax the people to go over and rebuild the bridges overseas; and our bridges are falling down and our infrastructure's falling down. Ron Paul, 1/30/2018
- [Sentiment Score: 0] Let me just say two things about Congressman Paul's history. Newt Gingrich, 1/19/2012
- [Sentiment Score: 14] I think if you want to be President of the United States, the purpose of being President of the United States is to create a better future, a brighter future, more safety, more prosperity, more jobs, better education. Rudy Giuliani, 12/9/2007
- [Sentiment Score: 14] I'm very proud of the fact that Marian Wright Edelman of the children's defense fund has come to me over and over again, and proud to have authored the legislation to deal with the whole child, that authored the first child care legislation in this country, to begin in the earliest days to make sure that parents have the assurance that there will be a quality place for their child to be, and an affordable place, an available place, and then to begin with early childhood education, to see to it that we'd have a good head start program. Christopher Dodd, 6/28/2007

Following the assignment of sentiment scores to individual sentences in the data set, I aggregated all data by primary season and political party. The average sentiment of each debate season by party is listed in Table 7.1. You will note that although individual moments from each debate might be very positive or very negative, the averages tend to hover slightly above neutral. It is also worth noting that there appears to be little difference between the average sentiment scores from campaign to campaign. While the individual sentences evaluated received ratings between –8 and 14, all aggregate

TABLE 7.1. Average Sentiment of Debate Season and Party

PARTY	DEBATE SEASON	AVERAGE SENTIMENT
Democratic	2008	0.47
Democratic	2016	0.50
Republican	2008	0.37
Republican	2012	0.40
Republican	2016	0.36

scores are between 0.35 and 0.47. However, the 2016 Republican primary is, indeed, more negative than those of prior years. However, it's worth evaluating whether this difference is statistically significant.

An analysis of variance (ANOVA) was used to evaluate whether there were statistically significant differences in the sentiment of each debate assessed. The results turned out to be highly significant ($F = 187, p > 0.001$), and so Tukey's honest significant difference (HSD) test was used to evaluate pairwise differences between each debate. Table 7.2 provides the results of the Tukey's HSD test. The results indicate that there was a significant difference in the negativity of debates by party. Republican primary debates tended to be more negative than Democratic debates. However, while this difference is statistically significant, the magnitude of difference is not large. The only finding that hints at the possibility of a longitudinal change in campaign negativity occurs between the 2012 and 2016 Republican primary debates. However, this result merely approaches significance ($p[adj.] = 0.054$), and the magnitude of difference, again, is not large.

Nevertheless, to evaluate whether this finding indicates a trend toward increasing negativity in GOP primary debates, I plotted the average sentiment score of each GOP primary debate over the course of the entire data set (Figure 7.1). The first thing that should be immediately apparent is that every debate, including those that occurred during the 2016 primary contest, had an average sentiment score of greater than zero. This means that the average sentiment of each debate was positive, just as we saw with the campaign season results. While Figure 7.1 does show a modest declining trend across the data set, it does not—in any way—indicate that the 2015–2016 primary debates were extreme outliers of negativity.

There is another presumptive hypothesis that must be tested to fully evaluate the common claims about 2016 presidential campaign negativity. This is the pervasive suggestion that Trump is uniquely negative. To evaluate this, I compared the average sentiment score of each candidate in each debate to determine whether there was a significant difference between the negativity of individual candidates at each contest. Given the difference

TABLE 7.2. Tukey's HST Post-Hoc Test Results for Primary Debates, by Season and Party. Boldface type and asterisks indicate significant results.

COMPARATORS	DIFFERENCE OF MEANS	LOWER	UPPER	P (ADJ.)
d2016-d2008	0.02	-0.03	0.08	0.78
r2008-d2008	**-0.1**	**-0.15**	**-0.06**	**0.00***
r2012-d2008	**-0.07**	**-0.12**	**-0.03**	**< 0.01***
r2016-d2008	**-0.12**	**-0.16**	**-0.07**	**0.00***
r2008-d2016	**-0.13**	**-0.18**	**-0.07**	**0.00***
r2012-d2016	**-0.1**	**-0.15**	**-0.04**	**< 0.01***
r2016-d2016	**-0.14**	**-0.19**	**-0.08**	**0.00***
r2012-r2008	0.03	-0.01	0.08	0.29
r2016-r2008	-0.01	-0.06	0.03	0.95
r2016-r2012	-0.04	-0.09	0.00	0.05

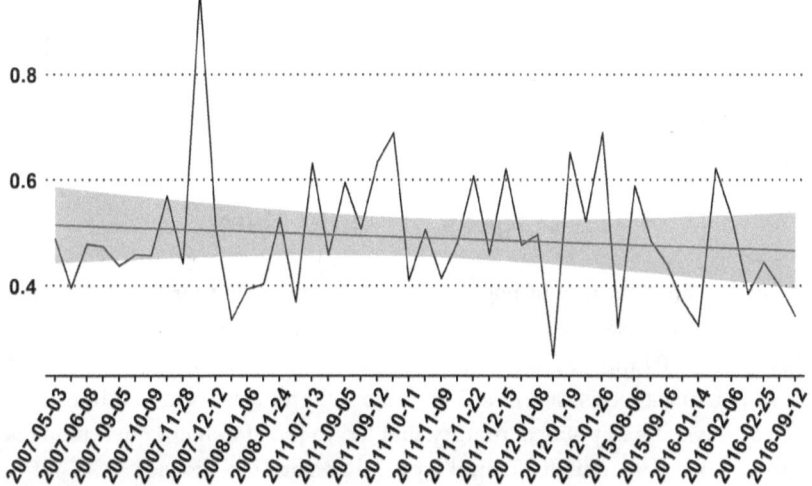

FIGURE 7.1. Average sentiment score and trend of GOP primary debates, 2007–2016. Note: Alternating debate dates omitted for readability.

in topics from debate to debate (e.g., foreign vs. domestic policy foci), it seemed most appropriate to compare candidates at the same debate. Certain topics might lead to more general negativity, and thus comparing across debates might skew the results.

As it turns out, there was no significant difference between Trump's and other candidates' negativity at each debate. In fact, the variance was shockingly narrow, with average sentiment scores diverging between 0.08 and 0.1. Ted Cruz and Ben Carson may represent the extremes (excluding Trump) of presumptive negativity during the 2015–2016 primary season. That is, Cruz is particularly well known for his negativity, whereas Carson is largely known for his affable drowsiness. However, at any given debate, the difference between Trump's and Cruz's or Trump's and Carson's average sentiment score is never more than 0.0999. An important caveat to this finding, however, is that negativity is certainly not the only measure of bad taste.

Ultimately, these data indicate that the negativity of presidential primary debates has remained relatively stable over the last eight years. It might be possible that evaluating a longer time frame could show a more significant decline in positivity. However, on its face, the claim that the 2016 presidential campaign was more negative than any previous campaign appears to be false. What's more: individual candidates (including Trump) do not vary widely in their negativity. These results are limited to the more moderated debate events, and it is possible that stump speeches or advertisements have gone more negative over this period. Nevertheless, several of the most derided examples of negativity in the 2016 campaign season do come from these primary debates, which therefore suggests that we should be able to observe an increasing negativity were it a feature of the larger electioneering discourse.

The Tragedy of "Little Marco"

To understand the role of negativity in the structuring structures of campaign rhetoric, it seems appropriate to look toward the example that opened this chapter: Trump's appeal to genital size as indicative of presidentialness. To fully explicate this case in a GAP idiom will require a broader interrogation of the shifts in political oratory that led to the aforementioned moment during a primary debate. Trump's penial declaration did not arise out of nothingness. It was a turn in a conversation. It was a response to an ongoing war of words with his primary competitors. In this case, the rebuttal is directed specifically at Marco Rubio, who was, so far as I can tell, the first presidential candidate to directly, albeit implicitly, connect the recurring issues of Trump's hand size with the question of his endowment.

Rubio announced his candidacy for president on April 13, 2015. He joined what would, over the course of the primary campaign, become seventeen Republican candidates. Although garnering a fair amount of media attention, Rubio's campaign never achieved a great deal of success. He finished third in the Iowa caucuses and second in South Carolina and Nevada. After losing his home state of Florida to Trump, Rubio suspended his campaign on March 15, 2016. Despite his lackluster performance, Rubio's case is an ideal one for our study of genre. Over the course of his campaign, he went from being pilloried for his overly scripted approach to breaking new ground with respect to electoral mudslinging. And here we have another example of the multiplicity of human (sub)systems. Like my earlier discussion of Burke's multitudes (chapter 2) or my analysis of people as process (chapter 4), the analysis here provides an example of the reciprocal unfolding that happens through successive rhetorical events. Specifically, early in the campaign Rubio was known for resisting the seemingly irresistible of pull of Trump's rhetoric and pursing a higher register of discourse. But, in the end, Rubio, too, was pulled into Trump's genre-ing processes and began modifying his responses to the emerging genre of "Laconic political oratory."

The notion of *Laconic speech* emerged in ancient Greece as a description of spartan Spartan discourse. Common examples feature what might now, anachronistically, be called *trash talk*. Descriptions of ancient Laconic speech center largely around prebattle parleys wherein sieging armies deliver terms to besieged Spartans, and they respond with threats. Leonidas's "Μολὼν λαβέ [Come and take them]," a reply to Xerxes' demands that his soldiers surrender their arms, is a common example. Although Plato's (1956) *Protagoras* suggests that Laconic speech may be merely a ruse, a technique for lulling interlocutors into complacency (342b–e), it is generally understood to be dull, elliptical, and acerbic. Some researchers in psychiatry and psychology have found that Laconic speech (especially alongside aphasia and logorrhea) are symptomatic of dementia and Alzheimer disease (Hier, Hagenlocker, & Shindler, 1985; Miklossy et al., 2003). While I make no particular mental health claims with respect to Donald Trump, "Laconic political oratory" seems to offer a particularly satisfactory description of his mode of political discourse.

This brings us back now to the Tragedy of Little Marco. As previously mentioned, Rubio was, for a time, stalwart in his refusal to adopt the conventions of the new and emerging genre of Laconic political oratory. However, he eventually gave way, and indeed some pundits blame his electoral losses on his shift in genre. Beverly Hallberg (2016) of the libertarian "news" site the *Federalist*, wrote, "Ironically, the once-labeled next 'Great Communicator' lost his way with voters because they (and admittedly his family) were 'embarrassed' by his rhetoric." In her article, she traces the shifts in accommodation from "Rubio the Robot's" use of overly scripted oratory to his embrace of "Trump Tactics" and finally to his too-little-too-late attempted recovery. While no articles in more traditional media outlets trace the rhetorical trajectory of Rubio's entire primary campaign, there is ample evidence to support Hallberg's analysis. Op-eds published in *USA Today*, *Bloomberg*, and the *Washington Post* decry his generic and scripted performance in presidential debates. Likewise, there was much ado in the media and punditsphere following Rubio's descent into Laconic political oratory.³

Ultimately, a careful analysis of Rubio's penis speech can provide us great insight into the function of genre as process and the role of negativity selection pressures therein. By most measures, Rubio is an accomplished orator. As a lawyer and successful politician, by the time of the 2016 Republican primary, he'd had ample time to hone his oratorical craft. Thus, we should expect to see a candidate fluent in the generic conventions of political oratory, one who excels in recognizing and responding to genre-ing processes in any given situation. And, indeed, we did see a high degree of generic sensibility in early candidate Rubio's debate performances. It was not exceptional rhetoric. Obviously, he failed to appropriately moderate the generic conventions of the particulars of the situation, and his overreliance on conventional response led to accusations of robotic scriptedness. He was too good at following genre conventions. He had, as Catherine Schryer (200) might describe it, "become habituated to these constellations of strategies . . . fail[ing] to see both the possibilities for or constraints on human action" (p. 460). In Bergsonian terms, his oratorical response was born in the "dead leaves" on the surface of his mind. However, Rubio's now infamous speech shows a very different rhetor, one attempting to leverage the memory of experience hard earned to adapt his oratory to an emerging genre.

On February 28, 2016, at Roanoke College in Salem, Virginia, Rubio offered what began as a seemingly traditional stump speech.⁴ However, that stump speech morphed slowly over the first ten minutes into a generic hybrid. That is, what began as a traditional response to the recurrent rhetorical situation of the stump speech eventually became a full-fledged act of Laconic political oratory. The progression, in this case, is particularly interesting. Rubio carefully attenuates his audience to what is to come. He prepares them to accept the shift in genre that only he and his campaign staff

---

3. See, for example, Jaffe (2016), Kreig (2016), or Hellman (2016).

4. While the complete video of this speech was available on YouTube (Roanoke College, 2016) until at least December 2017, it appears to have fallen victim to a Digital Millennium Copyright Act (DMCA) takedown notice. Additionally, as far as I can ascertain, no complete transcripts appear to have been made and archived. Fortunately, insofar as Marco Rubio was employed by the federal government as a senator at the time of his infamous speech, the text is in the public domain. Therefore, I have provided a partial transcript for posterity and your reference at http://www.sscottgraham.com/rubio-dick-speech.

know is coming. It is also clear from the video, once you know what's coming, how distasteful Rubio finds the whole thing.

Rubio's speech begins with the typical invocational epideictic of a stump speech. He thanks his audience and declares without hedge that he will be the next president of the United States. As anticipated, his confident declarations are rewarded with notable applause. He praises Virginia to the Virginians, and does the same for Salem, and Roanoke College. And, then at about two minutes in, Rubio begins to hint at the impending genre shift:

> Now, I like debates about ideas. I like debates about policy. We have spent a year talking about and debating policy and ideas. But, you cannot have a policy debate with someone that has no policies.

Here Rubio signals that he will be shifting away from the ostensibly proper subjects of a stump speech to the regrettably necessary attack on his opponent's character. Rubio has no choice, mind you. Trump's failure to advance any meaningful policy has prevented Rubio from addressing matters of greater importance.

After this warning, the more traditional register of presidential mudslinging follows for some time. Rubio declares Trump a "con man" and goes on to describe how he has defrauded his customers, his employees, and now the American voters. Rubio criticizes Trump's record on illegal immigration, outsourcing labor, and business management. Then, without much in the way of a segue, he makes his first, ever-so-careful, Laconic move:

> It's a scam. He says he's a strong leader. I saw him the other day at an event. He told a protester, "I want to punch you in the face." Let me tell you something. Donald Trump has never punched anyone in the face. This guy has been protected and sheltered his entire life, his whole life. OK. By the way this is the guy . . . do you know why he didn't go into the draft, didn't go into the military, because he had suffered an injury playing squash. It's a very dangerous game.

Here Rubio shifts from a traditional critique of his opponent's record into a clear assault on his masculinity. Trump is nothing more than a coddled elite and nothing like the strongman he pretends himself to be.

At this point, however, Rubio steps back from the Laconic immediately. He does not follow his emasculation of Trump with another acerbic jab. Quite the contrary; he criticizes his own speech for going low while reminding the audience he has no choice because Trump has no policy ideas worthy of critique.

> We cannot turn over the conservative movement to a con artist. This country needs a conservative movement that speaks to our people and solves our problems, and in a moment, I'm going to outline to you exactly what we're going to do when I'm President of the United States. Because unlike Donald Trump, I have real ideas, and real solutions to turn this country around. But give me a couple more minutes to have fun with it, and then we're going to get to the policy. I promise you.

In the midst of arguing that his and the audience's shared time would be better spent addressing policy, Rubio invites his audience to "have fun" with him, signaling that the Laconic phase is not yet over.

Then, after a more traditional takedown of Trump's failed for-profit university, Rubio pauses. This is no typical pause. It drags on longer than any other besides those where he waits for applause to die out. Watching the video, you can almost see him choking back the bile and girding his loins for what is about to come next, for what his campaign staff appears to have made him do. Pulling out his phone, probably only as prop, but possibly also to read a text message from his campaign manager demanding that he forge ahead, Rubio's fully Laconic phase begins. At first, he tries to launch directly into it, but just once more he has to remind himself and his audience that this is inappropriate (even though he will do it anyway):

> You guys know [Trump] likes to attack people personally, right? So, just give me one more minute because we've got to have fun with it. He likes to go on Twitter. . . . First of all he says I'm sweating all the time. It's hot in here. Am I sweating now? No. He doesn't sweat because his pores are clogged from the spray tan he uses. Donald is not going to make American great. He's going to make America orange. The next thing . . . The other thing he says. He's always calling me "Little Marco," and I'll admit, he's taller than me. He's like 6'2", which is why I don't understand why his hands are the size of someone who's 5'2". Have you seen his hands? They are like this. And you know what they say about men with small hands? . . . You can't trust them. You can't trust them.

And with that, Rubio's dick-speech sets up Trump for his subsequent dick-rebuttal. And the rest, as they say, is political history.

Both the immediate context of Rubio's Roanoke College speech and its larger context, as part of the ongoing Republic primary debate, allow us to see the benefits of a GAP approach. In the moment, at Roanoke College, Rubio creates a generic hybrid. He attempts to effect a satisfaction that merges two recurring genres (the stump speech and Laconic political oratory) with the particulars of the situation at hand. The processual nature of genre-ing is especially evident in Rubio's attenuation efforts. He knows that his oratorical history and long-standing resistance to Laconic genres have provided this situation the appropriate structuring structures to allow for a Laconic satisfaction. That is, his audience isn't ready for him to go low. Rubio has to, *in medias res,* forge a new fit. He has to invoke the new genre-ing processes of Laconic political oratory in the context of his stump speech so as to properly invite his audience into the unfolding situation and prepare them for satisfaction.

Ultimately, Rubio is only partially successful. He is not able to forge the fit he seeks. One jab—"Donald is not going to make American great. He's going to make America orange"—lands well and is met with enthusiastic laughter and applause. However, "You know what they say about men with small hands?" is not nearly so successful. The resultant applause is thin, and the laugher is awkward and forced. The young woman in the front row visibly face-palming as Rubio tries to extricate himself from his failed joke speaks volumes. Rubio fails to achieve a satisfaction, and while this one moment was not enough to end his campaign, it certainly did not help.

A GAP approach to genre theory also helps us better account for the macro-context of Rubio's speech. Despite a clear disinclination to shift away from more traditional oratorical genres to Laconic genres, he made the change. Rubio adapted to the genre-ing processes brought forth by Trump's long-standing use of the Laconic toolkit. After being called "Little Marco" one too many times, Rubio went for the low-hanging fruit of small hands = small penis and tried it out on a crowd of college students. In much the same way that I activated the memory of my departmental slight to implement the cut direct, Rubio activated the memory of his enduring slights so as to break with the powerful structuring structures of political oratory. While Rubio could not successfully forge a fit, Trump could. Indeed, Trump's success has created a situation that seems to shift the very genre of discourse around him. It shifts it in such a way that only he can fit the newly forged situation. It forced Rubio (at least) to go negative (despite his long-standing resistance) but failed to provide the possibility of success.

As discussed in chapters 4 and 5, the legacy of formalism when combined with pedagogical commitments often leads rhetoricians (even those working in Miller's idiom) to think of genre as constraint. The stabilized-for-now genre-ing processes place limits on the possible range of successful action. This is not wrong, but this is also not complete. In highly complex situations composed of multiple competing genre-ing processes, effecting a satisfaction can mean establishing which organizing structures take precedence. In essence, Trump's rhetoric trumps traditional political genres. His Laconic speech leverages the powerful organizing structures of reality TV and Twitter flame wars to supplant the traditional genre-ing processes of political oratory. He was not successful in establishing a satisfaction because he flouted convention. He was successful because he, and the media apparatuses that supported his rhetoric, forged a new fit, setting new standards for evaluation, standards that are altogether different from the genre-ing processes of non-Laconic political oratory.

In this analysis, Rubio is our canary in the coal mine. His status as an accomplished orator combined with his struggles in meeting the rhetorical demands of the primary campaign show the limits of any approach to genre that focuses excessively on conventional accommodation as rhetorical success or conventional violation as rhetorical failure. Furthermore, both Trump's and Rubio's rhetorics help showcase the extent to which neither genres nor fittingness necessarily pre-exist an unfolding situation. To be sure, organizing structures and genre-ing processes are given through history and recurrence, but at the same time a rhetor in the moment can invoke alternative organizing structures. During the primary campaign Trump deployed genre tactically. He violated the conventions repeatedly and effectively, and in so doing, eventually established new generic conventions that would exercise their own structuring effects on individual situations.

The Trump-Effect Effect ← Not a Typo

So, what do these dueling analyses tell us? On the one hand, it might appear that we have contradictory findings: the CR analysis demonstrates that there was no appreciable change in the negativity of primary debates over time, and yet the GOP analysis of the Rubio–Trump byplay seems to show a powerful negative pull. We might simply explain away the latter finding by declaring that the Rubio–Trump genital debate is merely an aberration, an outlier that does not meaningfully impact the aggregate shape of the overall campaign season. But I do not believe this is quite the case. Rather, I think the two analyses show us different—equally true—things about the 2016 campaign primary season.

Of course, some of these differences come from the affordances of each methodological orientation. As mentioned above, CR is well suited to telling us about the population of responses, and from that population of responses we might derive the true typical. In contrast, the intuitive approach embed-

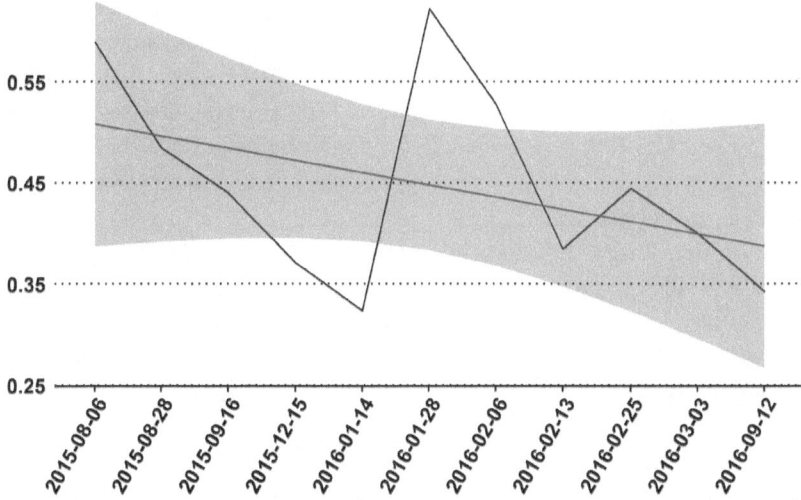

FIGURE 7.2. Average sentiment score and trend of GOP primary debates, 2015–2016

ded in GAP provides greater insight into the genre-ing processes themselves. We can better discern how Rubio *qua* rhetor was pushed and pulled as he crafted his oration. The particularities of his response (which is all we would get in a CR analysis) would elide the complexities of competing genre-ing processes in the moment. Ultimately, however, I believe the CR and the GAP analyses work together productively to help us identify an underappreciated phenomenon in the 2016 primary campaign: The Trump-Effect Effect.

While much has been made of the so-called Trump Effect, the CR analysis presented here does much to suggest that Trump may not be a uniquely powerful genre-ing force in contemporary political discourse. However, The Trump-Effect Effect—that is, the effect of discussing the Trump Effect as an effect—may exert rather more influence. Allow me to clarify: what I'm arguing here is that the popular discourse about the effect of Trump on political discourse may have had more of an effect on that discourse than Trump himself did. The GAP analysis of Rubio's speech hints in this direction. It shows Rubio pulled—apparently against his will—into Laconic speech. However, I would argue that Rubio's delayed adoption of Laconic moves suggests that it was the Trump-Effect Effect rather than the Trump Effect that caused his shift. Indeed, I think the broader view of Rubio's campaign clearly shows his revulsion for Trump and the oratorical conventions he represents.

As further evidence of the power of the Trump-Effect Effect, I offer Figure 7.2. Figure 7.2 is the final slice of Figure 7.1—that is, it extracts only the

2016 GOP primary campaign from the longer view of average negativity by debate. At this "zoomed-in" scale, you will notice a very interesting outlier on January 28, 2016. By and large, the 2016 GOP primary debates follow lock-step in line with the broader view of GOP primary debates over the past few cycles. That is, the average sentiment tends to hover between 0.3 and 0.5. Yet, suddenly, in late January, the average sentiment jumps from a seasonal low to nearly 0.6.

Essentially from the moment he descended the golden escalator and announced his candidacy, Trump became a figure of enduring media attention. Indeed, his speech announcing his candidacy quickly set the tone for his campaign and was the origin point of one of his most infamous pronouncements:

> When Mexico sends its people, they're not sending their best. They're not sending you. They're not sending you. They're sending people that have lots of problems, and they're bringing those problems with us. They're bringing drugs. They're bringing crime. They're rapists. And some, I assume, are good people. (*Time* Staff, 2015)

Whether this actually constituted a new low in overt racism in contemporary Republican presidential rhetoric or not is an open question. However, it is inarguable that this line has been treated as though it were a profoundly unique violation of electioneering conventions. And, of course, as Gunn notes above, this was only the first in a litany of boorish Trumpian lines that would garner sustained attention from the punditsphere and be presented as "new lows" in presidential rhetoric.

So, going into the January 28, 2016, election, we have a massive media rhetoric of the Trump Effect. Candidates and viewers alike are told over and over again that this is a uniquely bad moment in American political history. And, suddenly, Trump declines to attend a debate. He exempts himself from the discourse and the Trump-Effect Effect kicks in. This is not a case of Trump pulling discourse down but rather of the rhetoric of the Trump Effect allowing candidates to use his absence is a pretext for violating long-standing negativity conventions. Most contestants, at one point or another, acknowledge Trump's absence. Jeb Bush, for example, was sarcastically wistful, declaring:

> I kind of miss Donald Trump. He was a little teddy bear to me. [laughter] We always had such a loving relationship in these debates and in between and the tweets. I kind of miss him. I wish he was here.

However, remarks by Ted Cruz and Marco Rubio did more to acknowledge the Trump Effect as an effect, and not just as a function of the individual who would become president:

> CRUZ: Well, let me be clear, if Donald engages in insults or anybody else, I don't intend to reciprocate. I have not insulted Donald personally and I don't intend to. I am glad Donald is running. I'm glad he has produced enormous enthusiasm, and, every Donald Trump voter or potential voter, I hope to earn your support. I know everyone else on this stage hopes to earn your support. Now, there is a difference between personal insults and attacks—between going into the mud with ad hominems and focusing on issues and substance.
> RUBIO: Chris, let's begin by being clear what this campaign is about. It's not about Donald Trump. He's an entertaining guy. He's the greatest show on earth.

In the first instance, above, Cruz pivots from Trump's particular insults to a broader discussion of the discursive climate and establishes his aim to avoid divisive discourse, at least for this debate. Likewise, I take Rubio's claim that Trump is "the greatest show on earth" to be an acknowledgment more of the Trump-Effect Effect than of the skill of the man himself. In both cases, the candidates use the Trump Effect as an excuse to go high, because Trump has been branded by the media as the reason they needed to go low.

The Trump-Effect Effect is one particular example of an understudied but important phenomenon—the effect of genre-ing on genre-ing. That is, attempts to understand genre can, themselves, become part of the genre-ing processes. Indeed, Miller (2010) acknowledges this phenomenon in a chapter called "Should We Name the Tools? Concealing and Revealing the Art of Rhetoric." In an analysis focused on similar dynamics in an earlier presidential election, she draws our attention to how media meta-discourse can influence the discourse itself:

> As I write this, we are in the 2008 presidential election campaign, in which each major candidate represents a position under discussion here: one candidate promotes his campaign as the "straight talk express," and the other candidate's acknowledged eloquence puts him under suspicion. An election draws public attention to the powers of rhetoric. The editorial pages, political cartoons, television pundits, talk shows, YouTube offerings, and late-night comedians have been analyzing and satirizing the rhetorical effects of both candidates, making visual the strategies and styles of their

campaigns, alerting us to the ways we are being manipulated, and in some cases, naming the rhetorical tools explicitly. (Miller, 2010, p. 32)

This account, however, is an acknowledgment—not a finding. The broader aim of Miller's essay is to ask the normative question: *Should* we name the tools? Is it ethical to provide public insights into the techniques of dissimulation? The question she does not ask is the descriptive one: *how* is it that the naming of tools impacts public rhetorics?

At present, rhetoricians have only a limited understanding of this phenomenon, in one particular sphere—pedantry. Here, again, is the relevant passage from Burke's (1931/1984) *Counter-Statement*:

> The matter of conventional form has brought out the extremes of aesthetic acuity and aesthetic bluntness. The rise of conventions may be due to exceptional imaginativeness and accuracy; their preservation may be due to the most inaccurate and unimaginative kinds of pedantry. (p. 204)

This, of course, describes precisely the problem with Robo-Rubio in his early debate performances. But it also hints at the larger phenomenon of the Trump-Effect Effect and genre-ing genre-ing. The ways that efforts to understand genre can affect situated responses extend beyond pedantry. When genre analysis, itself, emerges as a force within genre-ing processes, it can catalyze both thoughtless piety (pedantry) and reactionary innovation.

Chasing Satisfaction

To close out this chapter, it is useful to look at another (nonpolitical) case of genre analysis leading to reactionary innovation. Byron Hawk's (2018) analysis of sound artists in *Resounding the Rhetorical* provides a remarkably similar account of innovators working to break with powerful genre-ing processes. Hawk offers an ethnographic account of artists making use of computers, mixing boards, acoustic samples, and effects pedals in live and recorded performances. The sound art studied in *Resounding the Rhetorical* is the improvisational work of ensembles who aim to create a unique ambient acoustical experience for audiences. Importantly, "sound art is not interested in the repetition of a musical genre or common meaning but in an experience of sound that hasn't been fully anticipated by the artists or the audience" (Hawk, 2018, p. 144). In the account, the acoustical rhetors gesture to genre-ing processes without showing fidelity. However, as Hawk notes, "the paradox of execution is that an anti-genre stance can still lead to the enaction of a genre" (p. 147). Audiences can hear how genre-ing processes continue to impact the situated response despite the artists' rejection of them. This is, perhaps, all the more acute among these particular sound artists, one of whom happens to hold a PhD in ethnomusicology. He is keenly aware of the common forms and genre-ing processes and so goes out of his way to flout them. However, from Hawk's account, it appears just as important that audiences know conventions are being flouted. So, the sound artists in the study gesture at conventions through partial adoptions and then intentional violation.

Ultimately, these analyses suggest that we may need to be ever more careful with how our genre-analytic work informs our best-practice recommendations and pedagogy. Compositionists across America know the pain of having to break students of the five-paragraph theme each year. A particular essay genre is overly formalized and concretized in pedagogy, and we see the equivalent of pedantry among even the best students. Much the same happens with the ever-present questions about the use of first-person pronouns or slavish devotion to the MLA 2014 citation format that a high school English teacher taught as gospel. It is easy, of course, to blame overworked high school teachers for these issues, but doing so distracts us from the real possibility that our own pedagogy commits these same errors. Formalism is alive and well in university-level technical communication, even in textbooks and articles that invoke the GASA tradition. However, this is not just about formalism. It's about appreciating the extent to which any genre analytic might prevent fully kairotic responses. Satisfying the rhetorical situation might also require appreciating how the rhetoric of genre impacts the practice of genre and, further, how the interrelationships between the two may change over time. And, as mentioned at the end of chapter 6, this is something that can only happen with diachronic methods. Thus, CR must become a critical tool not only for our study of rhetoric in the world but also for our study of rhetoric as a discipline.

CHAPTER 8

IMAGINING A UNIFIED FIELD

AN OVERARCHING THEME of this book has been my efforts to imagine a unified field—an integrated intellectual framework that links the many subareas of rhetorical studies. Tragically, the presumptive unity of our discipline has been fractured by the rhetoric around RNM and CR. Following the development of these areas, an unfortunate amount of scholarly energy is now devoted to advancing novelty claims, priority claims, and boundary claims regarding these two subareas. As a result, the titular question of this book becomes an all-too-common feature of occluded genres like peer review. Now, I fully appreciate that boundary work will always and invariably be an enduring feature of any discipline. Of course, in many respects, that's what it means to be a discipline. (Adherents to a discipline are those who have been disciplined.) Nevertheless, disciplinary boundary work in rhetorical studies has reached a certain fever pitch with the emergence and popularization of RNM and CR. And that boundary work is exacerbated by the enthusiasm of novelty claims surrounding these projects. When RNM and CR scholars claim that their work is heretofore unprecedented, they tacitly authorize that pernicious territorial question.

Ultimately, I suspect these issues are driven by problems of identification. Somewhere along the way, many rhetoricians have become more invested in their *-isms* than in the discipline itself. Put another way, their *-isms* have become *-ists*. Many rhetoricians harbor a more authentic identification based on subdisciplinary commitments. They are new materialists, compositionists, genre theorists, grounded theorists, cultural theorist, content analysts, technical communicators, digital rhetoricians, and scholars of public address. (OK, we lost the *-ists* there at the end, but you get the point.) For many, methodology and/or sites of inquiry have become identity. From my perspective, this causes two significant issues for the discipline: (1) When your methodology is your identity, every intellectual problem will be reduced to the particular framework and approach with which you identify. And (2) it becomes all too easy to read your approach as *the* approach. That is, your rhetoric becomes the One True Rhetoric, and other inquiry traditions are treated as heretical. This last issue is particularly problematic because when disciplinary boundary work is animated by doctrine and heresy, then interlocutors become more likely to use inconsistent arguments to warrant their claims.

This is the issue I point to in chapter 1 with my invocation of David Zarefsky's (1998) work in rhetorical historiography. Inconsistency is perhaps the least of the many problems that arise from the shifting perspective between rhetoric *qua* what and rhetoric *qua* how. Nevertheless, I fully realize that merely pointing out how askers of "Where's the rhetoric?" oscillate in their definition of rhetoric as part of differential boundary work will be insufficient to convince many that RNM and CR are, and have always been, fully rhetorical. And so, the last few hundred pages of bibliographic, archival, rhetorical-analytic, ethnographic, and computational inquiry have been my longhand version of

Here! Here is the rhetoric!

Ultimately, however, provocations and exhortations are not the tone with which *Where's the Rhetoric?* should end. Rather, my aim is a more positive—albeit perhaps dreamy and illusive—vision of a better disciplinary future. I'd rather see a future for rhetorical studies that does not center around the adversarial titular question of this book and reply by evidentiary assault. Instead, I will focus on providing a more conciliatory approach—one consonant with my dream of a more unified field.

I Found It! I Found the Rhetoric

Kenneth Burke has provided rhetorical studies many centrally important animating constructs. The pentad, terministic screens, and a rhetoric of scapegoats are among the best known. Over the pages of this book, I have worked to extend and expand our engagement with the Burke of Bergson's left-branch legacy and his influence on Miller's new materialist theory of genre. My commitment to these constructs notwithstanding, Burke's most important contribution to our discipline might be the metaphor of the parlor. Certainly, it's a tremendously useful way of explaining large swathes of rhetorical theory; but even more importantly, it helps us understand ourselves. It helps us understand what it means to be a discipline.

There are many approaches to defining a discipline. Internalist definitions of disciplines actively construct disciplinary boundaries around particular shared questions and approaches, but this way leads to enduring conflict between rhetoric *qua* what and rhetoric *qua* how. Personally, I'm rather fond of the sociological approach, which would essentially say that rhetoric is what rhetoricians do. A useful framework, but probably too tautologous for most to embrace. Fortunately, rhetoric has its own externalist approach to defining disciplinary boundaries (Burke's parlor), and I see no reason not to apply it reflexively. Even though the metaphor is widely known, it is worth revisiting Burke's prose here. In the *Philosophy of Literary Form* (1941), Bruke describes the "unending conversation" thusly:

> Imagine that you enter a parlor. You come late. When you arrive, others have long preceded you, and they are engaged in a heated discussion, a discussion too heated for them to pause and tell you exactly what it is about. In fact, the discussion had already begun long before any of them got there, so that no one present is qualified to retrace for you all the steps that had gone before. You listen for a while, until you decide that you have caught the tenor of the argument; then you put in your oar. Someone answers; you answer him; another comes to your defense; another aligns himself against you, to either the embarrassment or gratification of your opponent, depending upon the quality of your ally's assistance. However, the discussion is interminable. The hour grows late, you must depart. And you do depart, with the discussion still vigorously in progress. (pp. 110–111)

Although this passage is part of an extended analysis of dramatic forms, the footnote Burke (1941) appends to it marks it as his theory of disciplines: "it is in this 'unending conversation' that the assertions of any given philosopher are grounded" (p. 111). In its most common reading, the metaphor reminds us that disciplines are enduring conversations that persist despite periodic changes in interlocutors. However, in the light of our newfound appreciation for Burke's Bergsonian history, this passage can take on additional significance. The metaphor of the parlor essentially offers a new materialist theory of disciplines. It is the structuring structures which guide the processes of becoming that compose the discipline, not its atomistic components. Neither individual interlocutors nor any given line of argument make a discipline. Rather, it is the *duration*—to use Bergson's term—of the conversation. Lest there be any doubt that this account is committed to a more materialist theory of discourse, on the very next page Burke reminds us that material-economic structures ground our media of expression and configure the idiom of our discourse.

So, to be Burkean about disciplines is to say that I've found the rhetoric in RNM. It's here in this unending conversation that leads back to Bergson. The rhetoric of RNM is here in the greatly simplified illustration in Figure 8.1 of the citation history presented in chapter 2. The new representation is greatly simplified, as all abstractions must be. As the schematic indicates, the long history of the Bergsonian conversion can be understood as a bifurcation and reintegration. One conversation split into two and came back together again in the same parlor at the same party. Burke and Schütz capitalized on different moments in Bergson's oeuvre, which were then reintegrated in Miller's (1984) "Genre as Social Action." Likewise, Bergsonian insights in Whitehead and Deleuze were reintegrated in Latour's science-in-the-making. As the right side of the figure indicates, the work of *Where's the Rhetoric?* to establish the GAP framework has been intended as a further reintegration of Bergson's ideas.

Additionally, traditional rhetoric and RNM are not the only players in this enduring conversation. The reintegration of Bergsonian vectors in the development of RNM allows us to take advantage of important epistemological insights. The latest efforts in science studies handily move us past the positivist caricatures of science toward a new understanding of science-in-the-making, one that can be viewed as consonant with all abstractive inquiry. As a result, (1) we have an epistemological foundation for CR that avoids the ethical pitfalls of the positivist overcorrection, and (2) our intuitive and abstractive inquiry practices can be productively integrated in continuing conversation as part of a unified field.

Now, certainly, I find this intellectual history to be interesting in its own right. However, it is more than an idle curiosity. Rather, I argue that a broader recognition of Bergson's influence in these areas has the potential to pay large dividends for rhetorical inquiry—and not only in terms of disciplinary unity. Specifically, the GAP framework allows us to productively address long-standing problems in RGS. GAP offers a coordinated approach to multiple modes of inquiry including traditional rhetorical criticism, eth-

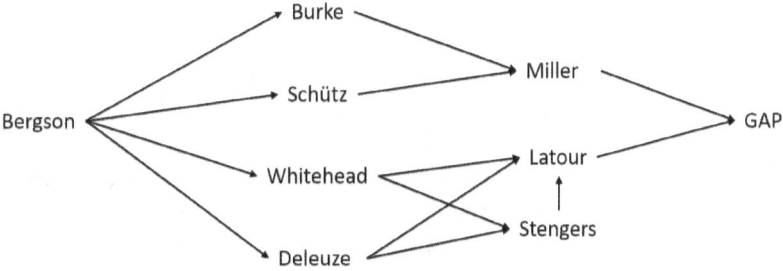

FIGURE 8.1. Bergsonian legacies in new materialisms, RGS, and GAP

nography, and computational methodologies. However—and this is critically important—GAP does not suggest that all rhetoricians need to make use of any particular method or combination of methods. Rather, the argument is disciplinary. The discipline of rhetorical studies will be most productively advanced through a combination of methodological approaches working in (even agonistic) dialogue with one another. Indeed, my argument is not so much that we need to be less critical with one another but rather that we save our intellectual efforts for debating approaches and findings as opposed to whether this or that subarea "belongs" in rhetoric or not.

A Useful Abstraction

Ultimately, the approach outlined in this book is one that aims at practicality and utility. His penchant for "useless" metaphysics notwithstanding, I would argue that Bergson's scholarship is at its most powerful when applied to situated action. A unified field is a nice friendly concept, but it's meaningless without a coordinated program of action. For Bergson, memory and its role in the intuition-abstraction dialectic is the wellspring of situated action, and so that is where I will return in closing *Where's the Rhetoric?* Over the last six chapters of this book, you may have noticed that each chapter included one or more terms broken out visually and presented—more or less—in the form of a dictionary definition. These terms are what I have identified as the book's primary insights. In breaking them out from the text, I hope to provide one final demonstration of the intuition-abstraction dialectic—this time with the aim of providing a solid foundation for situated action within a unified rhetorical field.

Just as the intuitive experiences of recurrent situations provide the fodder for abstraction in the form of identifying genre conventions, the intuitive experience of reading these pages provides the fodder for the following abstraction. I have used the convention of boldface terms to highlight the key moments that will form the basis for *Where's the Rhetoric?*'s final abstraction (below). Here I reinforce the key terms to provide an overarching representation of the intellectual work of this book. Thus, the following distillation is organized around the key concepts of the book, dividing them into key themes: (1) Inquiry Traditions, (2) Foundational Concepts, (3) Core Constructs, and (4) Meta-Methodological Resources. With the aid of this useful abstraction, I will close *Where's the Rhetoric?* by ruminating on new horizons of inquiry that might be made possible by a more unified field.

TABLE 8.1. Inquiry Traditions

Rhetorical New Materialisms (RNM): Any approach that grounds rhetorical inquiry in a relational metaphysics and a flat ontology. RNM construes sites of inquiry as products of sociomaterial interaction.

Computational Rhetoric (CR): Any approach that uses computation to create abstractions of rhetorical insights. CR is especially well suited to creating aggregate abstractions of comparatively large data sets.

Genre as Process (GAP): An approach to inquiry that focuses on genre-ing processes within sociomaterial situations. GAP is grounded in a relational metaphysics that investigates the role of structuring structures, including the abstraction of those structuring structures, in shaping situated action.

TABLE 8.2. Foundational Concepts

New Materialisms: A loosely related body of theoretical initiatives bound together by a diagnostic consensus that (1) Western thought has been inappropriately dominated by certain problematic dualistic ways of thinking; (2) these ways of thinking inappropriately focus attention on the relationship between "humans" and "nonhumans," as discrete ontological categories; and (3) these ways of thinking lead to unethical and oppressive ways of approaching the world and its inhabitants. Proposed solutions to the diagnostic consensus frequently involve replacing dualistic metaphysics with a relational model.

Dualistic Metaphysics: The universe is made up of more-or-less discrete entities that can be classified according to certain pre-existing types that exist in opposition with other pre-existing types: e.g., mind/body, nature/culture, science/society, humans/nonhumans.

Relational Metaphysics: The universe is not, as is so often assumed, made up of discrete objects that can be classified according to certain pre-existing types. Instead, all "entities" are complex systems of interrelated parts, nested in larger complex systems of interrelated parts, that cohere through active processes of becoming.

Processes of Becoming: The complex systems that make up the universe do not persist in a stable state, more or less as they always were. Rather, complex systems are perpetually active making and remaking themselves as subordinate and superordinate systems change around them.

TABLE 8.3. Core Constructs

Situation: A site of material-semiotic interaction from which motive emerges. Situations are, as the term suggests, the wellspring of situated action.

Situated Action: Following the move from dualistic to relational metaphysics and the corresponding emphasis on processes of becoming, new materialists often make a subsequent move from representation or epistemology to situated action. Under a dualist metaphysics, the driving questions about how humans interact with an ontological separate world center around issues of how humans use language to represent the world and thus how humans "know" the world. Under a relational metaphysics, attention to humans centers on how humans-as-complex-systems participate in the processes of becoming at specific sites of activity.

Genre: [no such thing]

Genre-ing: The processes of structuring activity that occur in situational hierarchies and guide situated action.

Memory: The activation of past images to enable situated action (as opposed to responsive motion).

Fit Forging: Action that effectively shifts the dynamics of an unfolding situation to fit the unfolding "response."

Satisfaction: The "final phase" of concrescence (Whitehead, 1978, p. 26). It "marks the transition of the present to the past" (Stengers, 2011, p. 297). It is the end of an event, that moment where the situation appears to cohere as complete.

Genre Innovation: The process of instantiating change in the structuring templates of recurrent situations. Genre innovation arises from perturbations in series of events over time. The new structuring templates of emerging genres arise from transforming disjunctive pre-existing structuring templates into novel conjunctive structuring templates. New genres become stabilized when they themselves begin to genre.

Meta-Genre-ing: When genre analytic activity, itself, becomes an influential force on situated action.

TABLE 8.4. Meta-Methodological Resources

Intuition: An experiential approach to metaphysical inquiry characterized by a general aim of identifying how abstract representations of reality distort our understanding of reality.

Abstraction: The process of distilling intuitive insights into formalized representations so as to better support future situated action.

Intuition-Abstraction Dialectic: The intuition-abstraction dialectic describes both the activity of situated actors and GAP inquiry. The individual methods of GAP (traditional rhetorical criticism, ethnography, and computational approaches) all rely on the dialectic to create useful representations that distill intuitive experiences.

CHAPTER 8

New Horizons of Inquiry

The analytic contributions of *Where's the Rhetoric?* have largely been organized around Miller's proposed suggestions for the next thirty years of genre inquiry. Specifically, I have engaged most directly with her suggestions that the interrelationships between genre and medium and the question of genre innovation should be central projects going forward. In tackling these questions, I have argued that the common construal of genre and medium or agency and structure as ontologically distinct entities stymies progress in each of these areas. Essentially, I have argued that the perceived gap between words and things—on the one hand—and agency and structure—on the other—need not be so debilitating for RGS or rhetoric more generally. Ultimately, I think my analyses of the tweetorial, the cut direct, and Brandon's hybrid e-game / greeting card all demonstrate the powerful utility of GAP's relational metaphysics for rhetorical inquiry.

Additionally, although the primary focus of chapter 7 was to demonstrate the efficacy of a hybrid traditional-CR approach to inquiry, the analysis also engages both of Miller's core concerns. Most directly, the chapter addresses the fraught nature of genre innovation. In genred discourses, innovation cannot occur without violation. That is, pre-existing conventions authorized by hierarchical structuring structures must be thwarted so as to offer a potentially new form. However, the perceived newness of a form is, in part, a function of attempts to analyze the genre-ing processes in question. My analysis of the arguably overanalyzed conventions of electioneering discourse show how similar responses can be interpreted as either fidelity or innovation. What's more, the analysis of Rubio's failures in contrast to Trump's successes demonstrates that fidelity and violation do not map quite as directly onto success and failure as is commonly assumed. With respect to medium, Miller was clear that future work in RGS that engages the interpenetration of genre and medium should not limit itself to "new" media. And certainly, she's correct that much has been made of the role of internet communication technologies in genre change and innovation. She's also quite correct that the entanglement of genre and medium occurs regardless of the novelty of the technology of transmission. My analyses of electioneering discourse focus on the oldest of media—the air, or, rather, speech.

Although this work has productively advanced genre with respect to Miller's proposed next thirty years, there remains, of course, much work to do in these areas. *Where's the Rhetoric?* is an initial demonstration of the potential of GAP. If other scholars in the discipline elect to take up the construct, and—in so doing—apply it to new sites and cases, I think we will begin to develop an even more satisfactory account of genre and medium and genre innovation. As Miller suggests, I think more work in the area of old media will be a key pathway forward. Too much is made of the internet, as though it were special, some sort of super-medium. I too am guilty of this with my focus on tweetorials and game/e-cards. Speech is also difficult because of its long-standing presumption of banality. While I think it's important to demonstrate that GAP is equally useful for both the newest and the oldest of media, scholarship on intermediary media may be the most productive.

One area that may lead to the greatest productivity is at the intersection of GAP and sound studies. In recent years, we have seen a proliferation of interdisciplinary scholarship in sound studies, a movement Jonathan Sterne (2012) describes as deeply committed to exploring "what sound does in a human world and what humans do in the sonic world" (p. 2). Rhetoric is increasingly becoming an important part of this conversation, especially following a 2013 manifesto for rhetoric and sound studies (Gunn, Goodale, Hally, & Eberly). Steph Ceraso's (2018) *Sounding Composition* is especially noteworthy here for how her approach to sound is consonant with a GAP framework. As she writes:

> My choice to use the word sounding in the title and chapter titles for this book is strategic. Sounding signifies that sound is being made or emitted from someone or something. The fact that sounding is a verb, that it implies action, is pertinent to the arguments I make in *Sounding Composition*. (p. 10)

Furthermore, my development of GAP has been enhanced by rhetorical sound studies (and its antecedents) in several places. Both Bank's rumination on the DJ and the scratch and Hawk's study of sound art contributed to my development of GAP. What's more, there is a deep history of theoretical work that has yet to be fully appreciated here. Bergson, Burke, and Schütz were all substantially engaged with music in the development of their theories. Indeed, OBB's rumination on the crescendo was a central insight for this book.

Additionally, GAP would be productively advanced through better engagement with cultural rhetorics. For many in rhetoric "the history of media" evokes a fairly limited notion of Western media forms centered on the development of paper, printing, radio, television, and the internet. Quite obviously, there are many different media—both historic and contemporary—used in many different cultural contexts the world over. One particularly interesting example that combines much of what is discussed in this book is Kristin Arola and Adam Arola's (2017) "An Ethics of Assemblage: Creative Repetition and the 'Electric Pow Wow.'" Through a Deleuze-inspired analysis of club DJing and First Nations electronic music, Arola and Arola develop a theory of "creative repetition" in assemblages that they describe as follows:

- A good assemblage is responsive, responding to situations and enacting new functions;
- a good assemblage is innovative and productive;
- a good assemblage is novel, opening up new ways of thinking, seeing, and living; and
- a good assemblage does all of this with a focus on the "we" as opposed to the "I," always considering, "Whom does this assemblage benefit?" (p. 211)

The parallels between their "creative repetition" and GAP are quite striking. No doubt this is partially due to Arola and Arola's tacit invocation of the right-branch Bergsonian tradition. However, the pathway to creative repetition may have been even easier to see here by virtue of the authors' engagement with indigenous acoustic forms. This further suggests that RGS's traditional anchorage in technical communication sites and genres may stymie inquiry into the nature of genre-ing processes themselves.

In addition to expanding sites of inquiry, I would also argue that the work of this book suggests that rhetoricians should continue to aggressively expand our computational toolkit. Although rhetoricians were early adopters on the pedagogical side of DH, we remain somewhat late to the party with respect to the active development of computational research technologies. As a result, those who engage in CR are largely limited to tools designed for other disciplines and purposes. While sentiment analysis was a useful framework for my relatively narrow research question about negativity in electioneering rhetorics, it is not broadly applicable, and it is easy to misuse. Many of the CR technologies available were designed by computer scientists, marketing specialists, and linguists. As such, they are often not well suited to answering rhetorical research questions.

Obviously, one clear exception to this is the work of Bill Hart-Davidson and Ryan Omizo. The Hedge-O-Matic and the Faciloscope are two tools designed by rhetoricians for rhetoricians. The Hedge-O-Matic takes a cue from RGS, focusing on one of its long-standing central concerns with respect to scholarly discourse—the role of the hedge (obviously). As Omizo and Hart-Davidson (2016) describe the tool:

The Hedge-O-Matic tokenizes raw text at the sentence level. Each sentence is then classified as either a hedge or non-hedge by a Support Vector Machine trained on a corpus of hedgey and non-hedgey sentences culled from academic science journals.

The Faciloscope is, perhaps, even more interesting from a GAP perspective. Essentially, the tool

> works by breaking a conversation down into three basic functional "moves" that participants make that move conversations along. It does this by interpreting every sentence-sized chunk of the conversation and classifying the results using a machine-learning algorithm trained to recognize the three moves. (Hart-Davidson, 2016)

By focusing on the move, the Faciloscope is centered firmly in a rhetorical (and even an RGS) tradition. So many of the available CR technologies tokenize by sentence or n-gram, artificial units of discourse not particularly related to the rhetor's decision-making process. Other approaches like topic modeling use what's known as a "bag-of-words" model, where the structure of discourse is completely eliminated from the analysis. While I would still argue that tokenized or bag-of-word analyses can be useful to rhetorical inquiry, it would be very interesting to imagine a whole suite of tools built around the move.

Beyond RGS, *Where's the Rhetoric?* suggests that there is much more work to be done with respect to excavating rhetoric's intellectual heritage. I have described myself as a rhetorical new materialist for nearly a decade. As a long-standing participant in the area, I like to think I'm fairly conversant with our intellectual history. However, I will admit right here and now that prior to this project I had never even heard of Henri Bergson. In fact, when I began my bibliographic and archival work, I thought that the common link between GASA and new materialisms was Whitehead. It was only through exploring the appropriation of Whitehead in Deleuze and Burke that I discovered that my initial intellectual history had not gone back far enough.

Of course, every scholarly project must adopt certain relatively more-or-less arbitrary limits, else it will never be completed. Indeed, attempting to account for the shared intellectual heritage of GASA and new materialisms while simultaneously making a case for CR strains the limits of what can be accomplished in a single monograph. As such, there were many exciting bibliographic and historiographic connections that I could not afford to chase down. Given my focus on RGS, I have only scratched the surface of

Bergson's oeuvre. It is deep and provocative all on its own. What's more, it finds extensive use of early Burke as well as the scholarship of Schütz. These trajectories have the potential to lead rhetoricians in many productive directions not necessarily relating to genre. I think we will be remiss if we do not explore them in greater detail.

APPENDIX

The appendix offers tabular displays of the data that compose the citation network represented in Figure 2.1. Where an individual work was cited more than four times in the data set, it is described in its own table (Tables A.1–A.4). The remaining citations are in an aggregate table (Table A.5).

TABLE A.1. Works That Cite Bergson's *Creative Evolution*

AUTHOR	TITLE	WEIGHT
Stephen	*Misuse of Mind*	10
Schütz	*Structures of Life-World*	10
Benda	*Le Bergsonisme*	10
Whitehead	*Process and Reality*	5
Burke	*Grammar of Motives*	5
Stengers	*Thinking with Whitehead*	5
Burke	*Permanence and Change*	3

TABLE A.2. Works That Cite Bergson's *Matter and Memory*

AUTHOR	TITLE	WEIGHT
Stephen	*Misuse of Mind*	10
Benda	*Le Bergsonisme*	10
Whitehead	*Process and Reality*	5
Stengers	*Thinking with Whitehead*	5
Deleuze	*Difference and Repetition*	4
Whitehead	*Science and the Modern World*	3

TABLE A.3. Works That Cite Bergson's *Time and Free Will*

AUTHOR	TITLE	WEIGHT
Stephen	*Misuse of Mind*	10
Whitehead	*Process and Reality*	5
Deleuze	*Difference and Repetition*	5
Schütz	*The Problem of Rationality*	5
Deleuze & Guattari	*A Thousand Plateaus*	5

TABLE A.4. Works That Cite Whitehead's *Process and Reality*

AUTHOR	TITLE	WEIGHT
Stengers	*Thinking with Whitehead*	10
Latour	*Reassembling the Social*	3
Whitehead	*Modes of Thought*	1
Latour	*Pandora's Hope*	1

TABLE A.5. Citation Relationships Among Lessor-Cited Works in the Bergson-Rhetoric-New Materialisms Scholarly Network

CITED WORK	CITING WORK	WEIGHT OF INFLUENCE
Attitudes Towards History	*Counter-Statement*	1
Blogging as Social Action	*Genre Innovation*	5
Difference & Repetition	*Never Been Modern*	3
Difference & Repetition	*Pasteurization of France*	3
Difference & Repetition	*Thinking with Whitehead*	5
Environmental Impact	*Genre as Social Action*	10
Environmental Impact	*Blogging as Social Action*	3
Environmental Impact	*Genre Innovation*	3
Genre as Social Action	*Blogging as Social Action*	5

APPENDIX

TABLE A.5. (*Continued*)

CITED WORK	CITING WORK	WEIGHT OF INFLUENCE
Environmental Impact	Genre Innovation	3
Genre as Social Action	Blogging as Social Action	5
Genre as Social Action	Genre Innovation	5
Grammar of Motives	Environmental Impact	5
Grammar of Motives	Genre as Social Action	5
Grammar of Motives	What can Automation	3
Laboratory Life	Never Been Modern	5
Le Bergsonisme	Attitudes Towards History	1
Misuse of Mind	Permanence & Change	10
Modes of Thought	Permanence & Change	3
Modes of Thought	Thinking with Whitehead	10
Never Been Modern	Reassembling the Social	5
Never Been Modern	What can Automation	3
Pandora's Hope	Reassembling the Social	5
Pasteurization of France	Laboratory Life	5
Pasteurization of France	Never Been Modern	5
Pasteurization of France	Reassembling the Social	5
Permanence & Change	Environmental Impact	5
Permanence & Change	Genre as Social Action	5
Problem of Rationality	Laboratory Life	1
Science in Action	Never Been Modern	5
Science in Action	Reassembling the Social	5
Science Modern World	Structure Sci Rev	1
Science Modern World	Process & Reality	5
Science Modern World	Thinking with Whitehead	10
Structure Sci Rev	Laboratory Life	3
Structure Sci Rev	Science in Action	3
Structure Sci Rev	A Humanistic Rationale	5
Structure Sci Rev	Thinking with Whitehead	5
Structures of Life-World	Environmental Impact	10
Structures of Life-World	Genre as Social Action	5
Thinking with Whitehead	Reassembling the Social	3
Thousand Plateaus	Thinking with Whitehead	5

REFERENCES

Allington, D., Brouillette, S., & Golumbia, D. (2016). Neoliberal tools (and archives): A political history of digital humanities. *LA Review of Books,* May 1. Retrieved from https://lareviewofbooks.org/article/neoliberal-tools-archives-political-history-digital-humanities/

Arola, K., & Arola, A. (2017). An ethics of assemblage: Creative repetition and the "electric pow wow." In K. Blake Yancey & S. J. McElroy (Eds.), *Assembling composition* (pp. 204–221). Logan, UT: Studies in Writing and Rhetoric.

Artemeva, N. (2004). Key concepts in rhetorical genre studies: An overview. *Canadian Journal for Studies in Discourse and Writing/Rédactologie,* 20(1), 3–38.

Artemeva, N. (2005). A time to speak, a time to act: A rhetorical genre analysis of a novice engineer's calculated risk taking. *Journal of Business and Technical Communication,* 19(4), 389–421.

Banks, A. J. (2011). *Digital griots: African American rhetoric in a multimedia age.* Carbondale, IL: Southern Illinois University Press.

Barad, K. (2007). *Meeting the universe halfway: Quantum physics and the entanglement of matter and meaning.* Durham, NC: Duke University Press.

Barnett, S. (2016). *Rhetorical realism: Rhetoric, ethics, and the ontology of things.* New York, NY: Routledge.

Barnett, S., & Boyle, C. (2016). *Rhetoric through everyday things.* Tuscaloosa, AL: University of Alabama Press.

Bartlett, T. (2020). "This Harvard epidemiologist is very popular on Twitter. But does he know what he's talking about?" *The Chronicle of Higher Education,* April 17. Retrieved from https://www.chronicle.com/article/This-Harvard-Epidemiologist-Is/248557

Beastie Boys, King, J., Dike, M., Simpson, M., & the Dust Brothers. (1989). The sounds of science. Recorded by The Beastie Boys on *Paul's Boutique*. Los Angeles, CA: Capitol Records.

Benda, J. (1912). *Le Bergsonisme ou un philosophie de la mobilitié*. Paris, France: Mercure de France.

Bennett, J. (2010). *Vibrant matter: A political ecology of things*. Durham, NC: Duke University Press.

Bergson, H. (1896/1911). *Matter and memory* (N. M. Paul & W. S. Palmer, Trans.). New York, NY: Macmillan.

Bergson, H. (1903/1946). Introduction to metaphysics. *The creative mind* (M. L. Andison, Trans.). (pp. 187–237). New York, NY: Philosophical Library.

Bergson, H. (1910/1960). *Time and free will: An essay on the immediate data of consciousness*. New York, NY: Harper and Brothers.

Bergson, H. (1911). *Creative evolution* (A. Mitchell, Trans.). New York, NY: Holt.

Bergson, H. (1911/1946a). *The creative mind* (M. L. Andison, Trans.). New York, NY: Philosophical Library.

Bergson, H. (1911/1946b). Philosophical intuition. *The creative mind* (M. L. Andison, Trans.). (pp. 126–152). New York, NY: Philosophical Library.

Bergson, H. (1911/1946c). The possible and the real. *The creative mind* (M. L. Andison, Trans.). (pp. 107–125). New York, NY: Philosophical Library.

Bergson, H. (2002). *Henri Bergson: Key writings* (K. A. Pearson & J. Mullarkey, Eds.). London, UK: A&C Black.

Bose, S. (2018). *RSentiment: Analyse sentiment of English sentences. R Package* (Version 2.2.2). [Computer software].

Bose, S., Saha, U., Kar, D., Goswami, S., Nayak, A. K., & Chakrabarti, S. (2017). RSentiment: A tool to extract meaningful insights from textual reviews. In S. Satapathy, V. Bhateja, S. Udgata, & P. Pattnaik (Eds.), *Proceedings of the 5th International Conference on Frontiers in Intelligent Computing: Theory and Applications* (pp. 259–268). Singapore: Springer.

Boyle, C. (2018). *Rhetoric as a posthuman practice*. Columbus, OH: The Ohio State University Press.

Boyle, C. (2019). Posthumanism and/as idle talk. *Rhetoric Review*, 38(4), 378–381.

Boyle, C., & Rivers, N. A. (2016). A version of access. *Technical Communication Quarterly*, 25(1), 29–47.

Brennan, T. (2017). The digital-humanities bust. *The Chronicle of Higher Education*, October 15. Retrieved January 6, 2018, from https://www.chronicle.com/article/The-Digital-Humanities-Bust/241424

Brown, J. J., Jr. (2015). Crossing state lines: Rhetoric and software studies. In J. Ridolfo & W. Hart-Davidson (Eds.), *Rhetoric and the digital humanities* (pp. 20–32). Chicago, IL: University of Chicago Press.

Burke, K. (1921, March 31). Untitled diary entry. Kenneth Burke Papers. Series 3. Box 1, Folder 33.

Burke, K. (1931/1968). *Counter-statement*. Berkeley, CA: University of California Press.

Burke, K. (1935). *Permanence and change: An anatomy of purpose*. New York, NY: New Republic.

Burke, K. (1984). *Permanence and change: An anatomy of purpose* (3rd ed.). Berkeley, CA: University of California Press.

Burke, K. (1941). *The philosophy of literary form: Studies in symbolic action*. Baton Rouge, LA: Louisiana State University Press.

Burke, K. (1937/1984). *Attitudes toward history*. Berkeley, CA: University of California Press.

Burke, K. (1945/1969). *A grammar of motives*. Berkeley, CA: University of California Press.

Burke, K. (1984). *Permanence and change: An anatomy of purpose* (3rd ed.). Berkeley, CA: University of California Press.

Burke, K. (n.d.-a) Perspective by incongruity [draft]. Kenneth Burke Papers. Series 3, Subseries 2. Reel 3, Side 0310.

Burke, K. (n.d.-b) Untitled fragment with quote from Benda's *Le Bergsonisme*. Kenneth Burke Papers. Series 3. Box 1, Folder 33.

Carter, S., Jones, J., & Hamcumpai, S. (2015). Beyond territorial disputes: Toward a "disciplined interdisciplinarity" in the digital humanities. In J. Ridolfo & W. Hart-Davidson (Eds.), *Rhetoric and the digital humanities* (pp. 33–48). Chicago, IL: University of Chicago Press.

Ceraso, S. (2018). *Sounding composition: Multimodal pedagogies for embodied listening*. Pittsburgh, PA: University of Pittsburgh Press.

Charney, D. (1996). Empiricism is not a four-letter word. *College Composition and Communication, 47*(4), 567–593.

Charney, D. (2015). Getting to "How do you know?" rather than "So what?" from "What's new?" *Technical Communication Quarterly, 24*(1), 105–108.

Condit, C. M. (1999). *The meanings of the gene: Public debates about human heredity*. Madison, WI: University of Wisconsin Press.

Coole, D., & Frost, S. (2010). Introducing the new materialisms. In D. Coole & S. Frost (Eds.), *New materialisms: Ontology, agency, and politics* (pp. 1–43). Durham, NC: Duke University Press.

Cooper, M. (2019). *The animal who writes: A posthumanist composition*. Pittsburgh, PA: University of Pittsburgh Press.

Crisan, A. [@amcrisan]. (2018, October 23). *How do researchers visualize data in #genomic #epidemiology? Myself, @jennifergardy, and @tamaramunzner wanted to know. So—we conducted a systematic review of #datavis in #genepi that's now out in @OxfordJournals Bioinformatics: https://doi.org/10.1093/bioinformatics/bty832 . . . (1/19)* [Tweet]. Twitter. https://twitter.com/amcrisan/status/1054737026363392001

Deleuze, G. (1966/1991). *Bergsonism* (H. Tomlinson & B. Habberjam, Trans.). New York, NY: Zone Books.

Deleuze, G. (1968/1994). *Difference and repetition*. New York, NY: Columbia University Press.

Deleuze, G., & Guattari, F. (1987). *A thousand plateaus: Capitalism and schizophrenia* (B. Massumi, Trans.). London, UK: Bloomsbury.

Dryer, D. B. (2015). "The fact that I could write about it made me think it was real": An interview with Carolyn R. Miller. *Composition Forum, 31*, Retrieved from http://compositionforum.com/issue/31/carolyn-miller-interview.php

Duncan, H. D. (1965/1984). Introduction. In K. Burke, *Permanence and change: An anatomy of purpose* (pp. xii–xlvii). Berkeley, CA: University of California Press.

Dyson, F. J. (1999). *The sun, the genome, and the internet: Tools of scientific revolutions.* Oxford, UK: Oxford University Press.

Edbauer Rice, J. (2005). Unframing models of public distribution: From rhetorical situation to rhetorical ecologies. *Rhetoric Society Quarterly, 35*(4), 5–24.

Frost, S. (2016). *Biocultural creatures: Toward a new theory of the human.* Durham, NC: Duke University Press.

Fuller, S. (2000). *Thomas Kuhn: A philosophical history for our times.* Chicago, IL: University of Chicago Press.

Feigl-Ding, E. [@DrEricDing]. (2020, January 24). 2/ "We estimate the basic reproduction number of the infection (R_0) to be 3.8 (95% confidence interval, 3.6–4.0), indicating that 72–75% of transmissions must be prevented by control measures for infections to stop increasing . . . [Tweet]. Twitter. https://twitter.com/DrEricDing/status/1220920013273608192

Feigl-Ding, E. [@DrEricDing]. (2020, January 25). *UPDATE: Transmission of #coronoavirus estimated at 2.6 by another research group (lower than the 3.8 initial reports). But 2.6 is still extremely bad —each infected person will infect 2.6 others. Even the authors admit #CoronaOutbreak containment will be very difficult. Thread:* [Tweet]. Twitter. https://twitter.com/DrEricDing/status/1221132573340061697

Geisler, C., Bazerman, C., Doheny-Farina, S., Gurak, L., Haas, C., Johnson-Eilola, J, . . . Yates, J. (2001). IText: Future directions for research on the relationship between information technology and writing. *Journal of Business and Technical Communication, 15*(3), 269–308.

Gibbons, M. (2018). The recalcitrant invention of X-ray images. *Technical Communication Quarterly*, 1–15.

Gieryn, T. F. (1983). Boundary-work and the demarcation of science from non-science: Strains and interests in professional ideologies of scientists. *American Sociological Review, 48*(6), 781–795.

Gottleib, S. [@ScottGottliebMD]. (2020, January 21). *THREAD: It doesn't appear China has shared samples of the novel #coronovirus but just published the sequence of different strains that have been recovered. This could hinder efforts to develop and validate screening tests in the West. China should share samples of the virus* . . . [Tweet]. Twitter. https://twitter.com/ScottGottliebMD/status/1219616181356843012

Graham, S. S. (2009). Agency and the rhetoric of medicine: Biomedical brain scans and the ontology of fibromyalgia. *Technical Communication Quarterly, 18*(4), 376–404.

Graham, S. S. (2015). *The politics of pain medicine: A rhetorical-ontological inquiry.* Chicago, IL: University of Chicago Press.

Graham, S. S. (2016). Object-oriented ontology's binary duplication and the promise of thing-oriented ontologies. In S. Barnet & C. Boyle, Eds. *Rhetoric, through everyday things.* (pp. 108–124). Tuscaloosa, AL: University of Alabama Press.

Graham, S. S. (2017). Data and lore in technical communication research: Guest editorial. *Communication Design Quarterly Review, 5*(1), 8–25.

Graham, S. S., & Herndl, C. (2013). Multiple ontologies in pain management: Toward a postplural rhetoric of science. *Technical Communication Quarterly, 22*(2), 103–125.

Graham, S. S., Kessler, M. M., Kim, S.-Y., Ahn, S., & Card, D. J. (2018). Assessing perspectivalism in patient participation: An evaluation of FDA patient and consumer representative programs. *Rhetoric of Health & Medicine, 1*(1–2), 58–89.

Graham, S. S., Kim, S. Y., DeVasto, D. M., & Keith, W. (2015). Statistical genre analysis: Toward big data methodologies in technical communication. *Technical Communication Quarterly, 24*(1), 70–104.

Graham, S. S., & Whalen, B. (2008). Mode, medium, and genre: A case study of decisions in new-media design. *Journal of Business and Technical Communication, 22*(1), 65–91.

Greene, R. W. (2004). Rhetoric and capitalism: Rhetorical agency as communicative labor. *Philosophy & Rhetoric, 37*(3), 188–206.

Gries, L. (2015). *Still life with rhetoric: A new materialist approach for visual rhetorics.* Boulder, CO: University Press of Colorado.

Gunn, J. (2018). Donald Trump's perverse political rhetoric. In R. Skinnell (Ed.), *Faking the news: What rhetoric can teach us about Donald J. Trump* (pp. 160–173). Exeter, UK: Imprint Academic.

Gunn, J., Goodale, G., Hall, M. M., & Eberly, R. A. (2013) Auscultating again: Rhetoric and sound studies. *Rhetoric Society Quarterly, 43*(5), 475–489.

Hallberg, B. (2016). How Marco Rubio lost his voice . . . and the election. *The Federalist,* March 16. Retrieved from http://thefederalist.com/2016/03/16/how-marco-rubio-lost-his-voice-and-the-election/

Haraway, D. (2016). A cyborg manifesto. In *Manifestly Haraway* (pp. 5–90). Minneapolis, MN: University of Minnesota Press.

Haraway, D. (1997). *Modest_Witness@Second_Millennium.FemaleMan_Meets_OncoMouse: Feminism and technoscience.* With paintings by L. M. Randolph. New York, NY: Routledge.

Harris, R. A. (2010). *Rhetoric and incommensurability.* West Lafayette, IN: Parlor Press.

Hart, R. P. (1984). *Verbal style and the presidency: A computer-based analysis.* Orlando, FL: Academic Press.

Hart, R. P. (2015). Genre and automated text analysis: A demonstration. In J. Ridolfo & W. Hart-Davidson (Eds.), *Rhetoric and the digital humanities* (pp. 152–168). Chicago, IL: University of Chicago Press.

Hart-Davidson, B. (2016). *Faciloscope: New tool in the facilitation toolkit for blogs and social media.* Institute for Museum and Library Services. Retrieved from https://www.imls.gov/blog/2016/07/faciloscope-new-tool-facilitation-toolkit-blogs-and-social-media

Hawhee, D. (2009). *Moving bodies: Kenneth Burke at the edges of language.* Columbia, SC: University of South Carolina Press.

Hawk, B. (2018). *Resounding the rhetorical: Composition as a quasi-object.* Pittsburgh, PA: University of Pittsburgh Press.

Hellman, J. (2016). Rubio apologized to Trump for "small hands" crack. *The Hill,* May 29. Retrieved from https://thehill.com/blogs/ballot-box/presidential-races/281636-rubio-apologized-to-trump-for-small-hands-comment

Henze, B. R. (2004). Emergent genres in young disciplines: The case of ethnological science. *Technical Communication Quarterly, 13*(4), 393–421.

Herndl, C. G. (1991). Writing ethnography: Representation, rhetoric, and institutional practices. *College English, 53*(3), 320–332.

Herndl, C. G., & Licona, A. C. (2007). Shifting agency: Agency, kairos, and the possibilities of social action. In M. Zachry & C. Thralls (Eds.), *Communicative practices in workplaces and the professions: Cultural perspectives on the regulation of discourse and organizations* (pp. 133–154). Amityville, NY: Baywood.

Hier, D. B., Hagenlocker, K., & Shindler, A. G. (1985). Language disintegration in dementia: Effects of etiology and severity. *Brain and Language, 25*(1), 117–133.

Hodgson, J., & Barnett, S. (2016). Introduction: What is rhetorical about digital rhetoric? Perspectives and definitions of digital rhetoric. *Enculturation,* November 22. Retrieved from http://enculturation.net/what-is-rhetorical-about-digital-rhetoric

Holsti, O. R. (1969). *Content analysis for the social sciences and humanities.* Reading, MA: Addison-Wesley.

Hu, M., & Liu, B. (2004). Mining opinion features in customer reviews. In A. G. Cohn (Ed.), *AAAI'04: Proceedings of the 19th national conference on Artificial intelligence* (pp. 755–760). Menlo Park, CA: AAAI Press.

Ingold, T. (2013) *Making. Anthropology, archaeology, art, and architecture.* London: Routledge

Jaffe, A. (2016). Donald Trump has "small hands," Marco Rubio says. *NBC News,* February 29. Retrieved from https://www.nbcnews.com/politics/2016-election/donald-trump-has-small-hands-marco-rubio-says-n527791

Jasanoff, S. S. (1987). Contested boundaries in policy-relevant science. *Social Studies of Science, 17*(2), 195–230.

Jensen, R. E. (2015). An ecological turn in rhetoric of health scholarship: Attending to the historical flow and percolation of ideas, assumptions, and arguments. *Communication Quarterly, 63*(5), 522–526.

Kelly, A. R., & Miller, C. R. (2016). Intersections: Scientific and parascientific communication on the internet. In A. Gross & J. Buehl (Eds.), *Science and the internet: Communicating knowledge in a digital age* (pp. 221–245). Amityville, NY: Baywood.

Kennedy, K., & Long, S. (2014). The trees within the forest: Extracting, coding, and visualizing subjective data in authorship studies. In J. Ridolfo & W. Hart-Davidson (Eds.), *Rhetoric and the digital humanities* (pp. 20–32). Chicago, IL: University of Chicago Press.

Kimball, M. A. (2013). Visual design principles: An empirical study of design lore. *Journal of Technical Writing and Communication, 43*(1), 3–41. https://doi.org/10.2190/TW.43.1.b

Kreig, G. (2016). Donald Trump defends size of his penis. *CNN,* March 4. Retrieved from https://www.cnn.com/2016/03/03/politics/donald-trump-small-hands-marco-rubio/index.html

Krippendorf, K. (1980). *Quantitative content analysis: An introduction to its method.* Beverly Hills, CA: Sage.

Kruse, K. M. [@KevinMKruse]. (2018, July 27). *I keep seeing this talking point in my mentions so, sure, let's address it* [Tweet]. Twitter. https://twitter.com/KevinMKruse/status/1022886356282945536

Kruse, K. M. [@KevinMKruse]. (2018, October 31). *No, that's completely wrong. Let's dig in* [Tweet]. https://twitter.com/KevinMKruse/status/1057654829290536960

Kruse, K. M. [@KevinMKruse]. (2018, November 3). *Now, my last bit of advice is probably the most important. Dunk on Dinesh D'Souza. I mean, people really do NOT like that guy. I went from 80k to 160k in two weeks just from a few threads on his nonsense* [Tweet]. Twitter. https://twitter.com/KevinMKruse/status/1058884680534159362

Kuhn, T. S. (2012). *The structure of scientific revolutions.* Chicago, IL: University of Chicago press.

Latour, B. (1987). *Science in action: How to follow scientists and engineers through society.* Cambridge, MA: Harvard University Press.

Latour, B. (1990). Technology is society made durable. *The Sociological Review, 38*(1_suppl), 103–131.

Latour, B. (1993a). *The pasteurization of France* (A. Sheridan & J. Law, Trans.). Cambridge, MA: Harvard University Press.

Latour, B. (1993b). *We have never been modern* (C. Porter, Trans.). Cambridge, MA: Harvard University Press.

Latour, B. (1999). *Pandora's hope: Essays on the reality of science studies.* Cambridge, MA: Harvard University Press.

Latour, B. (2001). "Retour sur <<Irréductions>>." *Canal U.* Retrieved April 4, 2020, from https://www.canal-u.tv/video/fmsh/retour_sur_irreductions_in_b_latour_pasteur_guerre_et_paix_des_microbes_la_decouverte_poche_n_114_2001_edition_originale_1984.28355

Latour, B. (2005). *Reassembling the social: An introduction to actor-network-theory.* Oxford, UK: Oxford University Press.

Latour, B., & Woolgar, S. (1979/2013). *Laboratory life: The construction of scientific facts* (2nd ed.). Princeton, NJ: Princeton University Press.

Leonhardt, D. (2020). A complete list of Trump's attempts to play down coronavirus, March 15. *The New York Times.* Retrieved from https://www.nytimes.com/2020/03/15/opinion/trump-coronavirus.html

Lipsitch, M. [@mlipsitch]. (2020, March 19). *OK lots of people think this is an intramural tiff. In the sense that we have been working @CCDD_HSPH for a decade and at @HarvardEpi for 25y to establish ID epidemiology as a field of excellence & we don't like a charlatan exploiting a tenuous connection for self-promotion, yes.* [Tweet]. Twitter. https://twitter.com/mlipsitch/status/1240847186247798784

Liu, B., Hu, M., & Cheng, J. (2005, May). Opinion observer: Analyzing and comparing opinions on the web. In *Proceedings of the 14th international conference on World Wide Web* (pp. 342–351). New York, NY: ACM.

Lopez-Mattei, J. [@onco_cardiology]. (2018, November 10). *I am an academic multimodality CV imager. I love doing CV imaging Tweetorials (threads with non-peer reviewed educational content). Check my Moments in @Twitter. I am an energetic activist for widespread pt access to cardiac CT/ MRI #AHA18 #cardiotwitter* [Tweet]. https://twitter.com/onco_cardiology/status/1061454932530872321

Lynch, P., & Rivers, N. A. (Eds.). (2015). *Thinking with Bruno Latour in rhetoric and composition.* Carbondale, IL: Southern Illinois University Press.

Mara, A., & Hawk, B. (2009). Posthuman rhetorics and technical communication. *Technical Communication Quarterly, 19,* 1–10.

Mays, C., Rivers, N. A., & Sharp-Hoskins, K. (Eds.). (2017). *Kenneth Burke + the posthuman*. University Park, PA: Pennsylvania State University Press.

McNely, B., Gestwicki, P., Gelms, B., & Burke, A. (2013). Spaces and surfaces of invention: A visual ethnography of game development. *Enculturation, 15,* http://enculturation.net/visual-ethnography

Mehlenbacher, A. R. (2019). *Science communication online: Engaging experts and publics on the internet.* Columbus, OH: The Ohio State University Press.

Meyer, R. (2016). How Twitter's new reply system will work: The @reply is dead. *The Atlantic,* May 24. Retrieved from https://www.theatlantic.com/technology/archive/2016/05/how-twitters-new-reply-system-will-work/484211/

Miklossy, J., Taddei, K., Suva, D., Verdile, G., Fonte, J., Fisher, C., . . . & McLean, C. A. (2003). Two novel presenilin-1 mutations (Y256S and Q222H) are associated with early-onset Alzheimer's disease. *Neurobiology of Aging, 24*(5), 655–662.

Miller, C. R. (1979). A humanistic rationale for technical writing. *College English, 40*(6), 610–617.

Miller, C. R. (1980). *Environmental impact statements and rhetorical genres: An application.* (Unpublished doctoral dissertation). Rensselaer Polytechnic Institute. Troy, NY.

Miller, C. R. (1984). Genre as social action. *Quarterly Journal of Speech, 70*(2), 151–167.

Miller, C. R. (1995). Rhetorical community: The cultural basis of genre. In A. Freedman & P. Medway (Eds.), *Genre and the new rhetoric* (pp. 67–78). London, UK: Taylor & Francis.

Miller, C. R. (2007). What can automation tell us about agency? *Rhetoric Society Quarterly, 37*(2), 137–157.

Miller, C. R. (2010). Should we name the tools? Concealing and revealing the art of rhetoric. In D. Coogan & J. Ackerman (Eds.), *The public work of rhetoric: Citizen-scholars and civic engagement* (pp. 19–38). Columbia, SC: University of South Carolina Press.

Miller, C. R. (2016). Genre innovation: Evolution, emergence, or something else? *The Journal of Media Innovations, 3*(2), 4–19.

Miller, C. R. (2017). The appeal(s) of Latour. *Rhetoric Society Quarterly, 47*(5), 403–462.

Miller, C. R., & Shepherd, D. (2004). Blogging as social action: A genre analysis of the weblog. *Into the Blogosphere.* Retrieved November 3, 2017, from https://conservancy.umn.edu/bitstream/handle/11299/172818/Miller_Blogging%20as%20Social%20Action.pdf

Miller, C. R., & Shepherd, D. (2009). Questions for genre theory from the blogosphere. In J. Giltrow & D. Stein (Eds.), *Genres in the Internet: Issues in the theory of genre* (pp. 263–290). Amsterdam, Netherlands: John Benjamins.

Mol, A. (1999). Ontological politics: A word and some questions. In J. Law & J. Hassard (Eds.), *Actor network theory and after.* Malden, MA: Blackwell / Sociological Review.

Mol, A. (2002). *The body multiple: Ontology in medical practice.* Durham, NC: Duke University Press.

Murray, E. [@EpiEllie]. (2018, November 10). *The results of my #tweetorial poll were pretty clear: from over 350 votes, 38% of you want to know about causal survival analysis. So, pull up a chair and let's talk time-to-event!* [Tweet]. Twitter. https://twitter.com/EpiEllie/status/1061415958634512386

Newton, C. (2016). Twitter begins rolling out its algorithmic timeline around the world. *The Verge*, February 10. Retrieved from https://www.theverge.com/2016/2/10/10955602/twitter-algorithmic-timeline-best-tweets

Omizo, R., & Hart-Davidson, B. (2016). Hedge-o-matic. *enculturation*, May 12. Retrieved from http://hedgeomatic.cal.msu.edu/hedgeomatic/

Pickering, A. (1995). *The mangle of practice: Time, agency, and science.* Chicago, IL: University of Chicago Press.

Pigg, S. (2014). Coordinating constant invention: Social media's role in distributed work. *Technical Communication Quarterly, 23*(2), 69–87.

Plato. (1956). *Protagoras* (B. Jowett, Trans.). New York, NY: Library of the Liberal Arts.

Prasad, V. [@VPrasadMDMPH]. (2018, May 14). *I bet our paper, out now, in @NatRevClinOncol will generate some controversy We argue it is NOW LUCRATIVE for Drug companies to test TOTALLY USELESS Rx Not that they do, but they aren't much better Let me take you through it, in this TWEETORIAL https://www.nature.com/articles/s41571-018-0030-2* [Tweet]. Twitter. https://twitter.com/VPrasadMDMPH/status/996172012585304064

Prasad, V. [@VPrasadMDMPH]. (2018, June 10). *As promised, a brief TWEETORIAL on why you should TWEET your criticism of a @NEJM paper rather than send a Letter to Editor (applies to others too), and ways NEJM could be better (aka more like @bmj_latest) Why sending a LTE to the NEJM is a waste . . .* [Tweet]. Twitter. https://twitter.com/VPrasadMDMPH/status/1005909411066286080

Quin, R. M. (2015). The evolution of advertising on Twitter, and what comes next. *audiense*, April 9. Retrieved from https://resources.audiense.com/blog/the-evolution-history-of-advertising-on-twitter

Rickert, T. (2013). *Ambient rhetoric: The attunements of rhetorical being.* Pittsburgh, PA: University of Pittsburgh Press.

Ridolfo, J., & Hart-Davidson, W. (Eds.). (2015). *Rhetoric and the digital humanities.* Chicago, IL: University of Chicago Press.

Roanoke College. (2016, February 28). *Marco Rubio live at Roanoke College* [Video]. YouTube. https://www.youtube.com/watch?v=3aVpyojzUbE [Removed for violating DMCA].

Robinson, K. (Ed.). (2009). *Deleuze, Whitehead, Bergson: Rhizomatic connections.* New York, NY: Palgrave-Macmillan.

Romono, J. (2017). Twitter's new thread feature takes us one step closer to longform tweeting. *Vox*, December 15. Retrieved from https://www.vox.com/culture/2017/12/15/16771922/twitter-new-threading-feature

Schiappa, E., & Keehner, M. F. (1991). The "lost" passages of *Permanence and change*. *Communication Studies, 42*(3), 191–198.

Schryer, C. F. (1999). Genre time/space: Chronotopic strategies in the experimental article. *JAC, 19*(1), 81–89.

Schryer, C. F. (2000). Walking a fine line: Writing negative letters in an insurance company. *Journal of Business and Technical Communication, 14*(4), 445–497.

Schütz, A. (1944/1996a). Fragments towards a phenomenology of music. In H. Wagner, G. Psathas, & F. Kersten (Eds.), *Alfred Schütz collected papers* (Vol. 4, pp. 243–276). Dordrecht: Kluwer Academic.

Schütz, A. (1958/1996b). The problem of social reality. In H. Wagner, G. Psathas, & F. Kersten (Eds.), *Alfred Schütz collected papers* (Vol. 4, pp. 3–74). Dordrecht: Kluwer Academic.

Schütz, A., & Luckmann, T. (1973). *The structures of the life-world* (R. M. Zaner & H. T. Engelhardt, Jr., Trans.). Evanston, IL: Northwestern University Press.

Scott, R. L. (1967). On viewing rhetoric as epistemic. *Communication Studies, 18*(1), 9–17.

Snow, C. P. (1959). *The two cultures and the scientific revolution.* Cambridge, UK: Cambridge University Press. [Reprint].

Stengers, I. (2011). *Thinking with Whitehead: A free and wild creation of concepts.* Cambridge, MA: Harvard University Press.

Stephen, K. (1922). *Misuse of mind: A study of Bergson's attack on intellectualism.* London, UK: Kegan Paul, Trench, Trubner.

Sterne, J. (2012). *The sound studies reader.* New York, NY: Routledge.

Teston, C. (2017). *Bodies in flux: Scientific methods for negotiating medical uncertainty.* Chicago, IL: University of Chicago Press.

Teston, C. B., & Graham, S. S. (2012). Stasis theory and meaningful public participation in pharmaceutical policy. *Present Tense, 2*(2), 1–8.

Teston, C. B., Graham, S. S., Baldwinson, R., Li, A., & Swift, J. (2014). Public voices in pharmaceuticals deliberation: negotiating "clinical benefit" in the FDA's Avastin Hearing. *Journal of Medical Humanities, 35,* 149–170.

Thieme, K. [@Katja_Thieme]. (2018, November 17). Here's the thing. If you—a computer scientist who has published exclusively on #compsci education—want to make some claims about how "the science of sex differences" is discussed on university and college campuses, you actually have to consider relevant #research. 1/ #citation [Tweet]. Twitter. https://twitter.com/Katja_Thieme/status/1063885882531373056

Thompson, S. A., & Mann, W. C. (1987). Rhetorical structure theory. *IPrA Papers in Pragmatics, 1*(1), 79–105.

Time Staff. (2015). Here's Donald Trump's presidential announcement speech. *Time,* June 16. Retrieved from http://time.com/3923128/donald-trump-announcement-speech

UserExperiencesWorks. (n.d.). *A magazine is an iPad that does not work* [Video]. YouTube. https://www.youtube.com/watch?v=aXV-yaFmQNk

Wallack, F. B. (1980). *The epochal nature of process in Whitehead's metaphysics.* Albany, NY: State University of New York Press.

Walsh, L., Rivers, N. A., Rice, J., Gries, L. E., Bay, J. L., Rickert, T., & Miller, C. R. (2017). Bruno Latour on rhetoric. *Rhetoric Society Quarterly, 47*(5), 403–462.

Whitehead, A. N. (1929/1978). *Process and reality: An essay in cosmology* (Corrected ed., D. R. Griffin & D. W. Sherburne, Eds.). New York, NY: Free Press.

Whitehead, A. N. (1968). *Modes of thought.* New York, NY: Simon and Schuster.

Whitehead, A. N. (1925/2011). *Science and the modern world.* Cambridge, UK: Cambridge University Press.

Wingard, J. (2018). Trump's not just one bad apple: He's the product of a spoiled bunch. In R. Skinnell (Ed.), *Faking the news: What rhetoric can teach us about Donald J. Trump* (pp. 39–52). Exeter, UK: Imprint Academic.

Winsor, D. (2006). Using writing to structure agency: An examination of engineers' practice. *Technical Communication Quarterly, 15,* 411–430.

Young, A. (2018). Rhetorics of fear and loathing: Donald Trump's populist style. In R. Skinnell (Ed.), *Faking the news: What rhetoric can teach us about Donald J. Trump* (pp. 21–38). Exeter, UK: Imprint Academic.

Zarefsky, D. (1998). Four senses of rhetorical history. In K. J. Turner (Ed.), *Doing rhetorical history: Concepts and cases* (pp. 19–32). Tuscaloosa, AL: University of Alabama Press.

INDEX

abstraction, 18, 52, 73, 90, 142–45, 187–88, 189 table 8.4
actor-network theory (ANT), 6–7, 31, 37, 66–67, 69
agency, 50n5, 54, 55, 56–57, 91–92, 93, 94–96, 99–101, 104, 108, 115–20, 124–29, 134–35, 158
"Agency and Automation" (Miller), 117
Althusser, Louis, 100, 110, 119
Ambient Rhetoric (Rickert), 7, 9, 38, 59, 99–100, 103–4
Animal Who Writes, The (Cooper), 7, 24, 39, 103
ANT. *See* actor-network theory (ANT)
Artemeva, Natasha, 97–98
atomistic metaphysics, 38–39
Attitudes Toward History (Burke), 26, 108
attunement, 9, 64, 98–100, 103, 105–6, 134
authority, 12n6, 66n2, 118–19, 138–40, 152, 156–57, 159

Banks, Adam, 89
Barad, Karen, 10, 38–39, 41, 105–6
Barnett, Scott, 7, 11n5, 41, 59
Bateson, Gregory, 105–6
Beastie Boys, 140
Benda, Julien, 26, 32–33
Bennett, Jane, 9–10, 24, 52
Bergson, Henri, 7, 16, 21–35, 23n2, 27 fig. 2.1, 60, 105, 108–12, 119–21, 139, 144, 148, 154, 185–87, 187 fig. 8.1

Bergsonism (Deleuze), 23, 25
Bergsonisme, Le (Benda), 26, 32–33
Berkeley, George, 23
Biocultural Creatures (Frost), 143
Bitzer, Lloyd, 54
blogging, 62, 88–89, 131–34
"Blogging as Social Action" (Miller & Shepherd), 71
Bodies in Flux (Teston), 7, 59
Bohr, Niels, 38
boundary work, 4–5, 9–10, 13–15, 35, 59–60, 138–39, 164, 183–84
Boyle, Casey, 6–7, 10, 24, 40–41, 59, 101–3, 105, 112
Brown, Jim, Jr., 11–12
Burke, Ann, 131
Burke, Kenneth, 3, 3n1, 7, 16, 21–22, 26, 30–33, 47–53, 60, 66–67, 70, 73–74, 90, 95–96, 106–9, 130–31, 140, 180, 184–86, 187 fig. 8.1
Bush, Jeb, 178

Callon, Michel, 31
Carson, Ben, 169–70
change, 116–22
Charney, Davida, 13, 137–38, 155–56
circulation model, 16
circulation studies, 132
Clark, Andy, 104
communism, 50

INDEX

computational rhetoric (CR), 1–3, 5, 11–15, 11n5, 139, 160, 164–65, 176–77, 181, 183, 188 table 8.1
Comte, Auguste, 138, 142
concrescence, 47, 56, 67, 69–70, 74–75, 109, 189 table 8.3
Condit, Celest, 2
conference paper, 97
constructivism, 8, 45, 48–49, 152
content analysis, 140, 145, 146, 148–51, 153, 155, 157, 159–60, 164–65, 184; quantification and, 152–55, 154 fig. 6.1
Coole, Diana, 6, 50, 50n5
Cooper, Marilyn, 7, 24, 31, 39–41, 103, 105–6, 112
coronavirus pandemic, 80–81, 162
Counter-Statement (Burke), 26, 49, 70, 73–74, 180
COVID-19, 80–81, 162
CR. *See* computational rhetoric (CR)
Creative Evolution (Bergson), 28, 34, 105, 109
creativity, 115–16, 124–29
Crisan, Ana, 86
critical Marxism, 50, 50n5, 51
Critique of Pure Reason (Kant), 23
Cruz, Ted, 167, 169–70, 179
cyborg anthropology, 38

"dad bloggers," 131–32
de-atomization, 95, 101–12, 145
Deleuze, Gilles, 7, 10, 23–25, 29, 41, 63, 67, 103, 139, 144, 186, 187 fig. 8.1
Deleuze, Whitehead, Bergson: Rhizomatic Connections (Robinson, ed.), 28
demarcation problem, 4
Dewey, John, 29–30
DH. *See* digital humanities (DH)
dialectical suspension, 117–18
Difference and Repetition (Deleuze), 24, 29
digital humanities (DH), 12n6, 13–15, 64
digital rhetoric, 11n5, 94, 184
DJing, 89
Dodd, Christopher, 167
D'Souza, Dinesh, 79, 82

dualistic metaphysics, 36, 45–47, 51, 67, 188 table 8.2
duration, 25–26, 43, 120, 135, 140, 186
dwelling, 100

"Ecological Turn in Rhetoric of Health Scholarship, An" (Jensen), 15–16
Edbauer-Rice, Jenny, 10, 15–16, 132–33
Edwards, Edwin, 162n2
Einstein, Albert, 23
élan vitale, 24
Emerging Genres in New Media Environments (Kelly & Miller), 63–64
empiricism, 13, 138, 156–58
enchantment ontology, 37, 39
entropy, 69, 132–34
epistemology: durable rhetorical, 155–60; modern and postmodern, 24; of recalcitrance, 159; science and, 156–58
error bars, 138, 138n1
ethnography, 122–23, 131, 135–36, 152–53
evolution, 130–31, 144–45
exactness, 138, 138n1, 141
experience: backdrop of, 56; in Burke, 73; communication and, 71; of continuity, 25; of genre, 139; modes of, 70; in Schütz, 42, 121–22

factishes, 66, 66n2
"fake news," 79, 82
Faking the News (Young), 163
Farrell, Thomas, 68
Fausto-Sterling, Anne, 7
Feigl-Ding, Eric, 81
fit forging, 129 fig. 5.1, 129–34, 189 table 8.3
formalism, 71–72, 175–76, 181
Foucault, Michel, 5, 7, 49, 119
Frentz, Thomas, 68
Frost, Samantha, 6, 50, 50n5, 101, 143
Fuller, Steve, 32

GAP. *See* genre as process (GAP)
genre: agency and, 118, 124–29; change, 135–36; as constraining, 96–97; creativity and, 124–29; gestalt shift, 116; hybridization, 116, 128–29; IText

INDEX 213

Working Group on, 62; in Miller, 34–35; new media and, 63–64; nonexistence of, 71–72; rhetorical situation and, 55–56; socialization and, 97
genre as process (GAP), 59–91, 83 fig. 3.1, 84 fig. 3.2, 85 fig. 3.3, 88 fig. 3.4; in Burke, 73; defined, 188 table 8.1; fit forging and, 130–31; from genre as social action to, 67–75; genre change and, 135–36; and modes of inquiry, 186–87; and rhetor-situation interaction, 94–95; satisfaction and, 90–91; and tweetorials, 75–90, 83 fig. 3.1, 84 fig. 3.2, 85 fig. 3.3, 88 fig. 3.4
genre as social action (GASA): boundary work and, 60; development of, 34; epistemology and, 65–66; materiality and, 53; medium and, 61–66; Miller and, 34, 53–54; and nonexistence of genre, 71–72; rhetorical new materialism and, 54–55; rhetorical situation and, 54; Schütz and, 43
"Genre as Social Action" (Miller), 21
genre-ing, 73–74, 88 fig. 3.4, 89, 125–28, 189 table 8.3
"Genre Innovation: Evolution, Emergence, or Something Else?" (Miller), 144
gestalt shift genres, 116
Gestwicki, Paul, 131
Gibbons, Michelle, 159
Gieryn, Thomas, 4
Gingrich, Newt, 167
Giuliani, Rudy, 167
glitches, 93–94
Goriunova, Olga, 93–94
Gottlieb, Scott, 81
Gottschalk Druschke, Caroline, 10
Grammar of Motives, A (Burke), 34, 48, 96, 106
Greene, Ronald, 117
Gries, Laurie, 7, 10, 40–41, 59, 133
Guattari, Felix, 24
Gunn, Joshua, 162

Hallberg, Beverly, 171
Haraway, Donna, 6, 10, 38
Harding, Sandra, 7
Hart, Roderick, 2, 12n6, 137–38

Hawhee, Debra, 3n1, 10, 48–49, 51–52
Hawk, Byron, 180–81
Heidegger, Martin, 59, 100
Henri Bergson: Key Writings (Ó Maoilearca), 23
Herndl, Carl, 7, 118–19, 152–53
hierarchical stabilization, 71
hierarchical structuring, 190
hierarchy, 69–71, 87, 88 fig. 3.4, 90, 115, 138, 141
historiography, 10, 16, 28, 36, 56.57, 113, 184, 193
Hodgson, J., 11n5
"Humanistic Rationale for Technical Writing, A" (Miller), 141
human-world entanglement, 95
Husserl, Edmund, 30
hybridization, genre, 116, 128–29

innovation, 41, 57, 60–63, 66, 95, 108, 115, 121–23, 134–35, 189 table 8.3
interactivity, 38–39, 128
interrater reliability, 149–50, 150n2, 151–52
"Intersections: Scientific and Parascientific Communication on the Internet" (Kelly & Miller), 77
Into the Blogosphere (Miller & Shepherd), 62
intra-activity, 37–40, 99, 105, 132
intuition, 189 table 8.4; abstraction and, 18, 142–45; aggregate, 155; in Bergson, 25–26, 29, 32, 120–21, 139, 154; in Berke, 33; defined, 139; quantification of, 149–52; in Russell, 23n2; science of, 145–55, 147 table 6.1, 154 fig. 6.1
IText Working Group, 61–62

James, William, 23, 29–30
Jasanoff, Sheila, 4
Jensen, Robin, 15–16, 113

kairos, 74–75, 104, 119, 181
Kant, Immanuel, 23
"keep Austin weird," 132–33
Kelly, A. R., 63–64, 77

INDEX

Kenneth Burke + The Posthuman (Mays, Rivers, & Sharp), 3n1, 7, 59
Kernen, Joe, 79
Kimball, Miles, 12
Krippendorff, Klaus, 149, 153
Kruse, Kevin, 79, 83 fig 3.1, 86
Kuhn, Thomas, 32, 42, 49, 52, 143

Laboratory Life (Latour & Woolgar), 31–32, 43–44
Laconic speech, 171
Latour, Bruno, 6–9, 26, 31, 43–45, 63, 65–66, 66n2, 67, 68n3, 156–57, 159, 187 fig. 8.1
Law, John, 7, 31
Licona, A. C., 118–19
Lipsitch, Marc, 81
Lopez-Mattei, Juan, 77
Lynch, Paul, 7

mangle, 158
Mann, William, 2
Marx, Karl, 50
Marxism, critical, 50, 50n5, 51
materiality, 8, 10, 25, 42, 47–48, 53–56, 64–65, 89–90, 93, 117
Matter and Memory (Bergson), 7, 23–24, 28, 45–47, 109
Mays, Chris, 3n1, 59
McNely, Brian, 131
Meaning of the Gene, The (Condit), 2
media, new, 62–63, 122–23
medium: and genre as social action, 61–66
Mehlenbacher, A. R., 63–64, 72–73, 77
Melonçon, Lisa, 2
memory, 109–12, 115–16, 189 table 8.3
meta-genre-ing, 189 table 8.3
metaphysics: atomistic, 38–39; dualistic, 36, 45–47, 51, 67, 188 table 8.2; relational, 36, 39, 51–52, 115, 188 table 8.2
Miller, Carolyn, 3, 7, 16, 21–22, 26, 30, 34–35, 43, 53–56, 60, 63–64, 68–74, 77, 88–90, 96, 106, 115, 117–22, 133–34, 141–45, 175, 179–80, 185–86, 187 fig. 8.1
Misuse of Mind (Stephen), 34

modernity, 38, 53–56
Modest_Witness (Haraway), 38
Mol, Annemarie, 6, 40, 67, 103, 105, 156
Moving Bodies (Hawhee), 3n1, 48, 51
multiple ontologies, 67
Murray, Ellie, 79, 81–83, 83 fig 3.1, 85 fig 3.3, 88 fig. 3.4

negativity, 165–70
new materialism(s): Bergson and, 30–31, 187 fig. 8.1; Burke and, 33–34; of Burke and Miller, 21; critical Marxism and, 50; defined, 36, 188 table 8.2; examples of, 37; otherness of, 6–11; science and, 143; Whitehead and, 30–31, 45–47. *See also* rhetorical new materialism (RNM)
new media, 62–63, 122–23
Nietzsche, Friedrich, 34

object-oriented ontologies (OOO), 6, 9
object-oriented rhetoric, 2, 10
Ó Maoilearca, John, 23–24
ontology: enchantment, 39; in Mol, 40; multiple, 67; object-oriented, 6, 9
"On Viewing Rhetoric as Epistemic" (Scott), 141
OOO. *See* object-oriented ontologies (OOO)
otherness: of new materialisms, 6–11
overdeterminism, 96–101

Pandora's Hope (Latour), 65–66, 68n3
Paul, Ron, 167
Pearson, Keith Ansell, 23–24
peer review, 9–10
Peirce, Charles Sanders, 155
percolation model, 16
permanence, 116–22
Permanence and Change (Burke), 7, 26, 33–34, 48–52, 60, 67, 106, 116, 140
"Perspectives on Cultural & Posthumanist Rhetorics" (Boyle), 101–2
Philosophy of Literary Form (Burke), 185
Pickering, Andrew, 156–58
Pigg, Stacy, 131–32
Plato, 10, 171

Politics of Pain Medicine, The (Graham), 7–8, 41, 59, 103
Popper, Karl, 32
positivism, 13, 65, 141–44
Posobiec, Jack, 85
"Possible and the Real, The" (Bergson), 120–21
posthumanism, 37, 40, 47, 52, 101–2
posthuman rhetoric, 2
postmodern epistemology, 24
postmodernisms, totalizing, 42–45
practice, 40–41
Prasad, Vinay, 78, 86–87
prehensions, 29
presidential election of 2016, 161–62, 166–68, 168 table 7.1, 168–69, 169 fig. 7.1, 169 table 7.2, 170–75
Principles of Human Knowledge (Berkeley), 23
process: in Bergson, 25, 28–29, 46; in Boyle, 41; in Burke, 51; genre as, 59–91, 83 fig. 3.1, 84 fig. 3.2, 85 fig. 3.3, 88 fig. 3.4; people as, 93–113; in Whitehead, 28–29, 31–32, 47, 70. *See also* genre as process (GAP)
Process and Reality (Whitehead), 7, 29, 32, 47, 107
process of becoming, 37–40, 43, 46–47, 52, 144, 188 table 8.2
Protagoras (Plato), 171
public affairs blog, 133–34

recalcitrance, 156–60
relational metaphysics, 36, 39, 51–52, 115, 188 table 8.2
reliability, 149–50, 150n2, 151–52
Resounding the Rhetorical (Hawk), 180
RGS. *See* rhetorical genre studies (RGS)
rhetoric: computational, 1–3, 5, 11–15, 11n5, 139, 160, 164–65, 176–77, 181, 183, 188 table 8.1; as in crisis, 1–2; genre as social action and, 54–55
rhetorical genre studies (RGS), 3, 12, 24, 60, 96–101
rhetorical new materialism (RNM), 1–3, 5, 7–11, 13; Bergson and, 35–42; boundaries of, 59–60; Boyle and, 41; de-atomization and, 102–3; defined, 188 table 8.1; examples of, 37; human-world entanglement and, 95; Miller and, 53; origins of, 21–22; overdeterminism in, 96–101. *See also* new materialism(s)
Rhetorical Realism (Barnett), 10
rhetorical situation: in Burke, 67–68, 90; computational rhetoric and, 11; dynamic, 123; and genre as social action, 54; materiality and, 55; in Miller, 34, 55–56, 71, 119–20; recurrent, 148, 155
"Rhetorical Structure Theory" (Thompson & Mann), 2
Rhetoric as Posthuman Practice (Boyle), 7, 24, 40–41, 103, 105
Rhetoric of Motive, A (Burke), 48
Rhetoric Through Everyday Things (Boyle), 7, 59
rhetor-situation interaction, 94–95, 98
Rickert, Thomas, 7, 9–10, 38, 41, 59, 98–100, 103–5, 112
Rivers, Nathaniel A., 3n1, 7, 10, 59
RNM. *See* rhetorical new materialism (RNM)
Robinson, K., 23n2, 28–29
Rubio, Marco, 170–73, 172n4, 173–75, 179
Russell, Bertrand, 23, 23n2

satisfaction, 74–75, 82–90, 83 fig. 3.1, 84 fig. 3.2, 85 fig. 3.3, 88 fig. 3.4, 90–91, 180–81, 189 table 8.3
Schryer, Catherine, 71, 96–97, 172
Schütz, Alfred, 26, 29–30, 32, 34–35, 42–43, 55, 68, 121–22, 187 fig. 8.1
science: Bergson and, 139; boundary work in, 4; in Comte, 138; dropping, 140–42; epistemic authority in, 156–58; of intuition, 145–55, 147 table 6.1, 154 fig. 6.1; in Latour, 156; in Miller, 142; new materialism and, 143; positivism and, 142–44
Science and the Modern World (Whitehead), 32
Science Communication Online (Mehlenbacher), 72
Science in Action (Latour), 156
Scott, Robert, 141–42
scratch, in DJing, 89
Sharp-Hoskins, Kellie, 3n1, 7, 59

Shepherd, D., 62–63, 71–72, 74, 88–89, 100, 118, 125, 133–34
Shulgin, Alexei, 93–94
situated action, 37, 43, 46, 50, 52, 57, 68, 73, 99, 120–22, 144–45, 149, 155, 160, 187, 189 table 8.3
situation: defined, 189 table 8.3. *See also* rhetorical situation; rhetor-situation interaction
sociosymbolic, 62–63
"Sounds of Science" (Beastie Boys), 140
Stengers, Isabelle, 31, 187 fig. 8.1
Stephen, Karin, 26, 34
Still Life with Rhetoric (Gries), 7, 59
Structures of the Life-World, The (Schütz), 42–43, 121
subjectivity, 104, 134

"Technology Is Society Made Durable" (Latour), 68n3
Teston, Christa, 7, 40–41, 59
Thieme, Katja, 79, 83 fig 3.1, 85–86
Thinking with Bruno Latour in Rhetoric and Composition (Lynch & Rivers), 7
Thinking with Whitehead (Stengers), 31
Thompson, Sandra, 2
Thousand Plateaus, A (Guattari & Deleuze), 24
threading, in Twitter, 76–77
Time and Free Will (Bergson), 25, 109–10
trash talk, 171
Trump, Donald, 80, 161–63, 166, 170–80

Tsing, Anna, 10
tweetorial, 75–90, 83 fig. 3.1, 84 fig. 3.2, 85 fig. 3.3, 88 fig. 3.4
Twitter. *See* tweetorial
2001 IText Working Group, 61–62

Verbal Style and the Presidency: A Computer-Based Analysis (Hart), 2
Vibrant Matter (Bennett), 9, 24, 52

WAGR. *See* writing, activity and genre (WAGR)
Wallack, F. Bradford, 33–34
Walsh, Lynda, 8–9
We Have Never Been Modern (Latour), 44
Whitehead, Alfred North, 7, 23, 23n2, 25–26, 28–31, 40–42, 45–47, 67, 69–70, 74, 103, 107–8, 120, 186, 187 fig. 8.1
Wilson, Woodrow, 23
Wingard, Jennifer, 162–63
Winsor, Dorothy, 118
Woolgar, Steve, 31–32, 43–44, 107
World War I, 23
writing, activity and genre (WAGR), 131
"Writing Ethnography: Representation, Rhetoric, and Institutional Practices" (Herndl), 152

Young, Anna, 163

Zarefsky, David, 184

www.ingramcontent.com/pod-product-compliance
Lightning Source LLC
Chambersburg PA
CBHW030136240426
43672CB00005B/155